Explore! Big Sur Country

Help Us Keep This Guide Up to Date

Every effort has been made by the author and editors to make this guide as accurate and useful as possible. However, many things can change after a guide is published—trails are rerouted, regulations change, techniques evolve, facilities come under new management, and so on.

We would love to hear from you concerning your experiences with this guide and how you feel it could be improved and kept up to date. While we may not be able to respond to all comments and suggestions, we'll take them to heart and we'll also make certain to share them with the author. Please send your comments and suggestions to the following address:

FalconGuides
Reader Response/Editorial Department
P.O. Box 480
Guilford, CT 06437

Or you may e-mail us at:

editorial@falcon.com

Thanks for your input, and happy trails!

Outfit Your Mind
falcon.com

Exploring Series

Explore! Big Sur Country

A Guide to Exploring the Coastline, Byways, Mountains, Trails, and Lore

Barry Parr

FALCONGUIDES ®

GUILFORD, CONNECTICUT
HELENA, MONTANA
AN IMPRINT OF THE GLOBE PEQUOT PRESS

FALCONGUIDES®

Maps created by Mapping Specialists, Ltd. © Morris Book Publishing, LLC
All photos courtesy of the author, Barry Parr

Library of Congress Cataloging-in-Publication Data is available.

ISBN-13: 978-0-7627-3568-6
ISBN-10: 0-7627-3568-6

Manufactured in the United States of America
First Edition/First Printing

To buy books in quantity for corporate use
or incentives, call **(800) 962–0973**
or e-mail **premiums@GlobePequot.com.**

To my son, Ivan, a fellow hiker since he was one week old.

On leaving Morro [Bay] I found myself definitely entering that little-known stretch of mountain country which borders the Pacific closely for a distance of about a hundred miles. For most of that distance there are no roads and few settlers, while the trails are rough, steep, and often so little travelled as to be difficult to follow. Further, no maps of the region were to be had. Many persons told me that I should never get through without a guide.
—J. SMEATON CHASE, 1913

The boardwalk above Moonstone Beach offers explorers an overview of sand, sea, and tide pools.

Contents

List of Maps

Acknowledgments

I greatly appreciate the time and effort that many people took to advise me on sections of this book. Among these are Susan Lotta and Suzanne Pierce Taylor of the Salinan Indian Council; Greg Bartlow and Robyn Buechel of the Monterey Peninsula Regional Park District; Blake Cooper, Mark Dobel, Jay Durant, Joe Durant, Jim Eva, Sam Eva, Phil and Pat Gordon, Ivan Parr, David Savoy, and Neil Toda. Thanks to Melissa Simcox for her help with keyboarding.

I also want to thank my three editors, Bill Schneider, Shelley Wolf, and Laura Jorstad; my proofreader, Steve Arney; and the cartographers at Mapping Specialists for their beautiful maps.

Chapter 1

Introduction to Big Sur

Big Sur is a wilderness with a dash of civilization. Renowned as a coastline where the Santa Lucia Mountains plunge into the Pacific from elevations exceeding 5,000 feet, Big Sur has a remote, rugged, somewhat otherworldly character. Mystery pervades its moods and scenes, confronts you at every turn. Big Sur probably contains more backyard-variety terra incognita than any other readily accessible place in California. Even those who know the area over a lifetime have to admit that there are extensive patches of ground right under their noses that they have never seen, and never will.

Only by using your imagination can you begin to fathom the magnitude and richness of Big Sur.

Consider, for instance, how the famous views along Big Sur's most heavily traveled corridor, Highway 1, conceal so much more than they reveal to the eye. The vast surface of the ocean, sweeping to a far horizon shaped by the curvature of the earth, conceals an unfathomable wilderness where sounding whales skirt dark submarine canyons, where great white sharks patrol the boundaries of undulating kelp forests. The rhythmic waves and currents, transmitted ceaselessly across thousands of miles of rotating planet, never stop.

Big Sur's characteristic cliffs and coastal terraces meet the Pacific south of Soberanes Point.

Then consider that shoreline. Although it stretches along Big Sur for nearly 100 miles, most of it within a few hundred yards of the road, it is for the most part as unapproachable to the average motorist as the shore of the lunar Ocean of Storms. From the high roadway we lose all perspective. As we glimpse the distant white breakers, it's easy to forget their awesome power and size; it is a shock to see one close-up, rising up before us, suddenly huge, and battering itself to oblivion against the rocks. Only the most accomplished kayakers brave this treacherous coastline, and even they can spare but fleeting glances for the countless rocks, sea caves, and tide pools where creatures and plants decimated elsewhere in California still thrive in all their pearly-shelled, feathery, bespined, and tentacled glory.

Consider next the massive slopes and cliff faces that rise from this wave-battered shoreline. We who drive along Highway 1 are keenly aware of them, gaping in our periphery vision. We pull over for a safer look, peer over the brink, and still see very little of these great, sheer surfaces. And yet there are many square miles of near-vertical real estate, virtually unexplored, lining the Big Sur coast. There are thousands of miniature worlds teeming with life, the private estates of beetles, bees, butterflies, and rodents, clinging flower gardens, tufts of grasses, succulent beds of flowers, hidden caves, raptors' eyries, seeping springs bedecked in fern and moss, and countless sun-warmed rocks where lizards bask unmolested, except by predators that approach on wings.

Turning inland from Highway 1, we can see the mountains rising and a succession of canyons cut into them. Occasional gaps frame distant summits, but there are few places along the highway where we can see what lies beyond that first ridge of the Santa Lucia Range. (*Lucia*, by the way, is always pronounced as the Spanish *loo-SEE-a*, never the Italian *loo-CHEE-a*.) To glean some idea of the extent and character of this hinterland of lush ravines, redwood forests, oak woodlands, chaparral, rugged gorges, and highlands of granite and limestone, you will need to hike the trails or drive the back roads. Don't expect a picnic jaunt. Back roads are steep, narrow, and rugged. Footpaths into the Ventana and Silver Peak Wildernesses regularly disappear into almost impenetrable brush, routinely leaving large tracts inaccessible and unseen for years at a stretch, until the next wildfire or ambitious trail crew opens them up again.

Big Sur has always inspired the imagination. Its mystery lives in its ambiguous name, a legacy of the Spanish who settled at Monterey, who dismissed it (though not without a high degree of respect) as El País Grande del Sur—the big country to the south—a land too rugged to civilize and deck out with the proper names of saints and kings. Even in our present age, Big Sur's remoteness and otherworldly atmosphere inspire an unusual profusion of spiritual retreats, New Age sanctuaries, monastic enclaves, writers, artists, and people who march to the beat of a different glockenspiel. Even the local race of fairy folk who

The redwood forests of Soberanes Canyon in Garrapata State Park cannot be seen from Highway 1 and are among the best surprises of the Big Sur coast.

purportedly dwell among these redwoods and highlands of Big Sur—diminutive humanoids known as the Watchers or Dark Watchers—are far less familiar to the general public than other legendary creatures of California, such as Bigfoot or Sasquatch of the northwest forests and the Lemurians of Mount Shasta.

The Santa Lucias support an incredibly diverse variety of natural habitats. This is a living biological laboratory, but you don't need to be a naturalist to appreciate the natural world of Big Sur. Just about everyone is hardwired to admire the contrast between a soaring, crashing coastline and a deep, quiet, heavily forested canyon mysteriously wheedling its way into the mountains. Most visitors likewise can readily appreciate a spot of whale-watching, or the glimpse of a condor, or the spectacle of elephant seals as massy as fully loaded plumbers' vans battling for a chance to mate. Throw in a bobcat, some otters at play, majestic redwoods, carpets of spring wildflowers, and maybe an elk or two, and even the most confirmed mall walker will concede that Big Sur is worth a look. How much more so to anyone actually keen on the outdoors!

Lay of the Land

There's always some disagreement about where Big Sur starts and ends, or how far inland it goes. Most people usually think of Big Sur as the rugged coast between Malpaso and San Carpoforo Creeks—and that sounds right to me, too. Hikers and backpackers typically include the immediate hinterland, especially the Ventana Wilderness (aka "the Ventana"). To the U.S. Postal Service, however, the modest Big Sur Post Office stands rooted above the valley of the Big Sur River. For practical reasons, local residents likewise refrain from smearing the *Big Sur* moniker all up and down the map. For them, this coast is a much more clear-cut succession of place-names that distinguish scores of commercial businesses, creeks, ridges, headlands, vanished settlements, and other land-marks; places like Pitkins Curve, Posts, Nepenthe, Partington Ridge, Torre Canyon, Krenkel Corner, Coastlands, Rain Rock, Fullers Beach, and Hurricane Point.

And then there's local writer Lillian Bos Ross, who perceptively observed, "Big Sur is a state of mind."

By anyone's definition, this book covers a region larger than Big Sur, embracing the coast between the Carmel River and Cambria, and the northern Santa Lucia Range that rises behind it. Roughly 100 miles long from north to south, and 25 miles wide, this region contains a great deal more than the superb scenery along cliff-hanging Highway 1.

This book is for people who want to linger in Big Sur and the Santa Lucias, to enjoy the trails, coves, vistas, campgrounds, and little cafes; to know a bit of the lore that has held so many in thrall. Whether you enjoy family camping, day hiking or backpacking, outdoor photography, mountain biking, soaking in a hot spring, long walks with your dog, or pampering at a fine restaurant or resort, Big Sur can accommodate you, and this book can direct you.

The Latest News on Big Sur

Want to know about Big Sur trail conditions, weather, road closures, or special tours? Two Web sites offer excellent, timely information on all facets of Big Sur, whether historical, natural, or topical:

- Pelican Network: www.pelicannetwork.net
- Ventana Wilderness Alliance: www.ventanawild.org

Summer fog rolls mysteriously into Mill Creek Canyon below the Nacimiento-Fergusson Road.

Wildlife-watching and wildflowers are among the best in the West. Outdoor enthusiasts delight in Big Sur's myriad waterfalls, deep canyons, undersea gardens, strange rock formations, swimming holes, and miles of trails and back roads, paved and unpaved. Travelers who appreciate history relish the rarefied atmospheres of the San Antonio mission, Partington Cove, and Point Sur Light Station, the matchless castle built by William Randolph Hearst in the mountains behind San Simeon, and the scores of haunting reminders of the American, Spanish, and Mexican settlers, and of the Costanoan, Salinan, and Esselen peoples who preceded them. Along with its artists and writers, Big Sur is home to many hard-to-define, one-of-a-kind destinations that delight travelers in search of the unusual and the esoteric. But even if you stray no farther than the terrace of Nepenthe restaurant, you are already well on the way to appreciating the beauty, magic, and mystery of Big Sur.

How to Use This Book

This book is a general guide. The chapters are arranged primarily by subject of interest. I use that system because birders looking for lagoons may not be interested in prime windsurfing spots, nor does a pilgrim in quest of a monastic retreat necessarily want to know how to obtain a license to hunt pigs on Fort Hunter Liggett.

All these topics, by the way, are covered here, along with myriad others. To navigate among the various sections of this book, please check either the extensive table of contents or the index in the back of this volume. These serve as a kind of map-and-compass guide through the (admittedly vast) range of topics I've covered here—pointing you in the right direction. As in Big Sur itself, some bushwhacking may still be required.

For navigating in the actual countryside of Big Sur, this book offers several touchstones to help you. Highway 1 is, of course, the main stem of this region. Many tourists never venture beyond it—nor need they, for it's a majestic roadway, one of the most beautiful in the world. Most of this volume centers on Highway 1, and I encourage you to check out the Highway 1 Mileage Log found at the end of chapter 2, Driving Highway 1. The Highway 1 Mileage Log is an exhaustive list of stops along the route, along with their exact mileages from both the Carmel River (at the northern end of Big Sur) and Cambria (to the south). Whenever you have a question about finding a particular destination in this book—be it beach, restaurant, park, town, or side road—turn first to this Mileage Log.

Likewise, the back of the book includes a Highway 1 Mileage Chart that cross-lists distances between many of the highway's most popular points. The distances can be determined from either direction.

Don't forget to reference the detailed foldout map found inside this book's back cover as well.

Chapter 2, Driving Highway 1, offers an overview of Big Sur's central artery. If you're looking to cruise this famous route, chapter 2 will tell you what

A Note About Addresses

Big Sur is a big region that considers itself a small town. Locals here navigate less by street addresses than by landmarks: "Just beyond the ridge," you'll hear, or "Take that road next to the white cross." It's not as confusing as it may seem—really!—given the linear nature of Highway 1. And it's just the way things work here. If you need help finding your way, ask an old-timer, or (again) consult this book's charts and maps.

to expect from the drive and will guide you along the way, pointing out scenic highlights and stopping off briefly here and there to take in some of the interesting sights.

Chapter 3, Destinations Along Highway 1, is a more detailed look at some establishments you may want to visit: parks and attractions, resorts and lodgings, restaurants, and campgrounds. Any one of these "destinations" might be the base from which you choose to explore Big Sur—or you may prefer to use this chapter to plan overnight stays at multiple spots along Highway 1.

Chapter 4, Driving the Back Roads, will take you inland through the heart of the region's rugged mountains with all they have to offer—including places to camp if you're so inclined.

Chapter 5, Hiking the Trails of Big Sur, takes a close-up look at forty-five of Big Sur's most popular and stunning hiking routes. Those interested in other forms of outdoor fun should find everything they need in chapter 6, More Outdoor Recreation Fun, which covers water sports, cycling, horseback riding, hunting, and fishing.

The final chapters (chapters 7, 8, and 9) give you an in-depth look at three of the reasons behind this area's enduring attraction: its nature, history, and culture. You'll read overviews of these facets of the region, learn some little-known Big Sur facts, and be clued in to additional spots you might like to visit.

The Maps

You'll find a FalconGuides® four-color foldout map provided at the back of this book as well as six black-and-white maps included in the interior of the book. The front side of our color map offers an overview of the northern part of Big Sur with an accompanying map legend and a hypsometric key. The reverse side includes the southern portion of Big Sur.

Our new color map contains detail, such as topography that shows both land and water features with the land elevation measured in feet. In addition, you'll find numerous activity icons on the color map highlight the hiking trailheads, overlooks, missions, beaches, and campgrounds. (Note: The beaches along the coast of Big Sur are too rough for swimming, with the exception of William Randolph Hearst Memorial State Beach in San Simeon.)

A few notes about reading the topography: The color map employs a technique called *hypsometry*, which uses elevation tints to portray relief. Each tone represents a range of equal elevation, as shown in the hypsometric key on the map. The map will give you a good idea of elevation gain and loss. The tones shown on the bottom of the key represent lower elevations while the tones toward the top represent higher elevations. Narrow bands of different tones spaced closely together indicate steep terrain, whereas wider bands indicate areas of more gradual slope.

If you'd like to supplement our maps with more detailed maps for back-country travel, you may want to obtain National Geographic's larger-scale map, or you may prefer the 7.5-minute series of topographic maps published by the U.S. Geological Survey (USGS). Electronic versions of these maps can be found online or as packaged software. USGS maps are derived from aerial photos and are extremely accurate when it comes to terrain and natural features, but because the *topos*, as they are known, are not revised very often, trails, roads, and other human-made features are often out of date. Even so, the 7.5-minute topo's fine depiction of topography is useful for seeing greater detail.

When to Go

Winter is the wet season, summer typically dry, and fall and spring transitional, but Big Sur remains a solid four-season destination. It can be a great vacation destination anytime. When making your plans, take other factors besides weather into account, such as road closures, seasonal crowding, local festivals, wildlife migrations, and, of course, your own intended activities.

Summer, from June to Labor Day, is the high season for tourists along the coast. Daytime traffic along Highway 1 can be heavy, especially on weekends. Expect afternoon traffic jams between Carmel and Point Lobos. Campgrounds are in full swing. You should book your lodgings well in advance and may need to make reservations for dinner. On the plus side, summer is also the high season for musical events at the Henry Miller Library. The guest season at the Tassajara Zen Mountain Center starts at the end of April and spans the summer.

The Santa Lucia Mountains display the classic colors of a California summer landscape: tawny yellow hillsides patched with the motley hues of green forest, woodland, and chaparral. Although afternoons tend to be warm on the coast, and often even hot in Big Sur Valley and on the higher slopes, fog typically rolls in from the sea during summer afternoons, an ethereal sight as it probes the redwood forests and upland canyons, but a chilling presence that can linger till midmorning. Whether befogged or crystal clear, the trails of Big Sur's Pacific slope offer excellent hiking during summer, a time when the interior mountains and valleys of the Santa Lucia Range can be uncomfortably hot.

Local Weather News

For local weather information, you can check the National Weather Service's Western Region Headquarters Web site (www.wrh.noaa.gov). To learn the forecast for the coastal (western) side of the Santa Lucias, search under "Monterey, CA"; for weather on the inland (eastern) side of the Santa Lucias, including the Ventana Wilderness, check "Paso Robles, CA."

Summer temperatures in the 100s in the San Antonio Valley and parts of the Ventana Wilderness are not unusual, and might well be welcomed by the crowds who come to play in the waters of Nacimiento and San Antonio Reservoirs. Given a bit of shade and free rein to wade, splash, and soak in cool water, a walk along Tassajara, Arroyo Seco, and other perennial streams of the interior can be blissful on a hot day. Hikers and backpackers who go deeper into the Santa Lucias during summer and early fall should be savvy as to which creeks and springs have dried up, and which trails are cleared and at least partially shaded. Some people enjoy that kind of adventure, but a sweltering afternoon's bushwhack through snake-infested chamisal is not everyone's cup of tea.

Fall brings to Big Sur what many consider to be the most delightful weather of the year, with milder temperatures in the interior, sunnier days along the coast, and beautiful light and clarity of atmosphere. The crowds diminish in the parks and along Highway 1, and weekday visitors may enjoy solitude on the popular coastal trails. In fall the big-leaf maples, willows, and sycamores tinge the canyons' prevailing green with yellow, while splashes of red single out Big Sur's most beautiful autumnal plant, poison oak. In October the Jade Festival attracts artisans, musicians, and jade dealers from far and wide to tiny Gorda. Most hunting seasons begin in autumn, affecting mainly the roads and trails of Los Padres National Forest. If you want to avoid hunters, save your autumn hikes for the state parks, where hunting is illegal.

The days grow shorter and crisper on the approach of December, bringing the first of many winter storms. Working in tandem with Mother Nature, the Forest Service closes many back roads to vehicular traffic (a boon to mountain bikers who don't mind traversing a slide or two). The wild gales that can blow into the Pacific slope during winter can be fierce. The season brings as much as 60 inches of rain (and even some snow), saturating steep hillsides and swelling rivers; but even as the clouds begin to pile up against the Santa Lucias, wood smoke from cozy cabins promises pleasant evenings. Snow falls on the highlands of the Santa Lucia Range, but the foothill grasses grow rank and green. Stopping for breakfast at a little cafe, the subjects of road closures, downed trees, and power outages inevitably crop up among the locals. Landslides periodically close Highway 1 and have in some years cut off the communities of Big Sur from the wider world for days and weeks at a time. Trees blow down throughout the backcountry, turning footpaths into obstacle courses. Scores of waterfalls materialize, some of impressive height, volume, and beauty.

But winter storms come in cycles, interspersed with occasionally lengthy stretches of crystalline-clear, mild days and chillier nights that are ideal for sightseeing, hiking, and bicycling. Though steep paths can be very slippery and very few of the swollen creeks are bridged, experienced backpackers with practiced stream-crossing skills might find winter the perfect season for extended

This shaded horse trail near Fern Pond at Garland Ranch Regional Park offers respite from the summer sun.

backpack trips into the wilderness. Winter also heralds the richest time for wildlife at Big Sur. From the edge of Highway 1, motorists can see the herds of massive elephant seals on the beaches near Piedras Blancas and pods of whales migrating south toward Mexico. On calm winter nights highway drivers are serenaded by bullfrogs. Condors, which live year-round in the remote Santa Lucias, save most of their visits to Big Sur Valley for winter. October through March is the best time to see monarch butterfly trees.

Spring creeps through the Santa Lucias from March through May, bringing longer stretches of good weather between the rainstorms. Wildflowers burst into view, remarkable in both variety and number. The streams that roared in March are purring by June, while the hills, so lately green, turn yellow over a couple of weeks. In March and April whales migrate north toward Alaska. Usually by April the Forest Service regrades and reopens the unpaved back roads. The running of the Big Sur International Marathon, on the last Sunday before May, heralds the start of a new tourist high season.

Spring wildflowers burst into bloom in March and April along the Indians Road, near Arroyo Seco.

Spring brings a flurry of backpackers and hikers into the backcountry, but those of us who visited in winter find ourselves sweating more in spring, picking off more ticks, waving away more flies, and more diligently seeking out patches of shade. The insistent droning of bees and cicadas hangs like heat on the afternoon air. Looking west from a high ridge in the Ventana Wilderness, that distant line of ocean fog looks tempting.

Public Land and Water at Big Sur

Although much of the Big Sur region is privately owned, the amount of acreage open to the public is extensive and expanding. Many jurisdictions overlap. What follows is a selective listing of some of the most well-known areas:

State Parks

With a mandate for preservation, recreation, and education, the state parks of the Big Sur region are big on hiking, camping, scenery, and interpreting history and nature. They restrict camping to established sites, reserve specific trails for bicyclists and equestrians, and prohibit hunting. Collecting is not allowed, except rocks in some cases. Dogs are typically restricted to developed areas and must be on leashes. Most state parks charge entrance fees, but a fee paid at one Big Sur State park will admit visitors to all other state parks along the Big Sur coast for that day.

Los Padres National Forest

The USDA Forest Service has a mandate to satisfy the demands of multiple use, including recreation, forestry, mining, grazing, and wood gathering. Local headquarters is the Monterey Ranger District office in King City. Rangers maintain some trails, regulate off-road vehicle use, close forest roads for winter, and grade them for reopening in spring. They publish maps and oversee designated campgrounds, typically through a private contractor. The Forest Service recreation areas at Pfeiffer Beach, Sand Dollar Beach, and Arroyo Seco all charge fees.

Hunting is permitted during appropriate seasons and with appropriate permits. Dogs typically are allowed to use national forest trails if they are under immediate voice control of the owner, although wilderness areas and some other locales specifically require leashes. Mountain bikes are allowed on many forest trails and roads, but not on the Coast Ridge Road, and not in any designated wilderness area. Campfires are seasonally restricted and require a valid campfire permit, issued free for the year. The Adventure Pass is not required at any roads or trailheads in this book.

Los Padres National Forest administers two designated wilderness areas in the Santa Lucia Range, the 240,024-acre Ventana Wilderness and the 31,555-acre Silver Peak Wilderness. No roads or mechanized gear are allowed in designated wildernesses. Dogs must be leashed, and parties are limited to twenty-five people and twenty-five stock. Wilderness permits are not required. More than sixty hike-in campsites are designated on the Forest Service map, though campsites, like trails, are only sporadically maintained and are routinely overgrown by chaparral that hides them until the next wildfire, or a chance trail crew, might reopen them. Backpackers should inquire about trail conditions before setting out.

In recognition of the unusual flora of the Santa Lucia Range, the Forest Service manages four special zones that protect rare and endangered plants: Alder Creek Botanical Area, Lion Den Springs Botanical Area, Southern Redwood Botanical Area, and the 2,787-acre Cone Peak Gradient Research Natural Area (RNA).

Big Sur National Wild and Scenic River

The North and South Forks of the Big Sur River, from their headwaters to their confluence, have federal status as a National Wild and Scenic River, protecting

19.5 miles and 6,240 adjacent acres from future dam building. This section of the river is approachable only by trail.

California Sea Otter State Game Refuge

Created in 1941, the refuge protects the southern sea otter along the coast from the Carmel River to Cambria.

California Coastal National Monument

Technically, this monument embraces all the islands, rocks, and exposed reefs along California's entire coastline, including Big Sur, from mean high-tide line out to a distance of 12 nautical miles. In practical terms at Big Sur, the monument offers a level of protection to coastal habitat and enables parties to explore many tide pools that are blocked from land access by private land so long as they approach by boat and remain below the mean high-tide line.

Monterey Bay National Marine Sanctuary

Reaching from north of the Golden Gate south to Cambria, and extending an average of 30 miles offshore, this ocean sanctuary is monitored to protect resources while allowing recreation and research.

Some of California's newest state park lands are at Arroyo de la Cruz.

Chapter 2

Driving Highway 1

Finding your way along Highway 1 is pretty straightforward. Perhaps you've seen that car commercial with a driver motoring down Highway 1, speeding neatly around the sharp turns, cliffs yawning threateningly, ocean crawling far below. The camera cuts to an interior. Vivaldi is playing, and there's a suave gentleman at the wheel, competent, self-assured, ruggedly handsome, clearly successful in life.

Suddenly, nagging uncertainty furrows his brow. Could he be lost?

Cut to a view of his dashboard GPS system; a light on the display is flashing. Then cut back to the driver, relaxing into a self-congratulatory smirk. He knows where he is now.

Well, *duh!*

You don't need a GPS to find your way down Highway 1. Heading south, that's the Pacific Ocean on your right. If the ocean is on your left, you're heading north.

Unfortunately, the logical conclusion may be that guidebooks to Highway 1 may also be superfluous. True enough, you *can* drive Highway 1 and enjoy it thoroughly without a guidebook. You'll still see the same fantastic views. You

For a classic ride down Highway 1, try a motorcycle or a convertible.

can pull over whenever you want. You can enjoy all the elements of a classic American road trip just by following your own instincts. And for most people, that's certainly plenty good enough.

So let's just say that this guidebook is not a question of need, but of enlightenment. Where it might come in handy is in offering some useful pointers for touring—like where to find coastal access, or an excellent lemon tart (which at Gorda they call a "lemon square"). A guidebook also helps answer practical questions: Can you visit the Esalen hot baths without taking a seminar? When and where can you see whales, otters, or condors? How can you tour Big Sur Light Station?

I feel that a guidebook's greatest glory lies in its most superfluous details. Who *needs* to know, for instance, that the caretaker of the Hunt Ranch once saw a formation of six flying saucers heading out to sea at the mouth of the Little Sur River? And yet I always glance at the skies whenever I cross the Little Sur Bridge. The more such stories you know, the more intimate you become with Big Sur. Collect enough of them, and you may get mistaken for a local.

What to Know Before You Go

Should I drive Highway 1 northbound or southbound?

Either way is fine, but all things being equal, driving from the north to the south is better. Certainly the views are finer for your passengers. Southbound drivers can pull out on ocean-side turnouts without crossing a lane. Also, fewer rocks fall in the southbound lane.

If you think you might have a fear of heights, however, the northbound direction might feel safer for you, since it's always farther removed from disconcerting drop-offs.

What's the speed limit?

Unless otherwise posted, the limit is 50 miles per hour along most of Highway 1 and 45 mph through the Big Sur Valley. Slow down even more when road and weather conditions require it, such as when you're in settled areas or passing road crews, bikes, and pedestrians.

Who enforces the law along Highway 1?

The California State Highway Patrol, mainly. Sheriff's deputies from Monterey and San Luis Obispo Counties also have legal jurisdiction in their respective counties. Rangers may issue traffic citations as they patrol state park and Forest Service roads.

Is Highway 1 a dangerous road?

Although it's narrow and winding, and there are cliffs, this is a perfectly safe road if you drive safely and courteously.

In particular, you need to stay alert for falling rocks, wildlife, bikes, pedestrians, and other drivers. Share the road. Please pass bikes and hikers with ample room and reasonable speed.

Highway Closures

Sometimes slides or road maintenance close Highway 1. On the north end of Big Sur, a permanent warning sign at Carmel River Bridge flashes news of closures. At the south end, emergency signs are posted as needed at the junction of Highway 1 and California Highway 46.

Before leaving home, call Caltrans (California Department of Transportation) at (800) 427-7623, or check its Web site (www.dot.ca.gov), for current highway conditions.

What's in a Name?

As it was being built, Highway 1 was known as the Carmel–San Simeon Highway. Planners envisioned it as part of a longer road called the Roosevelt Highway. Later it was named the Cabrillo Highway. Today almost everyone calls it Highway 1 or the Coast Highway.

The Federal Highway Administration's National Scenic Byways Program has declared Highway 1 an "All American Road." This is an honorific it shares with the likes of Alaska's Seward Highway, the Natchez Trace Parkway, the Beartooth Scenic Byway to Yellowstone, and the Las Vegas Strip. To qualify as an All American Road, a highway must be deemed unique in the United States and a worthy destination for a journey in and of itself. Highway 1 certainly measures up to those standards.

Rocks fall onto Highway 1 all year round. Watch for them, and also for the stopped traffic that they cause, especially on northbound, blind turns. Some parts of the highway are continually sinking, especially south of Lucia. Watch for road crews and obey their directives.

Keep your eyes on the road, not scanning the horizon for whales or studying your GPS device. Don't yack on the cell phone while driving (reception at Big Sur is a problem, anyway). Pull over if you want to see the views. There are plenty of pullouts. Give ample warning before slowing to pull off the highway.

Always pull over to let emergency vehicles pass. I also advocate pulling over to let delivery trucks and other working vehicles by.

Dim your high beams at night for approaching traffic or if you're following another vehicle.

Should I worry about the weather?

Certainly you should be more alert in bad weather. Severe winter storms cause landslides, mudflows, high winds, and flooding. Most slides occur on the steepest slopes, but the worst flooding hits the valleys, especially the stretch along the Big Sur River. Anticipate delays and closures, especially in winter.

Who maintains the road?

Caltrans (California Department of Transportation) is the outfit that does the job, and it's a big one. Like a bridge that has to be painted continuously, Highway 1 needs to be continually serviced and rebuilt by its road crews. Local residents make up most of the crews.

How often does Highway 1 have to close?

Scores of minor rockslides close sections every year. Most are quickly bypassed with traffic control as Caltrans clears rubble or makes repairs. Major slides that close the road for weeks or months at a time, however, are not unusual. Big storms in December 1955 and 1983 brought flooding and slides in many places, the latter storm closing Highway 1 for more than a year. The El Niño storms of 1998 caused the most widespread damage in the road's history.

How do Big Sur residents cope with long-term road closures?

Big Sur residents have developed interesting ways to deal with closures. Some have been known to cycle back and forth to the outside world by carrying their bikes across the slide. Others who need to commute will drive second cars hundreds of miles around the Santa Lucias to the other side of the slide, parking one on either side for the duration, and crossing on foot. Road closures are tough for business at Big Sur, but they go with the territory, and residents pride themselves on self-sufficiency.

Can I take my trailer or RV?

Highway 1 is plenty wide enough for trailers and RVs, and many campgrounds accommodate them. But be aware that few commercial areas have parking lots large and spacious enough to *easily* accommodate trailers. Trailers and RVs are not recommended on back roads.

Vehicles more than 20 feet long may not enter Point Lobos State Reserve during weekends, school vacations, holidays, or during the summer from Memorial Day through Labor Day. Trailers and motor homes towing vehicles are not allowed in the park.

Is gas available along the Big Sur coast?

Yes, at Carmel Highlands, Big Sur Center, Loma Mar near the top of Post Hill, Gorda, Ragged Point Inn, and San Simeon Acres. It's wise to tank up before you leave Cambria or Carmel, however.

Are towing and auto service available at Big Sur?

Yes, from Big Sur Garage & Towing, in the Village Shops at Big Sur Center. A member of AAA, it offers twenty-four-hour emergency services, RV towing, auto repair, and tires; (831) 667–2181.

Will my cell phone work on Highway 1?

Don't count on it. I have found many long stretches without reception.

There are public phone booths at Point Lobos State Reserve, Carmel Highlands General Store, Andrew Molera State Park, throughout Big Sur Center,

Historical Highway Closures

The following table shows only major closures. Highway 1 was not designed as a four-season highway. Until the mid-1950s the state of California closed it to through-traffic every winter, which is why no major closures are noted earlier.

Location	Date	Cause	Duration of Repairs
South of Lucia	Aug 1952	Earthquake	6 weeks
Partington Point	Dec 1955	Washouts	8 months
South of Big Sur	Jan 1963	Flooding	2 weeks
Cape San Martin	Jan 1965	Landslide	10 days
South of Big Sur	Jan 1969	Mudslides	3 months
Redwood Gulch	Jan 1982	Landslide	1 month
Various places	Jan 1983	Landslides	More than 1 year
Redwood Gulch	Mar 1986	Landslide	68 days
South of Lucia	Jan 1993	Rockslide	3 months
Hot Springs Creek	Mar 1995	Landslide	1 week
Gorda	Jan 1997	Landslide	1 month
Various places	Jan 1998	Landslides	3 months
Hurricane Point	Mar 1999	Landslide	3 months
South of Lucia	Feb 2000	Landslide	More than 3 months

Pfeiffer Big Sur State Park, Big Sur Station, Loma Mar, Deetjen's, Julia Pfeiffer Burns State Park (McWay Canyon), Lucia Lodge, Limekiln State Park Campground, Sand Dollar Beach Picnic Area, Gorda, Ragged Point Inn, and the Hearst Castle visitor center.

May I camp overnight in a highway turnout?

No. Tired motorists can stop for a nap, but if you want to camp, find a campground.

What are the two most obnoxious types of driver on Highway 1?

Exhaustive scientific research has proven that the two most pernicious driver types along Highway 1 are the bullheaded road hog six cars ahead of you and that bratty hotshot 6 inches from your back bumper.

What to do about them? Well . . . Veteran road warriors won't like it, but my advice is: *Pull over.* If you have someone behind you who wants to go faster, just pull over, even if you are going the speed limit. Likewise, if you're stuck behind a slowpoke who won't give way, pull over, admire the views, cool down, then continue. Take it easy. Let your trip down Highway 1 be a pleasure drive, not a race. If time is pressing, take U.S. Highway 101 instead.

A Straightforward Drive Down Highway 1

Many people like to drive Big Sur without detours or stopping to smell the roses. Although I prefer to linger, I have driven straight through on many occasions. It's easily done, and it can be fun, especially in a classic convertible. Following is a quick synopsis of Highway 1, its ups and downs, some of its quirks, and its scenery in passing.

Note that I discuss most of these places in greater detail in chapter 3, Destinations Along Highway 1, and elsewhere in the book. Check the index.

Note also that all mileages (both below and in the Highway 1 Mileage Log at the end of this chapter) are measured from the Carmel River Bridge in the north, and the junction of Highway 1 and Cambria's Main Street (the northernmost junction) in the south. Directional turnoffs are given as "east" or "west" of the highway; remember that whether you're traveling north or south, west is always toward the ocean, and east is toward the mountains.

Carmel River to Malpaso Creek

4.5 miles; road gently rolling with no exposure to cliffs. Traffic between Carmel and Point Lobos can be very heavy, even stop-and-go, on weekends and on late afternoon in summer.

Leaving the Carmel Crossing shopping complex behind, you cross the Carmel River to Odello Fields, so named for the family who farmed this land for generations. Deeded to Carmel River State Park in 1995, the fields are being restored to wetlands for wildlife.

If you drive this stretch at dawn or dusk, watch out for wild pigs as they cross the highway to root for food in the abandoned fields. Wild boar are not native here. They were introduced for hunting in the 1920s by George Gordon Moore, owner of the San Carlos Ranch, and soon spread throughout the Santa Lucias. Moore once told a friend of killing a boar that measured 9 feet from head to toe. He found eleven bullets embedded in the animal's fat. The moral of this story: Drive carefully.

As you climb gently out of the Carmel Valley, you'll pass Monastery Beach on the west, named for the striking Carmelite Monastery on an eastern hill, built in 1931 in a Mediterranean style. The Carmelite nuns are an order sworn to silence and seclusion, but their church is open to visitors. The hills behind are preserved as part of Palo Corona Regional Park.

Seen from the Bird Island Trail, the Carmel Highlands seacoast looks like a cross between the Mediterranean and the Caribbean Seas.

Passing the gated entrance to Point Lobos State Reserve, Highway 1 winds through Carmel Highlands, an exclusive residential area heavily wooded with Monterey cypress and pine. From a passing car, the older houses below the road appear fantastic, a fleeting vision of terra-cotta walls, white granite, green trees, and blue coves. There are few pulloff points, but you're not meant to stop and gawk here. Although it has a small but classy general store and some excellent lodging prospects (including the famous Highlands Inn), Carmel Highlands is not geared up for tourism, as Carmel is.

Driving over the Wildcat Creek Bridge and past Yankee Point (concealed by a subdivision), the highway bridge across Malpaso Creek is a good place to mark your official entrance into Big Sur. From the bridge, you can glimpse the abrupt canyon that made early travel across so difficult and gave this spot its name: Bad Crossing. Look west for little Malpaso Beach.

Malpaso Creek to Palo Colorado Road

6.5 miles; road gently rolling, with mild exposure to low bluffs. Traffic usually up to full speed.

Now the houses and trees thin out, and the road runs along a broad marine terrace with vistas of grassy hills to the east, coastal bluffs to the west, and the wide blue Pacific Ocean stretching to the horizon. This is a granite coastline of deep, sharp-edged coves and many offshore rocks. There is no main entrance to Garrapata State Park, just a sign and a sequence of pullouts with access to coastal trails. The greatest concentration of cars is around Soberanes Canyon, marked by a line of Monterey cypress and a weathered barn. Trails lead east into the hills and west to Soberanes Point.

Meandering between the distinctive hump of Whale Peak and a spur ridge of Palo Corona, Highway 1 passes a lonely outpost of the California Department of Fish and Game before crossing the Granite Canyon Bridge. At Doud Creek a trail leads to Garrapata Beach. You'll leave the state park at Garrapata Creek, crossing on a 150-foot arched span built in 1932. After a cluster of houses around Rocky Point, pass a steep drive leading down to the coast-side Rocky Point Restaurant.

Just beyond, at the junction of Palo Colorado Road, is the site of Notley's Landing, a village that once thrived on cutting redwoods and tanbark oaks along the upper Palo Colorado Canyon. The wild little town lived to drink and carouse on Saturday nights, but spent the rest of the week processing and shipping out timber and tanbark, which townsfolk dropped in a chute from the bluff to waiting schooners in a cove. The town died after the timber was depleted in the first decade of the twentieth century, though bootleggers made good use of the dog-hole port during Prohibition. All that remains is the 1898 Swetman farmstead on the east side of the road (private).

Palo Colorado Road to Point Sur Light Station

7.5 miles; road makes steep climb and descent from Hurricane Point, with great exposure on high bridges and higher cliffs. Traffic usually fast.

Before climbing to your first bracing stretch of world-famous Big Sur cliffs, you need to cross two famous deck arch bridges. The first, Rocky Creek Bridge, is often mistaken for the larger Bixby Bridge, just ahead. No slouch itself, the 239-foot arch of Rocky Creek Bridge stands 150 feet above its creek.

But the Bixby Creek Bridge is almost shockingly larger. You discover it suddenly after a long turn around the site of old Bixby Landing. The Old Coast Road, an unpaved remnant of the first wagon road to Big Sur, departs inland

When completed in 1932, the Bixby Bridge saved drivers from a long detour up Bixby Canyon to cross the little creek.

from the bridge's north anchorage. More than 700 feet long and 260 feet above the creek, Bixby Bridge is the longest concrete arch bridge in the world, and probably the third most photographed bridge in California (after the Golden Gate and the Oakland Transbay Bridges). The highway crosses on a curve, with exciting views of the crashing surf only 285 feet below the roadbed. It's a beautiful, stupendous piece of engineering, and a monumental problem for acrophobia sufferers.

The Beat novelist Jack Kerouac, who stayed in a cabin in Bixby Creek Canyon, neatly summed up the fearsome scene while looking up from the creek (a point of view restricted by private property): "The blue sea behind the crashing high waves is full of huge black rocks rising like old ogresome castles dripping wet slime, a billion years of woe right there, the moogrus big clunk of it right there with its slaverous lips of foam at the base—So that you emerge from pleasant little wood paths with a stem of grass in your teeth and drop it to see doom—And you look up at that unbelievably high bridge and feel death."

Directly from the south anchorage, the road winds upward into the cliff country around Hurricane Point, climbing 335 feet in a bit more than a mile. The front ridge of Sierra Hill, Hurricane Point is the second highest point along Highway 1 at Big Sur. Pull over and take a look down 560 feet to the moogrus ocean, dotted with ogresome castles and crawling with slaverous surf. I have heard reports that there are also a number of wrecked cars at the base of this cliff, but I've never gone down to look. (Besides, it's private property.) There's a fine view southwest over the sandy beach at the mouth of the Little Sur River to the great rock lighthouse at Point Sur. Standing on Hurricane Point, I am reminded of a snatch of an ancient Costanoan song (the only surviving fragment that I know of): "Dancing on the brink of the world . . ." This being the southern frontier of the Costanoan world, I wonder if a place like this might have inspired such a song.

Descending quickly to the Little Sur River near its mouth, you'll catch a glimpse upcanyon to a beautifully framed view of Pico Blanco, sacred to the Esselen and Costanoan peoples. This valley, the hills, beach, and lagoon are all part of a private cattle ranch.

Curving up and out of the Little Sur Valley, Highway 1 turns into one of its longest stretches of straight and flat road as it enters a broad coastal terrace. Beyond a sandy plain, the large rock of Point Sur, capped by the Point Sur Light Station, rises 360 feet above sea level.

Point Sur Light Station to Pfeiffer Big Sur State Park

7.5 miles; road rolls gently, mostly through forest with no exposure to cliffs. Traffic usually fast, but slows for settlement in Big Sur Valley.

Highway 1 turns inland just south of Point Sur, where the southern end of the Old Coast Road meets Highway 1, across the road from the entrance to Andrew Molera State Park. Leave the coast, heading upstream beside the Big Sur River and inside the state park for 3.3 miles, passing from open grassland to redwood forest. Exiting the park, you'll emerge in the old village area of Big Sur, known to locals as Big Sur Center.

Big Sur Center is not a densely settled town by any stretch. It's a modest gathering of restaurants, general stores, campgrounds, lodging, resorts, and other small businesses spread along Highway 1 and centered on the Village Shops. The health clinic, chapels, auto mechanic, and Captain Cooper School all gather at Big Sur Center. This is where most locals come to relax.

Point Sur Light Station, which is still in use, was built atop the great rock at Point Sur to help deter shipwrecks on this foggy cape.

The post office used to be here, too, but it moved some 4 miles ahead to Loma Mar, on Post Hill, after the big mudslide of 1972 buried it. Big Sur Center rebuilt here because the resort business needs to stay put alongside the Big Sur River. The focus here is on family vacations, as opposed to the couples-oriented lodging in the "high-rent district" up near Posts.

Big Sur Center ends where Pfeiffer Big Sur State Park begins. Oldest of the region's state parks, it's also the most popular with campers and day-use visitors, a haven of trails, swimming holes, and the classic camping experience, complete with campfire programs.

Pfeiffer Big Sur State Park to the Coast Gallery

6.1 miles; road climbs steeply to Posts, followed by rolling terrain, with spectacular exposure to high cliffs. Traffic should slow through settled areas, but is generally fast. Beware of cars turning off and onto highway.

Crossing the Big Sur River, Highway 1 girds for a steady climb of about 750 feet, in 2.4 miles, to Posts. Almost immediately on the east side of the road, you will see the large sign for Big Sur Station—also known as the Multi-Agency Visitor Center—a clearinghouse for information and the trailhead for the famous Pine Ridge Trail. Passing the Sycamore Canyon Road turnoff to Pfeiffer Beach on the west, you'll climb steadily to the tiny settlement of Loma Mar, providing a post office, restaurant, general store, gasoline, and other businesses.

Posts is just beyond, near the top of the hill. At close to 1,000 feet above sea level, Post Hill is the highest point on Highway 1. Posts is named for the longtime pioneer family whose house still stands at the junction. The nearby Post Ranch Inn and Ventana Inn together cater to a wealthier clientele than the folksier riverside resorts of Big Sur Center.

Highway 1 leaves the Big Sur Valley after Posts, but the community of Big Sur continues for another 2 miles. You'll regain ocean views without the immediate cliffs, long perspectives down a corrugated coastline. Curving in and out between sunny ridgelines and canyons dark with redwoods, the highway skirts Nepenthe, a restaurant and cultural landmark, and the Henry Miller Library tucked in redwoods behind a fence in Mule Canyon. At Castro Canyon, Deetjen's Big Sur Inn flashes past.

Are you ready to tackle some more curves and cliffs? Some of the best cliffs on the entire coast are found at Grimes Point, where, on a sudden turn after Grimes Canyon, the ocean reappears at the bottom of a stunning drop, 770 feet beneath the roadbed. Here's where you separate the plains dwellers from the mountain staters. This is not because of guts, mind you, but because when people aren't used to driving along a bulldozed ledge with a vast hole gaping just beyond the passenger's door—a hole where they can see the very curvature of the earth—they sometimes get distracted. White-knucklers should take heart, for just ahead is Lafler Canyon, where the Coast Gallery sits back from the cliffs upon a wide shelf.

The Coast Gallery to Esalen

8.2 miles; rolling terrain generally descending to Esalen, with exposure to high cliffs. Traffic usually up to full speed.

Now you enter the more remote middle section of Big Sur. Passing Torre Canyon, you'll round the nose Partington Ridge, where author Henry Miller had a home. The precarious-looking access drive to the ridge is private property.

Rounding the ridge, you'll enter Julia Pfeiffer Burns State Park. There are two principal creeks in this park, Partington Creek and McWay Creek, both of which have popular trailheads. Partington Creek flows under Highway 1 beneath an earthen embankment (not a bridge) with plenty of parking room on the shoulder. This is a popular trailhead for both the Tanbark Trail and the short path to intriguing Partington Landing. As you drive the next 2-mile stretch to McWay, pay extra attention for pedestrians, because there are a lot of tight turns, a narrow shoulder, and a well-used whale-watching vista point and trailhead en route. The state park's entrance station is at McWay Creek, a popular picnic and hiking area. The most famous sight here is McWay Falls, which drops into a cove near Saddle Rock, a very easy stroll from the parking area.

Leaving the state park, cross back to private property at Anderson Creek, where a former highway builders' camp housed convict laborers. Henry Miller and a colony of artists later took over the facility. From here the highway makes a fairly straight and level run down to Hot Springs Creek, followed by the turnoff to the Esalen Institute, a private institute offering seminars, lectures, and classes pertaining to the Human Potential Movement, and home of the famous hot springs on a cliff above the breakers.

Esalen to Lucia

9.7 miles; rolling terrain, with great exposure to high cliffs. Traffic usually up to full speed.

Skirting John Little State Reserve, which offers no public access, Highway 1 offers distant views to blockish Dolan Rock, believed to be a boundary marker between Esselen territory and the Salinan district of Quiquilit. Though it appears insignificant on the map, on the ground you can see that it makes a fine marker between two unfriendly peoples, since it's very obviously visible for miles, and approach by land is steep and difficult. The old coastal trail that passed here kept high on the ridge.

The first major creek south of Dolan Rock is Big Creek, a scientific preserve managed by University of California as the Landels-Hill Big Creek Reserve. It's hard to appreciate the beauty of the double-arch bridge that crosses the mouth of Big Creek until you drive a mile or so farther down Highway 1, where you can look back from a turnout north of Gamboa Point. It appears very frail and frighteningly exposed to the ocean. In winter and spring you can also see an unnamed waterfall falling to the strand in the foreground.

At Lopez Point the coastline bends very sharply inland to Lucia, a tiny community perched on a steep slope. The highway here runs east–west for a short stretch. Looking south across the bight shaped by Cape San Martin (known to locals as Lucia Bay), you can easily see Pacific Valley, a beeline of 8 miles across the water. Not all of Lucia meets the eye from Highway 1. The Benedictine monks in the New Camaldoli Hermitage enjoy the solitary life on the hill above.

Lucia to Gorda

13 miles; rolling with many abrupt cliffs, great potential for falling rocks, and sinking roadbed. Traffic generally up to full speed.

Highway 1's own version of Scylla and Charybdis live just south of Lucia, where the road squeezes past Rain Rock, a crumbling wall covered in a kind of cable mesh. Meanwhile, as the mountain keeps falling onto the road, the roadbed keeps slipping into the ocean. Both problems seem to keep Caltrans in perpetual beans and gravy.

After running this dynamite-blasted gauntlet, Highway 1 makes a quick dash across the mouth of Limekiln Creek. The lime mined and processed up the creek was once shipped from Rockland Landing, a dog-hole port at the mouth of the creek. The coast, the creek, and the kilns are all preserved now as Limekiln State Park, a favorite for its redwood forests, waterfalls, trails, and easy shoreline access.

Beyond the border of the state park, Highway 1 passes into Los Padres National Forest. A 2-mile dash down the pavement brings you to the Nacimiento Road (east), the only paved road to cross the Santa Lucias from Big Sur. Kirk Creek Campground occupies a shelf on a bluff above the ocean; there's a trail to the rocky beach. Neighboring Mill Creek served as another desperate dog-hole port, where once longshoremen hoisted freight ashore from lighters with cable and windlass. Today it provides easy road access to the rocky shore, a put-in site for small ocean craft, and a fine picnic spot.

At Pacific Valley, the largest coastal terrace since Point Sur, Highway 1 settles in to a long, flat straightaway. Although the land on both sides is fenced, the Forest Service grants access through several stiles and gates, all linked by an extensive, unmarked web of footpaths. The tiny residential settlement at the north end of the valley is the former Pacific Valley Center Store, which closed

There are many beautiful coves along Highway 1. This is Jade Cove.

after burning. The settlement at the south end is the Pacific Valley Ranger Station; it dispenses information, but serves mainly as a fire station and guard post. Also on the east side of the highway, about a mile farther, you will find Plaskett Creek Campground, the Pacific Valley School (site of the annual Jade Festival), and the unpaved Plaskett Ridge Road. The coast side of Pacific Valley is especially interesting. Sand Dollar Beach is a large public beach. Adjacent Jade Cove is renowned for its cobbles and veins of nephrite jade.

Before leaving the breakers for another climb to the cliffs, Highway 1 dips to Willow Creek, where a short spur leads to rocky Willow Creek Beach on a cove popular with surfers. In the days of the Willow Creek mining boom, schooners used to land mining equipment at the creek mouth.

Ascending from the Willow Creek Bridge to Cape San Martin, Highway 1 passes the unpaved Willow Creek Road. As you round the corner toward

Gorda, look for the yurts of Treebones Resort on the eastern hillside. Founded during the Santa Lucia gold rush in 1887, the laid-back hamlet of Gorda gets its water from springs in the hillside behind, yielding a petite windfall of flowing water, fountains, and exotic gardens.

Gorda to San Carpoforo Creek

13.4 miles; rolling terrain climbing and then falling to San Carpoforo, with great exposure to cliffs. Traffic usually up to full speed.

Highway 1 drops to near sea level as it crosses Alder Creek, and then begins another climb, passing the Villa Creek and Cruikshank trailheads that lead inland to the Silver Peak Wilderness. Making a hairpin turn at Redwood Gulch, the southernmost grove of coast redwoods, the highway climbs to more than 800 feet above the ocean before descending slightly to Salmon Creek. As they head into this hairpin turn, motorists visiting during winter or spring will be treated to a startling view of Highway 1's biggest waterfall, Salmon Creek Falls. (Northbound motorists don't see it unless they pull over and look behind them.) Salmon Creek Falls is a rare sight—a double falls, where two streams meet and combine in midplummet. If you park in the turnout and walk back for a closer look, the roar of water, the drenching cloud, the rocks, and the oaks might remind you of a Sierra Nevada cataract.

Now passing through drier chaparral and scrub, Highway 1 enjoys its final flirtation with the great cliffs of Big Sur before dropping down to the gentler landscape around San Simeon. It's another spectacular session for motorists, who climb to more than 800 feet above the sea just before crossing from Monterey into San Luis Obispo County. The cliffside descent is over when you arrive at Ragged Point Inn, a large tourist development on a high, flat point of land that protrudes into the Pacific. It's surrounded by bluffs with spectacular views up and down the coast.

Beyond, Highway 1 descends quickly to San Carpoforo Creek, crossing it near sea level. (The Forest Service recently bought land on both sides of the highway near here, but won't promote public access until it can finish surveys.) San Carpoforo Creek and its deep canyon to the east emphatically mark the southern end of Big Sur. This is where explorer Gaspar de Portolà in 1769 and author J. Smeaton Chase in 1911 both turned inland to avoid Big Sur's cliffs. Writing of his journey, Chase observed that the creek's name is commonly butchered both in writing (*San Carpoco, San Carpojo, Zanjapoco,* or *Zanjapojo*), and in local pronunciation (*Sankypoko* or *Sankypoky*). All have merit, but regardless of what you call it, you are now leaving Big Sur.

21.1 miles; gently rolling, with almost no exposure to cliffs. Traffic can be fast, but sometimes clogs up around elephant seal vista points and Hearst Castle.

For its final jaunt into Cambria, Highway 1 rolls easily down a broad coastal terrace, flanked by low bluffs and beaches on the seaward side, and with full view of the Santa Lucia Range at a short distance inland. This superb grazing country, once ranched by Mission San Miguel, was later carved into Rancho Piedra Blanca and Rancho San Simeon. George Hearst bought them for his private ranch in the 1860s, and the Hearst Corporation (www.hearstranch conservation.org) still owns 128 square miles of land, right up to the eastern edge of Highway 1. It is closed to the public.

San Simeon State Park has recently acquired nearly all the land west of the highway from San Carpoforo Creek to Cambria. Despite some small breaks for San Simeon and other properties, this spectacular stretch of about 20 miles contains the longest coastline of any California state park. Crossing Arroyo de la Cruz on a low bridge, Highway 1 zooms past the Piedras Blancas Lighthouse to a 1.5-mile stretch of rocky beach colonized by elephant seals. Traffic typically slows here during winter breeding season, so beware of rubberneckers. At the south end, Arroyo Laguna Beach is famed among windsurfers.

The old village of San Simeon lies just west of Highway 1. When Hearst Castle was under construction on the hill above in the 1920s, building materials and priceless treasures were shipped to San Simeon's little harbor, the best-protected anchorage on the coast between Monterey and Morro Bay. A pier and beach are now protected as William Randolph Hearst Memorial State Beach. The Hearst Corporation still owns the village proper and maintains the right to develop it along plans originally designed by Julia Morgan, the architect of Hearst Castle. Historic Sebastian's Store is another local landmark. South of town is San Simeon Acres, a compact, modern assortment of motels, restaurants, and shops that caters to crowds visiting the castle.

After passing the developed section of San Simeon State Park, popular among campers, beachcombers, hikers, and birders, Highway 1 arrives at the outskirts of Cambria, by far the largest town since Carmel. Moonstone Beach, along Cambria's shoreline, proffers both sand and tide pools. For the charming center of Cambria, where you can find all amenities in abundance, turn east at a traffic light onto Main Street.

Highway 1 Mileage Log: From Carmel River or Cambria

Miles from Carmel River (heading south)	Destination	Miles from Cambria (heading north)
0.0	Carmel River Bridge	97.5
0.6	Carmel Meadows (Ribera Road); west	96.9
1.0	Missionary Beach; west	96.5
1.2	Carmelite nunnery; east	96.3
1.9	Point Lobos State Reserve; west	95.6
2.7	Carmel Highlands store; east	94.8
3.1	Highlands Drive; east	94.4
4.1	Yankee Point Drive; west	93.4
4.5	Malpaso Creek Bridge	93.0
5.2	north boundary, Garrapata State Park	92.3
6.6	Soberanes Canyon trailhead; east	90.9
6.9	Whaleback Peak; west	90.6
7.8	California Department of Fish and Game; west	89.7
8.0	Granite Creek Bridge	89.5
9.2	Marker 19, to Garrapata Beach; west	88.3
9.4	Garrapata Creek Bridge	88.1
10.4	Rocky Point turnoff; west	87.1
11.0	Palo Colorado Road; east	86.5
12.5	Rocky Creek Bridge	85.0
13.0	Old Coast Road turnoff; east	84.5
13.1	Bixby Bridge	84.4
14.3	Hurricane Point; west	83.2
16.4	Little Sur River	81.1
18.5	Point Sur Light Station gate; west	79.0
18.9	Point Sur Naval Facility gate; west	78.6
21.5	Old Coast Road turnoff; east	76.0
21.5	Andrew Molera State Park; west	76.0
22.7	Highbridge Waterfall trailhead; east	74.8
23.3	Captain Cooper School entrance; east	74.2
24.0	River Inn Resort; west	73.5
24.0	Village Shops, Big Sur Center; west	73.5
24.3	Big Sur Campground and Cabins; west	73.2

(Continued)

Miles from Carmel River (heading south)	Destination	Miles from Cambria (heading north)
24.4	Riverside Campground and Cabins; west	73.1
24.7	Ripplewood Resort; west	72.8
24.7	Glen Oaks Motel and Restaurant; east	72.8
25.1	St. Francis of the Redwoods Catholic Church; west	72.4
25.3	Fernwood Park Resort; west	72.2
26.0	Pfeiffer Big Sur State Park; east	71.5
26.2	Big Sur River Bridge	71.3
26.4	Big Sur Station (Multi-Agency Facility); east	71.1
27.2	Sycamore Canyon Road (Pfeiffer Beach turnoff); west	70.3
27.7	Big Sur Post Office and store (Loma Mar); east	69.8
27.8	Loma Mar (gas station, bakery, restaurant); west	69.7
28.3	Old Post Ranch (turnoff to Ventana Inn); east	69.2
28.3	Post Ranch Inn turnoff; west	69.2
28.4	Coastlands; west	69.1
29.0	Nepenthe; west	68.5
29.3	Henry Miller Library (Graves Canyon); east	68.2
29.7	Deetjen's (Castro Canyon); east	67.8
32.1	Coast Gallery; Boronda Trail; east	65.4
33.2	Torre Canyon Bridge	64.3
34.0	DeAngulo trailhead; east	63.5
34.3	Partington Ridge Road (private); east	63.1
35.1	Partington Canyon (Partington Landing and Tanbark Trail trailheads)	62.4
36.0	Large Vista Point (west); fire road trail to Tin House (east)	61.5
37.1	McWay Creek; Pfeiffer Burns State Park main entrance; east	60.4
37.6	Anderson Creek Bridge	59.9
38.7	Burns Creek Bridge	58.8
39.3	Buck Creek Bridge	58.2
40.3	Esalen Institute; west	57.2
40.7	Lime Creek Bridge	56.8
41.8	Dolan Creek Bridge	55.7

Miles from Carmel River (heading south)	Destination	Miles from Cambria (heading north)
42.9	Rat Creek Bridge	54.6
43.4	Dolan Rock (offshore)	54.1
45.0	Big Creek Bridge	52.5
46.8	Gamboa Point; west	50.7
47.3	Vicente Creek Bridge	50.2
49.1	Lopez Point; west	48.4
50.1	Lucia	47.4
50.6	New Camaldoli Monastery entrance; east	46.9
52.2	Limekiln State Park	45.3
54.1	Vicente Flat trailhead; east	43.4
54.1	Kirk Creek Campground; west	43.4
54.2	Nacimiento Road; east	43.3
54.5	Mill Creek Bridge	43.0
57.2	Pacific Valley, public stile 1; west	40.3
57.9	Prewitt Loop trailhead (north end); east	39.6
58.5	Pacific Valley Station and Prewitt Loop Trail (south end); east	39.0
59.4	Sand Dollar Beach parking and picnic area; west	38.1
59.5	Plaskett Creek Campground; Pacific Valley School; east	38.0
59.6	Plaskett Ridge Road; east	37.9
60.0	Jade Cove turnout; stile on west	37.5
61.5	Willow Creek Bridge and Beach	36.0
62.0	Cape San Martin; west	35.5
62.1	Willow Creek Road and Treebones Resort turnoff; east	35.4
63.0	Gorda	34.5
65.5	Alder Creek Bridge	32.0
66.2	Villa Creek Bridge	31.3
66.8	Cruikshank trailhead; east	30.7
67.8	Redwood Gulch; Nathaniel Owing Memorial Redwood Grove; east	29.7
69.5	Soda Springs Trail; east	28.0

(Continued)

Miles from Carmel River (heading south)	Destination	Miles from Cambria (heading north)
71.0	Buckeye Trail (next to old ranger station on north side of highway)	26.5
71.1	Salmon Creek Bridge and trailhead	26.4
73.6	Monterey–San Luis Obispo County line	23.9
75.0	Ragged Point Inn	22.5
76.4	San Carpoforo Creek Bridge	21.1
80.8	Arroyo de la Cruz Bridge	16.7
82.7	Piedras Blancas settlement	14.8
84.1	Piedras Blancas Light Station; west	13.4
85.1	northern elephant seal vista point; west	12.4
85.4	middle elephant seal vista point; west	12.1
86.4	southern elephant seal vista point; west	11.1
87.5	Arroyo Laguna Bridge	10.0
89.2	northern turnoff to old San Simeon; west	8.3
90.2	W. R. Hearst Memorial Beach turnoff; west	7.3
90.2	Hearst Castle entrance; east	7.3
93.3	San Simeon Acres (north end of motel strip)	4.2
93.7	San Simeon Acres (south end of motel strip)	3.8
94.8	San Simeon Creek Road; east	2.7
95.1	San Simeon Creek Bridge	2.4
95.3	Washburn Day Use Area; east	2.2
95.7	north end of Moonstone Beach Road; west	1.8
97.5	Main Street, Cambria; turnoff to the east	0.0

Chapter 3
Destinations Along Highway 1

The traditional focus of Big Sur recreation is family-oriented outdoor fun: hiking, fishing, nature study, splashing in a creek, sightseeing, and so on. Private resorts located along the Big Sur River pioneered local tourism. The string of state parks and federal recreation areas that spread down the coast in the twentieth century had a dual mandate: outdoor fun and natural preservation.

A more recent trend in tourism at Big Sur caters to couples on a higher budget, and with more urbane tastes. In addition to being a family vacation spot, Big Sur is now advertised as a romantic getaway, a haven for pampered guests. This newer breed of Big Sur vacationers may be no less keen to hike and sightsee than traditional vacationers, but at the end of the day, they want to return to a self-contained resort with spa, sophisticated dining, and stylish lodging facilities. Post Ranch Inn and Ventana Inn exemplify this newer trend in Big Sur vacations. At these resorts, located far up Post Hill from the Big Sur River, grand vistas of ocean and mountain trump river frontage and redwood forest. Fortunately, this upmarket trend has not replaced the traditional folksy, family-oriented focus of Big Sur. It just adds another dimension.

Many of the hikes that are mentioned in this chapter are described in more detail in chapter 5, Hiking the Trails of Big Sur; see the index or table of contents to find these fuller descriptions. Keep in mind that the Big Sur coastline is very dangerous for swimmers and waders. (Hearst Memorial Beach is one exception.) Experienced surfers, divers, and kayakers do enter the water, of course, but it is your responsibility to judge your own abilities, and to use common sense.

The Big Sur Chamber of Commerce has an excellent Web site showcasing Big Sur lodging, restaurants, campgrounds, parks, beaches, and more: www.big surcalifornia.org.

Parks

Carmel River State Beach

Beaches, wildlife-watching, picnics, hiking, historical sites, photography, nature study, tide pools, horseback riding, river canoeing, diving, kayaking. No fishing. Dangerous surf warning.

The Carmel River has long been an important landmark. It was the center of the world for the Rumsien (a Costanoan triblet) for thousands of years. When voyager Sebastián Vizcaíno came ashore here for game and water in 1602, he named it Río del Carmelo. Explorer Gaspar de Portolà camped here, and Father Junípero Serra chose it for his mission headquarters. The state park buffers the Carmel River's outlet with a 1.5-mile stretch of shoreline. The surf is treacherous for swimming or wading. The brackish lagoon behind the beach provides food and lodging for local and migratory birds. Trails along both shores prove popular with birders, hikers, and horseback riders. Kayakers sometimes paddle on the river when it runs high.

Locals divide the beach into three sections. Carmel River State Beach, reached from Scenic Drive in Carmel, lies north of the river and includes some sand dunes. During dry months the river channel is blocked with a sandbar and you can walk the length of the park, but when the river flows full enough to break through, Carmel River Beach is cut off from its sister beaches to the south.

Middle Beach stretches from the Carmel River south to a small, rocky, granite headland. The closest approach is a pedestrian gate on Ribera Road in the Carmel Meadows subdivision. The highest point of the park is Cross Hill, where Portolà placed a large cross as a landmark to attract attention from a Spanish supply ship. When the Spanish returned, they found that the native Rumsien, having watched the Spaniards' strict obeisance before it, were themselves placing food offerings before it. A modern cross commemorates the original.

Monastery Beach, also known as San Jose Creek Beach, is southernmost. There's plenty of parking on the shoulder of Highway 1. A fence blocks direct access to Point Lobos State Reserve from the beach. The Carmel Trench of the Monterey Submarine Canyon drives close to shore here, allowing whales and other deep-sea creatures to approach, and no doubt over the centuries feeding the local sea-monster stories of the adjacent Point Lobos Peninsula. Scuba divers find Monastery Beach a convenient entry point for exploring this drop-off. A ghostly lady in a tattered gown is said to walk this sector of Highway 1 at night. (831) 649–2836; www.parks.ca.gov.

Point Lobos State Reserve

Fee area. Hiking, guided walks, wildlife-watching, photography, nature study, historical museum, natural history exhibits, beaches, diving, kayaking, picnics. Dangerous surf warning.

Point Lobos is the granite peninsula that forms the southern shore of Carmel Bay. Landscape painter Francis McComas called it "the greatest meeting of

Point Lobos marks the southern edge of Carmel Bay.

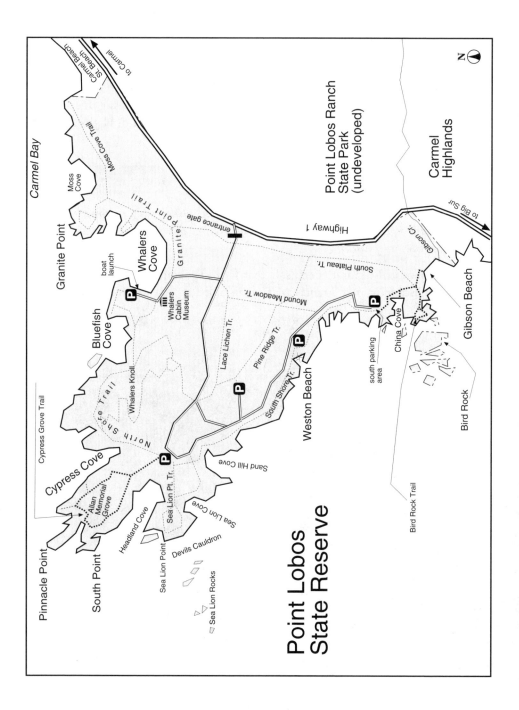

Point Lobos
State Reserve

land and water in the world," and indeed it is a hauntingly beautiful landscape of narrow coves, rough seas, monumental headland, and mysterious forest. Sea life and kelp forests abound in its waters, and visitors can spot whales and otters from the shore. Its offshore rocks nurture colonies of baying sea lions that gave the place its name—El Punta de los Lobos Marinos, literally "sea wolf point." It's a place of mystery, myth, and inspiration for countless storytellers, artists, filmmakers, and writers, including Robert Louis Stevenson, who used the dramatic physical setting for Spyglass Hill in *Treasure Island*. During summer, especially on weekends, the park can be very crowded.

Point Lobos was part of an 1839 land grant to Marcelino Escobar, who called it Rancho San José y Sur Chiquito. Legend says that Escobar's heir, José Abrigo, lost it in a game of dice to a soldier named Castro. True or not, it never amounted to much as cattle pasture. The rock and sea proved more valuable. The harbor at Whalers Cove served successively as home port for Chinese fishermen, Portuguese whalers, and Japanese abalone divers. A shellfish cannery stood on its shore. Whalers Cove also served as a harbor for shipping coal from Malpaso Canyon and stone quarried from its own granite shoreline. The Whalers Cabin Museum recalls all these maritime enterprises. Today all sea life is protected by state law, and only certified divers can explore the rich submarine gardens of Whalers Cove and nearby Bluefish Cove.

Park roads take you to within strolling distance from any point in the park, including Whalers Cove, but to see most interesting sights, you need to hike. None of the trails is very long or strenuous, but if you link two or more, you can make a more demanding hike. For an overview of the park, ascend Whalers Knoll, where Portuguese whalers once kept lookout for migrating behemoths. Hikes along the north shore, Granite Point, and Moss Cove Trails provide fine views of Carmel and its bay and the Monterey Peninsula. The Sea Lion Point Trail delivers exciting views of the churning sea in the channel known as Devils Cauldron. All of the coastal hikes are good for otter-watching. The two most scenic walks in the park are along the Cypress Grove and Bird Rock Trails; each is shorter than a mile, round trip.

Malpaso Beach

Most locals claim that Malpaso Creek marks the northern end of Big Sur. Until it was bridged, its deep cleft posed a real problem for travelers—hence the name of *Bad Crossing*. See for yourself by walking the path to the little cove and beach at the mouth of the creek. At low tide you will also find some tide pools and a narrow cave that you can squeeze through to an even tinier beach. The informal, unmarked path to Malpaso Beach leaves from the south end of Yankee Point Drive.

Across the highway from the park entrance, Point Lobos Ranch State Park climbs up into the Santa Lucia foothills. As yet undeveloped, it will one day add greatly to the variety and length of hiking possibilities in the Point Lobos area. Route 1, Box 62, Carmel, CA 93923; (831) 624–4909; www.parks.ca.gov, www.pointlobos.org, or http://pt-lobos.parks.state.ca.us.

Garrapata State Park

Hiking, fishing, wildlife-watching, tide pools, beaches, picnics, photography, nature study, mountain biking. Dangerous surf warning.

This park has neither a visitor center nor a main entrance, but Highway 1 passes through it for about 4 miles on a marine terrace. Even just driving through, the scenery is nice, with wide-open views of the low coastal bluffs. Still, there's more than meets the eye from the road, where you'll receive no clue that thick redwood forests grow just a few hundred yards inland from the grasslands and scrub that line the highway. Only by parking on the shoulder and walking through one of the openings in the fence can you get a closer look at Garrapata's rocky shore, wide beach, high ridges, and lush forests. The Park Service marks these gates with numbered posts, starting at the north end with 1 and ending with 19 in the south.

Serious hikers can make a strenuous 4-mile loop incorporating the Soberanes Canyon and Rocky Ridge Trails, enjoying far-reaching views and a lush redwood forest. For easier views, you can walk up Whale Peak, a distinctive hogback that rises abruptly from the west side of Highway 1. The easiest walks follow along the marine terraces around Soberanes Point. These bluffs make good platforms for viewing otters, whales, birds, and pinnipeds, while fishermen play out long lines from the bluffs into the deep granite channels. Mountain bikers have one option in this park: the Rocky Ridge Trail. For all these trails, park at turnouts on the east side of the highway near the row of trees and an old barn, remains of the old Soberanes homestead. This area lies between marker 7 and marker 11, but the barn itself is at marker 8.

Garrapata Beach is unsafe for swimming or wading, but it makes a beautiful spot for beachcombing or a picnic. It also offers some tide pooling at low tide. To get there, park at the turnout at marker 19, about 0.2 mile north of Garrapata Bridge. Go through the gate and follow the trail to the bluff. From there, a stairway leads to the beach. Another trail skirts 0.6 mile along the edge of the bluff, meeting Doud Creek at the halfway point, where you can cross the creek to continue north along the bluffs, or cut down to the beach on another short path.

Walkers should keep in mind that *garrapata* is the Spanish word for "tick." Poison oak is also common. (831) 624–4909; www.parks.ca.gov.

Rocky Point Open Space

Wildlife-watching, photography.

Monterey County owns this small parcel of rocky coast at the bottom of the short but steep road down from Highway 1 to the adjacent Rocky Point Restaurant. Looking south across the bight, many people mistake the large, graceful arch for Bixby Bridge. In fact, it's Rocky Creek Bridge. Bixby is hiding behind a hill.

Point Sur Light Station State Historic Park

Fee area. Historical site, guided walk, wildlife-watching, photography, nature study.

Sitting atop a massive volcanic rock that juts 361 feet above the Pacific, Point Sur Light Station casts a beacon that can be seen 24 miles out to sea, and from higher ridges of the Santa Lucia and Santa Cruz Mountains up to 50 miles away. Lonely night drivers winding along Highway 1 between Hurricane Point and Molera State Park find themselves playing a kind of hide-and-seek vigil with its haunting, periodic flashes. Poet Robinson Jeffers described it as a "phantasmagoric situation on a round rock three or four hundred feet high."

A functional symbol of the dangers of this remote, perilous coastline, the Point Sur Light Station served as home to four lighthouse keepers (simultaneously) and their families from 1889 to 1974. It is now fully automated and a part of the California State Park system. At scheduled times volunteer docents lead visitors by foot to the top of the rock for a tour of the lighthouse and other historical buildings. One of the most sublime vista points anywhere on the Pacific coast, the rock itself provides spectacular views of ocean and coastline, a broad, graceful sweep of white sand beach (part of Rancho El Sur), and a striking perspective of Pico Blanco aloft in the Santa Lucias. With binoculars it's ideal for spotting pelagic birds, whales, and sea otters.

Life atop this rock was challenging. Water had to be pumped up to a cistern atop the rock from a well on the flats. All building materials, including the sandstone building blocks cut from the Santa Lucias, had to be winched up to the top of the rock by steam-powered tramway. Until the narrow access road was built in 1900, supplies came mostly by sea and had to hoisted up from the rolling deck of a skiff. When keepers decided to plant their own vegetable garden, they first had to haul their own soil up. One kept a dairy cow for fresh milk; others tied their chickens to the rock to keep them from blowing away. A picket fence surrounding the dwellings kept children from falling overboard. The children went to school in a one-room schoolhouse built next to Highway

1, and their teacher also lived on the rock. No doubt one of the most trying aspects of living at Point Sur was the steam whistle, which blew a five-second blast every thirty-five seconds, day or night, whenever the fog rolled in.

The Central Coast Lighthouse Keepers are restoring the buildings. Their docents lead visitors through the lighthouse, climbing the spiral stairway to the lantern room and surrounding outside catwalk. A rotating aero beacon currently serves in place of the original 10,000-pound Fresnel lens, which was moved for temporary safekeeping to the Maritime Museum in Monterey. (Shipped from France, the lens was delivered here by mistake, gladly received, and quickly installed, though it was in fact ordered by Pigeon Point Lighthouse, up the coast in San Mateo County.) The residential buildings stand on the crest of the rock, along with the still-furnished blacksmith and carpentry shop. The largest building, the triplex, housed three of the four resident families and is said to be haunted at night by a teenage girl who suffers from a hacking cough, despite having been dead for the better part of a century.

Another residence serves as the state park visitor center, where a small display recounts the history of the *Macon*, a navy dirigible that crashed south of here in February 1935. Seven hundred eighty-five feet in length and filled with helium, this remarkable airship carried a crew of eighty-three and a small squadron of reconnaissance biplanes that could be launched and retrieved in midair by the *Macon* crew. As lighthouse tenders watched helplessly from this rock, the great airship, battered by a squall, fell to the ocean and sank in forty minutes. All but two of the crew were rescued. Divers have recently located the wreckage and brought up remnants, some of which (including dinner plates) are on display here.

Docents lead three-hour tours (fee) year-round on Saturday at 10:00 A.M. and 2:00 P.M., and Sunday at 10:00 A.M. From April through October they add a fourth tour on Wednesday at 10:00 A.M. and 2:00 P.M. In July and August they add a fifth tour at 10:00 A.M. on Thursday. From April through October docents also lead special moonlight tours that introduce some Point Sur ghost stories; phone for times. Tours are limited to forty people, and there are no reservations. Show up outside the locked gate on Highway 1, 7.9 miles north of Big Sur Station and 18.5 miles south of the Carmel River Bridge. Big Sur Station #1, Big Sur, CA 93920; (831) 625–4419; www.parks.ca.gov, www.light housefriends.com, or www.pointsur.org.

Andrew Molera State Park

Fee area. Hiking, camping, guided walks, wildlife-watching, photography, nature study, horseback riding, historical sites, picnics, beaches, kayaking, canoeing, river sports, mountain biking, surfing. Dangerous surf warning.

Big Sur's largest state park protects the mouth and lower valley of the Big Sur River. Although Highway 1 cuts through the park for 3.2 miles, its most magnificent features—spectacular Molera Beach and the views from Molera Point headlands—are accessible only by hiking, biking, riding a horse, or floating the river. A rich variety of natural habitats, including redwood forests, meadows, the Big Sur lagoon, a spectacular beach, high ridges, coastal bluffs, rocky shoreline, and riparian woodlands, makes this 4,766-acre park a prime destination for naturalists, birders, and wildlife-watchers. Hikers and cyclists can stay at the walk-in (or bike-in) Trail Camp, 0.3 mile from the central parking area.

The central parking area has a restroom, picnic area, and ranger kiosk. It's a short stroll to the Molera Ranch House Museum, the Molera Stables, and the

Pico Blanco rises on the horizon above beach-bound equestrians in Andrew Molera State Park.

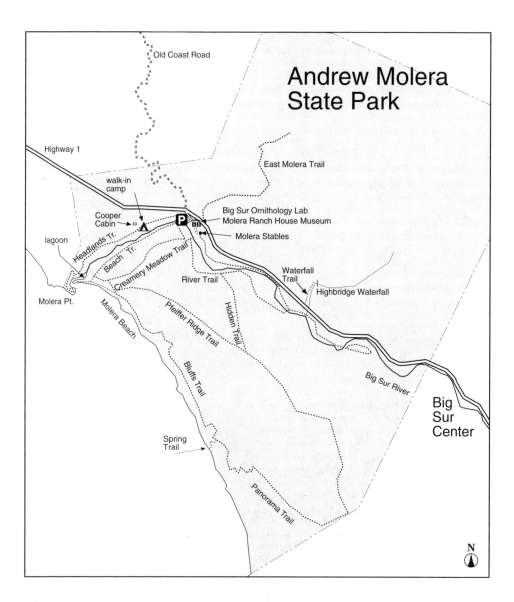

Ventana Wilderness Society's Big Sur Ornithology Lab. Dogs must be leashed, and are restricted to the main parking area and the unpaved road to the Molera Ranch complex. On summer weekends the rangers offer public programs with a historical or nature-oriented theme. Morning visitors to the ornithology lab can sometimes watch bird banding. The Molera Ranch House Museum (also known as the Big Sur Cultural and Natural History Center) opens weekends from 11:00 A.M. through 3:00 P.M., when docents are available.

Equestrians can rent mounts at Molera Stables and take guided tours of various length and difficulty, but all rides go to Molera Beach. Walk-ins and beginners are welcome, and private trips are available. (831) 625–5486 or (800) 942–5486; www.molerahorsebacktours.com.

The Big Sur River flows through the heart of the park. You can cross the river on a small plank bridge from the central parking area during low-water times, but the bridge is removed during the rainy season, when you must wade or forgo crossing. (There are plans to build a permanent footbridge.) During warm months when the river is lazy, families come for splashing and inner tubing. When the Big Sur runs high, canoeists put in at the central parking area for a 1.2-mile trip (one way) to its mouth. A sandbar blocks the mouth of the river during dry months. Sea kayakers launch from Molera Beach.

More than 20 miles of trails lead to all corners of the park. Molera Beach, wild and windswept, is a favorite among beachcombers—but be aware of incoming tides. The Headlands Trail to Molera Point is also popular for its awesome views.

Other easy trails follow the Big Sur River upstream through game-rich woodlands and redwood forests. An ambitious loop follows the Ridge Trail up Pfeiffer Ridge, returning via the Panorama and Bluff Trails. Far less well known are the trails east of Highway 1: the challenging Molera Trail, which zigzags through chaparral to a high point on the Coast Ridge, and the Waterfall Trail. Mountain bikes are restricted to the Ridge Trail, Beach Trail, and Creamery Meadow Trail. You may walk your bike along the path to Trail Camp. Big Sur Station #1, Big Sur, CA 93920; (831) 667–2315; www.parks.ca.gov.

Pfeiffer Big Sur State Park

Fee area. Hiking, guided walks, camping, lodge, stores, restaurant, gift shop, swimming holes, river sports, wildlife-watching, picnics, campfire program, historical sites, backpacking, nature study, photography, field sports.

This is Big Sur's oldest, busiest, and most developed state park. For generations of California kids, this is the place that comes to mind when someone mentions *Big Sur.* Its campground has all the feel of a classic American summer vacation: the tang of campfire smoke, the hiss of Coleman lanterns, the exquisite joy of spending all afternoon by the river building cobble dams and sailing leaf-and-acorn boats. In season there are guided walks, ranger programs, and nighttime campfire programs. There's even a softball field next to the large picnic grounds. Pfeiffer Big Sur State Park has extensive redwood forests, oak woodland, chaparral, meadow, and riparian zones, nurturing a host of animals and birds, including condors, water ouzels, cougars, bobcats, deer, raccoons, skunks,

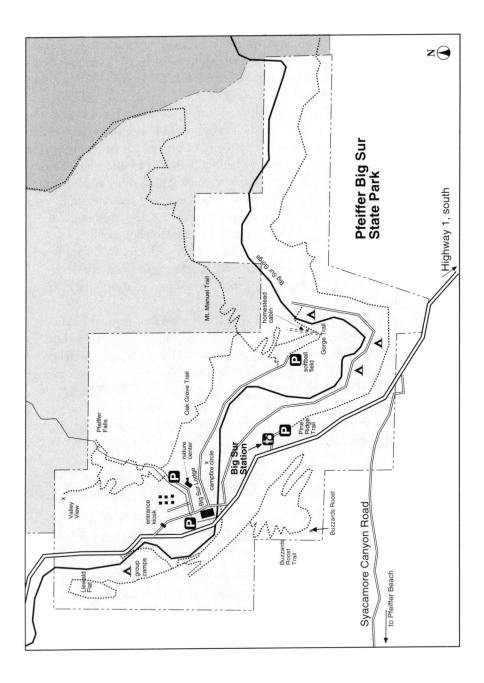

Pfeiffer Big Sur State Park

N

Highway 1, south

Syacamore Canyon Road

to Pfeiffer Beach

Mt. Manuel Trail

Big Sur Gorge

homestead cabin

Gorge Trail

softball field

Oak Grove Trail

Pfeiffer Falls

nature center

Big Sur Lodge

campfire circle

Big Sur Station

Pine Ridge Trail

Valley View

entrance kiosk

group camps

Liewald Flat

Buzzards Roost

Buzzards Roost Trail

and squirrels. The Ernst Ewoldsen Memorial Nature Center, open seasonally, provides a good overview of local wildlife.

The Big Sur River is the center of attention. One of the most beloved of Big Sur swimming holes sits smack at the head of the campground, where the narrow gorge opens wide and the last bridge crosses the river. Scrambling up the gorge is a rite of passage for generations of kids, their chance to explore, climb rocks, and look for new pools to conquer with a splashing cannonball. I hate to play the nagging adult here, but do be careful when you go up the so-called Gorge Trail, which is more like a 0.3-mile (one-way) scramble over and around roots, rocks, and river. The rocks are slippery, the constricted cascades run swift and deep, and the river swells when it rains upstream. Know your limits, turn around when you encounter rock walls too high to climb safely, wear your stream shoes, and don't you *dare* splash your sister.

Not everyone who stays at this park is a camper. Big Sur Lodge offers very comfortable motel-style cabins, as well as a swimming pool, restaurant, ice cream counter, and gift shop. There is a year-round grocery store at the lodge and a summer-only store in the campground. Condors often roost during winter in the large snag just outside the lodge lobby. The current lodge is a direct descendant of Pfeiffer's Ranch Resort, a tourist hostelry run by Florence Pfeiffer, whose family sold the land for a state park in 1933.

Leashed dogs are allowed in the campground and day-use areas only. Bicyclists may use the roads, but not the trails. There are campsites set aside expressly for cyclists passing through the park.

Pfeiffer Big Sur is a hiker's park. Trails range from the easy, self-guided nature trail to the unrelenting climb up Mount Manual, where hikers are rewarded with fine views across the Ventana Wilderness. The Pfeiffer family homesteaded this area in 1869, and one of their original homestead cabins still stands above the river, a short walk from the Gorge Trail. Of the middle-range hikes, the most popular goes to Pfeiffer Falls, in the midst of the redwoods. The Oak Grove Trail and Buzzards Roost Trail climb through a variety of terrains, from redwoods to chaparral. Big Sur Station #1, Big Sur, CA 93920; (831) 667–2315; www.parks.ca.gov.

Big Sur Station (Multiagency Facility)

Information, restrooms, trailhead parking.

The main building houses offices for the California Department of Parks and Recreation, (831) 677–2315; the USDA Forest Service, (831) 667–2423; and Caltrans (831) 667–2173. Rangers staffing the front desk can consequently answer most questions that you might dredge up about roads and recreation at Big Sur. They also sell maps and books. The Pine Ridge Trail starts from this point, and there is plenty of parking for backpackers. If you are taking your dog along this trail into the national forest, you are permitted to cross through Pfeiffer Big Sur State Park with your dog on a leash.

Pfeiffer Beach

Fee area. Beach walking, picnics, wildlife-watching, fishing, surfing, tide pools. Dangerous surf warning.

Backed by bluffs and shielded from the ocean (in part) by a flotilla of rocks and sea stacks, this spectacular beach is arguably the finest-looking readily accessible strand along the Big Sur coast. Waves have worn a large cave right through the largest rock, a marvelous sight when the setting sun lights it up. There are some tide pools on the north end of the beach. Swimming and wading are dangerous. Your dog is welcome on Pfeiffer Beach.

To get there from Highway 1, turn off at Sycamore Canyon Road, which is short but too narrow for trailers and RVs. This is the heart of Pfeiffer country. The old ranch house, a private home, still stands in a side canyon. Pfeiffer Beach is part of Los Padres National Forest, but its management is contracted to a private company, which collects a parking fee.

Julia Pfeiffer Burns State Park

Hiking, guided walks, environmental camping, creek play, wildlife-watching, picnics, historical sites, picnics, nature study, photography, diving, kayaking, tide pools. Dangerous surf warning.

This precipitous park clings to a slope that rises from sea level to more than 4,000 feet over a distance of about 2 miles. The coast is lined with granite and metamorphic bluffs, while deep stream canyons, wooded with redwood and tanbark oak, tumble down from the mountains. It's hard to think of such rugged property in commercial terms, but it has sustained both cattle ranching and logging operations, as well as a remarkable shipping port at Partington Landing. The park's underwater portion attracts experienced divers, but its most famous feature is McWay Falls, which drops from a bluff into the surf. Highway 1 enters the park at Partington Creek on the north end and exits 2.5 miles south, just before Anderson Creek.

Highway 1 crosses Partington Creek on a wide embankment, where there is plenty of shoulder space for parking. On the west side Partington Landing Trail leads steeply down to the rocky shore, where a tunnel bores through the ridge to the tight little harbor. On the east, the Tan Bark Trail winds up through the enchanting redwood forests of Partington Creek's canyon.

Pfeiffer Beach is one of the few strands at Big Sur that has a road going right to it.

Park headquarters comprises a parking area, trailhead, and picnic grounds along cascading McWay Creek. The little Canyon Trail leads 0.3 mile upstream to a lovely waterfall in the redwood forest. The longer Ewoldsen Trail makes a more ambitious semi-loop through a wider range of habitats, with views.

Downstream, the paved, wheelchair-accessible Waterfall Trail slips 0.1 mile under Highway 1 to a cliffside viewpoint overlooking McWay Falls. The creek drops 80 feet over a metamorphic bluff into a luminous green cove bounded by a white beach and conspicuous Saddle Rock. From this junction the Overlook Trail leads north about 200 yards to the garden terrace of the McWay Waterfall House. Once owned by Lathrop Brown and his wife, Helen, the house was demolished when the couple gave their property to the state in 1962, leaving nothing but a fenced garden with spectacular views up and down the coast, along with a few thriving exotic plants. If you turn south from the McWay Falls viewpoint, the Overlook Trail rounds the wooded ridge to a cypress-shaded level spot above Saddle Rock, once an Esselen encampment and now the site of two environmental camps. Big Sur Station #1, Big Sur, CA 93920; (831) 667–2315; www.parks.ca.gov.

Limekiln State Park

Fee area. Hiking, beach, camping, creek play, wildlife-watching, picnics, historical sites, nature study, photography, tide pools, fishing. Dangerous surf warning.

Limekiln Creek cuts a canyon so narrow through the coast-side cliffs that if you sneeze with even a modicum of extravagance while driving across the Highway 1 bridge, you might well miss it. It's worth the little detour, however, if only for the vista of Cone Peak from below the bridge. No other view along Big Sur gives so profound a notion of the scale of these mountains: The 3.2-mile bee-line between your sea-level position and the 5,155-foot summit is the steepest coastal gradient in the continental United States. And it looks it.

Limekiln State Park is worth visiting for many other reasons, too. The cobble beach, which offers one of the jolliest rock faces to be seen anywhere, was once an almost ludicrous "harbor" known as Rockland Landing. The landing shipped out tons of lime, mined and processed in limekilns just upstream. The park campground starts behind the beach, a splendid locale, except a little disconcerting when cars fly past on the bridge high overhead.

Upstream trails all delve into bosky redwood forests, initially crossing the main stream on sturdy wood bridges. The Hare Creek Trail splits right (southeast) where Hare Creek enters Limekiln Creek after its 3.6-mile plunge from the flank of Cone Peak. (The trail explores only about 0.3 mile of its cascades.) Turning right (northeast) up Limekiln Creek, you have a choice of two destinations: Limekiln Falls, and the ruins of the four old limekilns. Highway 1, Big Sur, CA 93920; (831) 667–2403; www.parks.ca.gov.

Kirk Creek Beach

Picnics, photography, wildlife-watching, tide pooling, surfing.

Unless you are camping at Kirk Creek Campground, park at the side of Highway 1. The trail to the beach used to leave from the north end of the campground, but that was wiped out in a slide. The new trail leaves from between campsites 9 and 10, on the south loop, dropping in 0.3 mile to a rocky shore. You could work your way north from there to the beach, but it would be safest and easiest at low tide.

Mill Creek

Photography, picnics, tide pools, fishing, surfing, wildlife-watching, kayaking.

With a little road connecting it to Highway 1, this old dog-hole port is a put-in point for kayakers and surfers. The Forest Service maintains some picnic tables here.

Pacific Valley

Picnics, hiking, wildlife-watching, nature study, fishing, photography, tide pools. Dangerous surf warning.

A network of easy trails crisscrosses this largest marine terrace on the Big Sur coast. The bluffs and grasslands are Forest Service land, but since the grazing of cattle was allowed until 2005, the paths are a mixture of use trails and cattle trails, and fences are in place. Eight public stiles and gates along the west side of Highway 1 provide easy public access. These stretch from stile 1 just north of Pacific Valley Center (a private residence) to the Jade Cove turnout in the south, a road distance of 2.6 miles. Sand Dollar Beach (see below) and Prewitt Ridge Loop trailheads are also located in Pacific Valley. The Pacific Valley Ranger Station is not a visitor center, but rangers can provide assistance and information.

Sand Dollar Beach

Fee area. Picnics, hiking, wildlife-watching, nature study, fishing, photography, tide pools, surfing. Dangerous surf warning. (See map on p. 162.)

The longest easily accessible public beach along the Big Sur Coast offers tide pooling, fishing, and beachcombing. Park in the Forest Service lot (fee) and take the short path (wheelchair accessible) to the beach overlook. Stairs lead down to the sandy crescent, where the breakers roll in with serious intent. There is a picnic area and a restroom.

Willow Creek

Picnics, surfing, tide pools, fishing, wildlife-watching, kayaking.

More cobble than sand, this popular surfing beach is linked by a short road to Highway 1 next to the Willow Creek Bridge. It's a favored put-in point for kayakers and surfers. The Forest Service maintains a picnic area.

Redwood Gulch

Nature study, hiking.

A 0.2-mile walk inland from the shoulder parking area brings you to the Nathaniel Owings Memorial Redwood Grove, the world's southernmost cluster of *Sequoia sempervirens*. The trees are not the finest specimens that you can see because they are nearing the limit of their natural growth area.

Salmon Creek Falls

Photography, nature study, hiking, picnics.

During the wet seasons no place at Big Sur reminds me more of the Sierra Nevada than Salmon Creek Falls. Although you can see it from the highway, a trifling 0.2-mile walk to the jumble of enormous boulders, oaks, and bay trees at its base will engulf you in its glorious roar and mist. Two streams pour over the lip, joining midway down to make a single waterfall.

William Randolph Hearst Memorial State Beach

Swimming, fishing, kayaking, hiking, boogieboarding, tide pools, picnics, nature study, surfing.

This well-developed two-acre park has the safest swimming beach of any along the Big Sur and San Simeon coastlines. The water is chilly, but the hook of San Simeon Point helps shield the little bay (San Simeon Cove) from northern swells. The 795-foot-long strand is a popular fishing spot, with great views of the Santa Lucia Mountains. The park has a bait, tackle, and grocery store. There are also barbecue grills, restrooms, and a picnic area. Vendors on the beach rent kayaks and boogieboards. The adjacent village of Old San Simeon is home to historic Sebastian's Store. 750 Hearst Castle Road, San Simeon, CA 93452; (805) 927–2020; www.parks.ca.gov.

Hearst San Simeon State Historical Monument

Historical site, museum exhibits, scheduled film showings, guided tours (day and evening), gift shops, food service, photography, picnics, RV and trailer parking.

The largest waterfall visible from Highway 1, Salmon Creek Falls roars wildly in winter and spring.

Better known as Hearst Castle, this palatial mansion and surrounding estate look nothing like a castle. It looks more like a Mediterranean dream-cathedral surrounded by Roman villas—actually guest houses, each a mansion in itself. William Randolph Hearst's grandiose flamboyance and indifferent mixing of styles are themes that run throughout his estate, and especially through the vast, priceless, but still kind of motley collection of artwork, furniture, vases, tapestries, books, sculptures, and pieces of old European buildings dismantled and shipped to the docks at San Simeon. It's a quintessentially American monument, right down to the ketchup bottles on the Great Hall dining table.

Hearst called the mansion La Casa Grande (the Big House), and the hill that it stands upon La Cuesta Encantada (the Enchanted Hill). Architect Julia

William Randolph Hearst Memorial State Beach provides the most protected waters along the Big Sur–San Simeon coast, but even there the waves can be rough and cold.

Morgan designed a complex of several buildings containing 165 rooms, surrounded by eight acres of terraced gardens and pools. Work continued from 1919 to 1947, but it's still unfinished. Hearst's parties were legendary, attracting the rich and famous, including Hollywood stars and such movers and shakers as Winston Churchill, Charles Lindbergh, Howard Hughes, and President Calvin Coolidge.

The visitor center contains a good introduction to the life and times of William Randolph Hearst, his career as a publisher and politician, and of course his lifelong love affair with La Cuesta Encantada. Buy your tickets when you arrive before touring the museum or, better yet, reserve them in advance. Even though the fleet of buses is continually shuttling visitors up and down the hill, tours fill up early.

Piedras Blancas Light Station

When it was lit in 1875, Piedras Blancas Lighthouse stood a full 115 feet above its base. No other California lighthouse stood taller, though two (Point Arena and Pigeon Point) were of equal height. After a storm wrecked the lantern house in 1949, the Coast Guard cut it down to its present height of 74 feet and replaced the first-order Fresnel Lens with a rotating aero beacon. The original lens was later moved to Cambria, where it now stands outside the Veterans Building on Main Street.

A crew of three keepers and their families lived at the light station in the early years, with another keeper hired on in 1906 to tend the fog signal. The original residence buildings have since been moved or torn down, and the present structures date from the 1960s. After the light was automated in 1975, even the keepers departed. The Coast Guard transferred ownership of the light station to the Bureau of Land Management in 2001. The BLM plans to restore the lighthouse, and offers tours (fee). Inquire after the schedule and tickets from the National Geographic Theater at Hearst Castle Visitor Center; (805) 927–6811.

Piedras Blancas was named in 1542 by Juan Rodríguez Cabrillo for the guano-encrusted white rocks just off the point. (In 1911 author J. Smeaton Chase noted that locals called it Peter's Blankets.) Because whales pass so close to shore here, whalers built a whaling station in 1864, nearly wiping out the species. The whale population has since recovered, and today you can sometimes glimpse one swimming through the narrow channel between the white rocks and the mainland. Piedras Blancas Light Station, P.O. Box 129, San Simeon, CA 93459; www.ca.blm.gov. Friends of the Piedras Blancas Lighthouse Lens, P.O. Box 1688, Cambria, CA 93428-1688; (805) 927–0459.

There are five basic tours to choose from:

- **Tour 1** is an overview of the estate. You will visit the esplanade, gardens, Neptune Pool, Casa de Sol (a guest house), the Roman Pool, and five ground-floor rooms in Casa Grande—the Assembly Room, Refectory, Billiard Room, Morning Room, and Hearst's private theater.
- **Tour 2** goes upstairs in Casa Grande. You will see the Doge's Suite, Cloister Rooms, libraries, Gothic Suite, and Gothic Study before descending to the pantry and kitchen. You also see the Roman and Neptune Pools.
- **Tour 3** features the Casa del Monte (a guest house), the north wing of Casa Grande, the north terrace, the Neptune and Roman Pools, and a video presentation on the construction of the estate.

- **Tour 4** provides an overview of the gardens and visits the Neptune and Roman Pools, the Neptune Pool dressing rooms, the Hidden Terrace, the wine cellar, and the largest and most elaborate of the guest cottages, Casa del Mar (April through October only).
- The **Evening Tour** explores the gardens, wine cellar, both levels of Casa del Mar, the Hidden Terrace, the Neptune and Roman Pools, and the Neptune Pool dressing rooms (spring and fall only).

Tours 1 through 4 last slightly under two hours, while the Evening Tour runs a bit longer. All require walking up to 1.5 miles, and all have some stairways. (Special arrangements can be made to accommodate handicapped visitors.) Each tour starts with a bus shuttle to the top of the Enchanted Hill (look for escaped zebras from Hearst's private zoo en route) and includes a showing of a film on the life of William Randolph Hearst in the National Geographic Theater at the visitor center. *Note:* Privately owned vehicles are prohibited from driving directly to the castle or on San Simeon Creek Road and farther on to Fort Hunter Liggett.

The ticket office is open daily from 8:00 A.M. to 3:00 P.M. Reservations are recommended, especially during summer. 750 Hearst Castle Road, San Simeon, CA 93452; www.parks.ca.gov. For tour reservations, call (800) 444–7275 or (805) 927–2020; international reservations, (916) 414–8400, ext. 4100; recorded information, (805) 927–2020; tour information, (800) 444–4445; ranger, (805) 927–2010 or (805) 927–2054.

San Simeon State Park

Beaches, tide pools, hiking, camping, campfire programs, photography, nature study, kayaking, picnics, historical sites, surfing, windsurfing, kiteboarding, boating, fishing, photography. Beware of heavy surf.

When it was created in 1932, San Simeon State Beach comprised a mere sixty-nine acres near San Simeon. Today, with the newer name *San Simeon State Park*, it preserves the longest coastline of any California state park, reaching about 20 miles from San Carpoforo Creek to Cambria (with breaks for private property at San Simeon and other places). For convenience when touring, think of this park as having a developed southern section and an undeveloped northern coastal strip.

The older, developed section of the park lies just south of San Simeon Acres. There you find the campgrounds, boat launches, official beach access, and trails. Unless you're camping, the focal point of your visit will be two day-use areas on Highway 1 just south of San Simeon Creek. A day-use parking area for

Large herds of cattle still graze the pastoral Santa Lucia Mountains behind San Simeon State Park.

San Simeon Beach lies on the west side. On the east side the Washburn Day Use Area has a picnic ground, restrooms, and a trailhead. Walkers can cross under Highway 1 to San Simeon Beach at the mouth of San Simeon Creek, which is blocked from the sea during the dry season by a sandy berm. From that same trailhead a wheelchair-accessible boardwalk heads in the other direction, inland, to a good birding marsh. Even kids will enjoy clomping across the marsh on a bridge. The boardwalk connects with the 3.2-mile San Simeon Nature Trail, which makes a wide loop around the back of Washburn Campground, with nice views of the pastoral Santa Lucias. There are a couple of short uphill sections. At one point the trail passes some vernal pools and mima mounds.

South of San Simeon Beach, the state park continues to follow the shoreline all the way to Santa Rosa Creek and Beach, in Cambria. Although it has alternating sections of sand, rocky shore, and even a marshy lagoon, most of this stretch is known as Moonstone Beach. Access is from Moonstone Drive, which forks from Highway 1 at a signal in Cambria and rejoins it at a second signal, also in Cambria. A row of motels lines the inland side of Moonstone Drive, but the coast side is clear. A mile-long boardwalk traces the top of the low coastal bluff, a delightful route for a stroll. There are tide pools and a range of birding habitats (including Santa Rosa lagoon at the south end) to explore. Beach-combers can search for translucent agates, known locally as moonstones. Leffingwell Landing Day-Use Area, on the north end, has a picnic area and a put-in spot for hand-launch boats and kayaks.

Recently acquired from the Hearst Corporation, the undeveloped part of San Simeon State Park follows the coastline west of Highway 1 from San Carpoforo Creek in the north to San Simeon Creek in the south. Most of it is closed off by barbed-wire fencing erected when it was Hearst Ranch. This fence does not stop the public from using some of the beaches, but the state park service discourages access in most areas until it can survey the natural and historical wealth of the area, and create a development plan (which will no doubt preclude development in most areas). This process will take years. In the meantime use common sense and courtesy, and avoid trampling any plants or disturbing wildlife.

The most popular stretch of coastline in this section hosts the famous elephant seal colony, between old San Simeon and the Piedras Blancas Lighthouse. Public viewing points allow visitors to look down on the beach at the beasts. Do not approach them.

San Carpoforo Beach is popular among surfers. It's accessible by a path from a turnout on Highway 1 just south of the San Carpoforo Bridge. Another use trail takes you to the beach at Arroyo de la Cruz (or Royal Cruise, as locals used to call it when author J. Smeaton Chase passed by in 1911). There's a hole in the fence on the south end of the Arroyo de la Cruz Bridge on Highway 1 and a large parking area on the shoulder. Arroyo Laguna Beach is probably the most celebrated windsurfing spot on the California coast. Users traditionally scale the fence or gate at the wide parking area near the Arroyo Laguna Bridge. (805) 927–2020; www.parks.ca.gov.

Resorts and Lodging

There are wide differences among Big Sur vacation resorts. Resorts along the Big Sur River in Big Sur Center retain an old-fashioned, family-oriented quality. They are small to modest in size. Rope swings, inner tubes, fishing poles, swimming holes, lounge chairs, and picnic supplies set the tone for fun.

The two resorts at the top of Post Hill (Ventana Inn and Post Ranch Inn) are internationally recognized properties that routinely win awards from upmarket travel publications. Marketed as romantic getaways, they feature spas, luxurious refinement, superb dining, inspiring views, and heavy-duty billing statements.

Everything else at Big Sur falls between these two extremities.

The following list of resorts and lodging covers only Big Sur, from north to south. There are many more motels and hotels in Carmel, Carmel Highlands, San Simeon Acres, Cambria, and beyond.

Big Sur Center

Big Sur River Inn

Founded in the 1920s under the name *Apple Pie Inn*, this classic holiday resort is famed for chairs set in the gentle current of the Big Sur River. There are swimming holes, a deck for lounging, and a lawn area on the riverbank. Guests enjoy a heated swimming pool and nearby restaurants and stores. Locals and guests gather for live music on Sunday afternoons. (831) 667–2700 or (800) 548–3610; www.bigsurriverinn.com.

Big Sur Campground and Cabins

Set in a redwood grove next to the Big Sur River, this friendly resort offers basic tent cabins where pets are allowed. There are a few wooden cabins, most furnished with kitchen and fireplace. While the kids play on the playground and basketball court, parents can use the laundry and store. (831) 667–2322.

Riverside Campground and Cabins

Cabin guests enjoy a setting in the redwoods near the Big Sur River. There's a playground for the kiddies and a laundry. (831) 667–2414; www.riversidecamp ground.com.

Ripplewood Resort

This resort has a store and cafe, as well as cabins on both sides of Highway 1. The cabins on the west side are close to the Big Sur River, but all are set amid the redwoods. (831) 667–2242; www.ripplewoodresort.com.

Glen Oaks Motel

Opened in 1956, this attractive redwood-and-adobe motel has a pleasant garden setting. There are two separate cottages for rent in the redwoods. (831) 667–2105; www.glenoaksbigsur.com.

Visitors to River Inn can sit on the bank, or in the middle, of the Big Sur River.

Fernwood Resort

In addition to a restaurant, tavern, campground, and store, Fernwood has a motel row along the highway. One room has a hot-tub deck. (831) 667–2422; www.fernwoodbigsur.com.

Big Sur Lodge

Located inside Pfeiffer Big Sur State Park, the lodge replaces the original Pfeiffer's Ranch Resort, built in 1910. The current buildings date from the 1960s. The main lodge building contains the restaurant, grocery store, gift shop, and front lobby. The "cottages" are up the hill in a clearing, surrounding a heated swimming pool and conference center. You can request units with fireplace and kitchen. 47225 Highway 1, Big Sur, CA 93920; (831) 667–3100 or (800) 424–4787; www.bigsurlodge.com.

Post Hill to Deetjen's

Post Ranch Inn

Surrounded by ninety-eight acres of the old Post Ranch, this modern resort is at once luxurious and unobtrusive, natural and exceedingly refined. Built atop a narrow, wooded ridge more than 1,000 feet above the Pacific, the guest rooms blend into the spectacular landscape. Each is architecturally unique. Partially hidden behind and beneath landscaped gardens, some rooms face the sea. Others look northwest from the woods to the granite crags of the Ventana Cones. All have fireplace, private deck, and luxurious bathroom spa. Guests have use of two swimming pools, the Sierra Mar restaurant, a small gym, the Post Ranch Mercantile store, a central spa, and a host of private services and activities that include massage, yoga sessions, instruction in tai chi and meditation, body and facial treatments, and guided hikes. The opportunity to explore this stunning property, enjoying views and locales of Big Sur that are not widely known or photographed, is in itself a treat. Needless to say, this is a very expensive place. The front kiosk admits nonguests with restaurant reservations, or if they intend to take an afternoon tour. (831) 667–2200 or (800) 527–2200; www.post ranchinn.com.

Ventana Inn and Spa

More like a village than a hotel, this casual but elegant resort embraces a host of facilities, including the Ventana Campground, a gallery store, the Allegria Spa Boutique, and a magnificent restaurant called Cielo. Guest rooms are in a separate area, connected by a beautiful path that is lit at dusk, permitting one of the Santa Lucias' loveliest nighttime strolls. (Guests don't have to walk, of course; they can drive and park.) Guest rooms offer mountain, ocean, or canyon views, and some have fireplace. Suites, houses, cottages, and villas are also available. Guests have use of a heated pool, saunas, private hot tubs, a small library, a Zen garden (for massages), a fitness room, and a host of spa services that include body and facial treatments, massage, reflexology, Reiki, and craniosacral therapy. Hikers are well placed near the gated entrance of the Coast Ridge Road, which is closed to bikes and nonresident vehicle traffic. In terms of expense, Ventana Inn ranks second only to Post Ranch Inn. (831) 667–2331 or (800) 628–6500; www.ventanainn.com.

Deetjen's Big Sur Inn

Homage to a time and place innocent of building codes, Deetjen's is a one-of-a-kind hostelry. Rambling through the redwoods on Castro Creek, this delightful hodgepodge of cottages, houses, and quaint garden paths is listed in the National Register of Historic Places and run by a nonprofit agency. It was built

Grandpa Deetjen's portrait still presides over the dining room at his famous, cozy, and somewhat eccentric inn.

(with the occasional help of prison laborers) by an independent Norwegian named Helmuth Deetjen, who arrived in Carmel from Bergen by way of Heidelberg and the University of Paris. There he met and married a Carmel girl, Helen Haight. When they built their own home at Big Sur in the 1930s, "Grandpa" Deetjen put his strong interests in woodworking and metaphysics to good use. The buildings were inspired by Grandpa's memories of old Norway. The Deetjens provided lodging to travelers, including artists and writers. An English widow, Barbara Blake, leased the barn in 1939 and created the decidedly "old English" restaurant you see today. Grandpa Deetjen died in 1972, but his inn carries on. His portrait hangs in the restaurant. Rumor has it that Grandpa's ghost also puts in occasional appearances. He's still hospitable, except to guests who don't mind their manners. (831) 667–2377; www.deetjens.com.

Big Sur's South Coast

Lucia Lodge

Imagine a motel perched on a cliff in the middle of nowhere, with banana trees and a picket fence, and you begin to get a picture of Lucia Lodge. Built in the late 1930s to serve travelers on the new Highway 1, this is the most remote lodging on the Big Sur coast. A store and restaurant are attached. (831) 667–2391; www.lucialodge.com.

Treebones Resort

Located just north of Gorda (turn right at the Willow Creek Road and follow the sign), Treebones is unique. Guests stay in yurts—round tents inspired by portable Mongolian lodges. They are comfortably fitted with large beds, sink, and heater. The main building has a gift shop, heated pool, sauna, and morning waffle bar for guests, who can also make use of the laundry and Ping-Pong table. A central bathhouse provides showers and toilets. Nightly barbecue. 71895 Highway 1, Big Sur, CA 93920; (877) 424–4787; www.treebonesresort .com.

Gorda Springs Cottages

The minuscule village of Gorda sprang into existence during the Willow Creek gold rush, but the present resort traces its roots to the opening of Highway 1 in the 1930s. Gorda gets its water from local springs that make unexpected appearances in varied, pretty ways around the landscaped property. Each cottage offers ocean views and a private patio. Some have Jacuzzi or fireplace. Gorda Springs also has a grocery store, a deli, shops, a gas station, and the Whale Watcher Café. Across the highway you can explore a short trail to the bluff. There are even some pet llamas. (805) 927–4600 or (805) 927–3918; www.bigsurgordasprings.com.

Ragged Point Inn

With a store, restaurant, gas station, and motel, Ragged Point is a full-service stop at the southern edge of Big Sur. Guests are lodged in a building atop a cliff, about 350 feet above the sea. The upstairs rooms on the ocean-facing side have balconies, and the downstairs rooms have private decks.

The grounds offer majestic scenery too good for anyone to pass up. Behind the lodge in the back gardens, follow the fence around the edge of the high bluffs for excellent views up and down the coast. A steep path, the Cliffside Trail, switchbacks down to a rocky northern cove. In wet seasons you can see two waterfalls, including 300-foot Black Swift Falls, the highest on the Big Sur coast. (805) 927–4502; www.raggedpointinn.net.

The tiny lodge at Lucia sits on a cliff above the Pacific.

Restaurants

The following list of places to eat (or *to dine*, if you prefer a fancier term to match fancier prices) covers only Big Sur. You will find many other restaurants in Carmel, Carmel Highlands, San Simeon Acres, Cambria, and beyond.

Rocky Point Restaurant

In this magnificent setting next to Rocky Point Open Space, down the steep driveway west of Highway 1 and just south of Garrapata Creek Bridge, you can dine inside or out. Open daily for breakfast, lunch, dinner, and drinks with a view. (831) 624–2933; www.rocky-point.com.

Big Sur Center

Big Sur River Inn

This strapping, friendly Big Sur institution serves breakfast, lunch, and dinner daily, either indoors around a huge stone fireplace or on the wooden deck overlooking the Big Sur River. There's live entertainment on Sunday afternoon. (831) 667–2700 or (800) 548–3610; www.bigsurriverinn.com.

Habanero Burrito Bar

The counter staff inside the Big Sur River Inn General Store can whip out a quick, fresh burrito to go. (831) 667–2700.

Big Sur Village Pub

Located in the Village Shops on the west side of Highway 1, this cozy British-style pub is especially popular among locals. It serves specialty beers and pub food. (831) 667–2355.

Big Sur Roadhouse

You'll find roadhouse decor but a Californian–Latin American menu at this eatery, open for dinner Wednesday through Monday. (831) 667–2264.

Ripplewood Café

This small, friendly cafe on the east side of Highway 1 has a nice fireplace, tables, and counter seats. It's open for breakfast and lunch. The attached grocery store offers coffee and sandwiches to go. (831) 667–2242; www.ripple woodresort.com.

Redwood Grill Restaurant

Part of the Fernwood Resort, this friendly, funky place serves lunch and dinner. (831) 667–2129; www.fernwoodbigsur.com.

Fernwood Tavern

The rustic pub at the Fernwood Resort has a large-screen TV inside and a woodsy deck in back. The live music starts about 9:30 on Saturday night and is popular with locals and visitors. (831) 667–2422; www.fernwoodbigsur.com.

Trail's Head Café

Located in the lodge at Pfeiffer Big Sur State Park, this is no rustic camper's eatery, but a good restaurant open for breakfast, lunch, and dinner. Dine outdoors in pleasant weather, or indoors (perhaps near the cozy cast-iron stove) on

Popular among locals, Ripplewood Café is a homey place for breakfast.

chillier days. There's an ice cream counter and espresso cafe attached. (831) 667–3111; www.bigsurlodge.com.

From Loma Mar to Lafler Canyon

Big Sur Center Deli

This grocery store next door to the post office has a counter for sandwiches and deli food. (831) 667–2225.

Big Sur Bakery and Restaurant

Located on Highway 1, this is where locals and savvy travelers come for take-out bakery items for breakfast, though eating at the counter with coffee is also pleasant. The place serves lunch and dinner Tuesday through Sunday, and brunch middays on weekends. Pizza is a big draw. (831) 667–0520; www.big surbakery.com.

Sierra Mar Restaurant

This award-winning restaurant at award-winning Post Ranch Inn is sheer bliss for sophisticates with deep pockets and discriminating tastes. Set on the edge of a ridge that plunges 1,149 feet down to the Pacific, Sierra Mar offers arguably the most naturally dramatic table seating of any California restaurant. The artwork and architecture are also lovely. Dinner features a four-course prix fixe menu (California cuisine) that changes nightly and a celebrated wine list. Also open for lunch. Reservations are a must. (831) 667–2800; www.postranchinn.com.

Cielo

The restaurant at Ventana Inn is a big, grand, beautiful affair with 50-mile views of ocean and mountain from the windows and outdoor terraces. The menu is splendidly creative, if pricey, and the chef emphasizes fresh, seasonal ingredients. The restaurant is open for lunch and dinner; the bar stays open through midnight. (800) 628–6500 or (831) 667–2331; www.ventanainn.com.

Café Kevah

On a terrace just below Nepenthe, this casual outdoor terrace offers casual brunch and light lunch. Order before sitting. It's open March through December, weather permitting. (831) 667–2344; www.nepenthebigsur.com.

Deetjen's Big Sur Inn

One of the most romantic interiors in California, the dining rooms of Deetjen's are redolent of a rambling, old English West Country pub, without being "cute." Lit by candlelight, warmed by hearth fires, the restaurant seems to loiter in a different century. A rum smuggler or highwayman in cocked hat would not seem out of place at the little bar. The food and drink are exceptional. It serves breakfast and dinner. (831) 667–2378; www.deetjens.com.

The South Coast

Lucia Restaurant

The restaurant's open for lunch or dinner, but the wonderful breakfast is only for guests staying at the lodge. On a cold night with a blaze in the fireplace, Lucia Lodge is the very essence of coziness. On a fine, clear day, take a seat on the deck and you can watch for breaching whales or pods of dolphins. Below the restaurant, the Rock Slide Lounge offers a full-service bar and views of the Pacific. (831) 667–2391; www.lucialodge.com.

Nepenthe

This magical place is, for many, the epitome of Big Sur, that perfect meeting of the wild and the urbane. It's all here: art, music, and literature; good food and drink; an enchanted oak woodland, billowing velvety mountains, the immense blue ocean and sky, and a horizon so vast that you can detect the curved edge of the earth itself. It's a rare place on this planet that serves both hamburgers and metaphysical speculation. (The restaurant also serves beer and wine, which go good with philosophy, sports, or whatever.)

And then there's its timeless style. Richard Burton and Elizabeth Taylor danced here while filming *The Sandpiper* in 1963, and it still feels like 1963 at Nepenthe. It's not old-fashionedness; it's style. The cool jazz that plays in the background. The clink of glasses and murmur of conversation. The name itself, *Nepenthe*, which means "respite from sorrow" in Greek.

Two sculptures help set the tone. Gaunt and moody, staring down at the parking lot from the roof of the Phoenix Shop, the *Dark Angel* was carved by local sculptor Buzz Brown. A character named Ray Ramsy

Writhing oaks and sculpted hills set the scene for Nepenthe.

won it in a card game and gave it to Nepenthe. At the top of the stairs, at the patio entrance, you meet the *Phoenix*. Its sculptor, Edmond Kara, carved it from a downed oak that he found at the bottom of Mule Canyon. (Nepenthe's ridge is framed by Mule Canyon to the north and Graves Canyon to the south, so in a sense the dead oak has risen in the world.)

Before Nepenthe, a log cabin stood atop this hill. Among the people who lived there was Henry Miller. Orson Welles bought it for his bride, Rita Hayworth, but sold it soon after to the Fassett family. The Fassetts hired an architect named Rowan Maiden, a disciple of Frank Lloyd Wright, to design the restaurant. Graced with balconies and a patio, his airy glass-and-redwood structure set an enduring mood. Of its 1949 opening, one observer wrote that crowds of "solid citizens" and "sandaled and jeaned and corduroy-shorted writers and painters and musicians and sculptors" came together to toast the Fassetts and launch Nepenthe.

Despite its fame, Nepenthe remains the kind of vital community center where costumed locals still gather for the annual Halloween Bal Masque to dance on the terrace and raise funds for the Big Sur Fire Service. (831) 667–2345; www.nepenthebigsur.com.

Treebones Resort Barbecue

This nightly barbecue features ribs, chicken, tri-tip, and salmon. Call for reservations. 71895 Highway 1, Big Sur, CA 93920; (877) 424–4787; www.tree bonesresort.com.

Pacific Market Deli

Located in the general store at Gorda Springs, this eatery lets you pick up sandwiches, soups, and salads and nosh right there among Gorda's gardens. (805) 927–3918.

Whale Watcher Café

This friendly establishment at Gorda Springs has a counter with stools, and tables both indoors and outside. The food and drink are excellent, and the desserts (made on the premises) superb. It's open for breakfast, lunch, and dinner. (805) 927–1590; www.bigsurgordasprings.com.

Ragged Point Inn Restaurant

This glass-walled restaurant looks out on a lush, cultivated garden and dining patio with space heaters for chilly days. The dinner menu features California cuisine. Breakfast and lunch are also served. (805) 927–5708; www.ragged pointinn.net.

Camping Along Highway 1

These campgrounds along Highway 1 are listed north to south. All have potable water and charge fees to camp, unless otherwise stated.

Andrew Molera State Park Trail Camp

Campsites: 24
This walk- or bike-in campground is 0.3 mile from the central parking area. It offers primitive camping, but it does have potable water. No reservations, no showers. (831) 667–2315.

Riverside Campground and Cabins

Campsites: 45
A privately run resort on the Big Sur River in Big Sur Center, this facility has river access for fishing, inner tubing, and swimming. There's a nearby store and restaurant. You'll also find a playground, a laundry, hot showers, and water and electrical hookups for RVs. (831) 667–2414; www.riversidecampground.com.

Big Sur Campground and Cabins

Campsites: 81

This, too, is a privately run resort on the Big Sur River in Big Sur Center with river access for fishing, inner tubing, and swimming. You'll find an on-site store, a laundry, a playground, a basketball court, hot showers, water and electrical hookups for RVs, and a dump station. (831) 667–2322.

Fernwood Resort

Campsites: 60

This privately run resort on the Big Sur River in Big Sur Center boasts river access for fishing, inner tubing, and swimming, as well as direct access to state park hiking trails. A rare albino redwood grows near the campground entrance. There are tent sites, tent cabins, bathhouses, a horseshoe pit, a volleyball court, water and electrical hookups for RVs, and an adjacent store, tavern, and restaurant. (831) 667–2422; www.fernwoodbigsur.com.

Pfeiffer Big Sur State Park

Campsites: 218

This huge campground along the Big Sur River offers easy access to fishing, inner tubing, and swimming. There are nearby trails and a restaurant, and you can enjoy campfire programs, a store, showers, an RV dump station, trailer space, and bike camps. Group camping is available on the west side of Highway 1. For reservations, call ReserveAmerica at (800) 444–7275.

Ventana Campground

Campsites: 80

In the redwoods of Post Canyon below Ventana Inn, which owns and runs it, this facility has hot showers and a camp store. (831) 667–2712; www.ventana wildernesscampground.com.

Julia Pfeiffer Burns State Park

Environmental Campsites: 2

At these two primitive walk-in sites 0.3 mile from the McWay Day Use Area parking lot, you'll need to bring your own water, but there are pit toilets. For reservations, call ReserveAmerica at (800) 444–7275.

Limekiln Creek State Park Campground

Campsites: 33

Here next to the beach, you'll find handy trails, hot showers, and space for some trailers. For reservations, call ReserveAmerica at (800) 444–7275.

Supplies

You can find groceries and camping supplies at the following stores. Some sell local publications, and others have video and DVD rentals. The list is arranged from north to south, and all are on Highway 1 (except the two in old San Simeon). Note that there are many other stores in Carmel, San Simeon Acres, Cambria, and beyond.

Carmel Highlands
• Carmel Highlands General Store: (831) 624–7851.

Big Sur Center
• Big Sur River Inn General Store: (831) 667–2700.
• Ripplewood General Store: (831) 667–2242.
• Fernwood General Store: (831) 667–2422.

Pfeiffer Big Sur State Park
• Country Store at Big Sur Lodge; the park also has a campground store, open only in summer. (831) 667–3100 or (800) 424–4787.

Loma Mar
• Big Sur Center Deli and Grocery: next to the post office. (831) 667–2225.

Lucia
• Lucia General Store: (831) 667–2391.

Gorda
• Pacific Market General Store: (805) 927–3918.

Ragged Point Inn
• General Store: (805) 927–5708.

Old San Simeon
• Sebastian's Store: (805) 927–4217.
• Virg's San Simeon Landing: bait and tackle, groceries, and more, at William Randolph Hearst Memorial State Beach. (805) 927–4676 or (800) 762–5263.

Kirk Creek Campground

Campsites: 33

This Forest Service campground is located on a terrace overlooking the Pacific, adjacent to Kirk Creek Beach, and near Nacimiento-Fergusson Road and Vicente Trail. There's trailer space, as well as hike-in and bike-in sites. Managed by Parks Management Company; www.parksman.com.

Plaskett Creek Campground

Campsites: 45

At this Forest Service campground near Pacific Valley, Jade Cove, and Sand Dollar Beach, you'll find hike-in and bike-in campsites, RV spaces, but no dump station. No reservations are accepted, except for the three group sites. Call Parks Management Company at (877) 444–6777; www.parksman.com.

Treebones Resort

Campsites: 5

Near Gorda, Treebones offers some ocean-view, walk-in campsites for tenters. Pets are allowed. 71895 Highway 1, Big Sur, CA 93920; (877) 424–4787; www.treebonesresort.com.

San Simeon Creek Campground

Campsites: 134

Near Hearst Castle in San Simeon State Park, this campground boasts campfire programs, restrooms with flush toilets, showers, trailer and RV spaces, a dump station, and hike-in or bike-in camps; firewood is offered for sale by the campground host. Reservations are recommended from March 15 through September 30. (800) 444–7275.

Washburn Campground (San Simeon State Park)

Campsites: 68

Smaller and more primitive than San Simeon Creek Campground, Washburn occupies higher ground about a mile up the park road. There are vault toilets and a dump station; reservations are recommended from March 15 through September 30. (800) 444–7275.

Chapter 4
Driving the Back Roads

Compared with Highway 1, Big Sur's back roads see relatively few motorists. Their maintenance is of low priority. Instead of rushing to clear or fix storm damage on a back road, county road departments and Forest Service crews will typically just close the road until the rains taper down in spring, usually by March or April. Even in good weather you can expect to find downed trees, ruts aplenty, stream fordings, rocks, and even boulders on the back roads, especially unpaved ones. If you go, be prepared for little adventures.

Most back roads are unsuitable for trailers and RVs, but two-wheel-drive sedans are perfectly capable of managing all *paved* backcountry roads. To be sure, they may be steep, single-lane, winding, and exposed to spectacular drop-offs, but these are driver issues, not vehicle issues. It should go without saying that you need to be a careful, capable driver.

High clearance is advisable for all vehicles on unpaved roads. Dirt road conditions change all the time. Four-wheel drive may sometimes be necessary; at other times on the same road, two-wheel drive may be perfectly adequate. To reduce chances of an unpleasant surprise, inquire locally about conditions before you take the road.

Avoid driving unpaved roads in wet weather. Respect private property, and slow way down when passing other vehicles, people, or private property. Stay on established roads. Make sure that your tank is full and your tires good before you leave, and that you bring a spare and all the fixin's. If you really want to do it right, bring a saw for clearing downed trees and a shovel for clearing minor obstacles or filling mud puddles. (For major obstacles, of course, just turn around and go back. Let the professionals deal with it.)

Drive slowly enough to stop for oncoming traffic on blind turns, and sound the horn if you need to. If you see a car coming, pull over as far to the right as you can. If two cars meet where there's no room to turn out, the car heading downhill should back up. Let common sense and courtesy prevail, however.

Fort Hunter Liggett has special rules for public entry. *Note:* There are only three public entrances to this military reservation: at Jolon, on the Nacimiento-Fergusson Road, and at the northern end of Milpitas Road. All visitors need to show photo identification to the sentry, and drivers also need to show proof of car registration and insurance. Sentries will issue a pass and instructions to display it. They may deny entrance during security alerts. You may drive and walk only in areas designated by military authorities. Bicycling, hiking, camping, picnicking, and swimming are prohibited on the base, except to hunters and fishermen who have obtained special permits from the Outdoor Recreation Office.

Which back roads do I most recommend? For the general public I pick three, all *paved*, and all usually manageable for two-wheel-drive sedans. Each is described in more detail later in this chapter:

- **Nacimiento-Fergusson Road,** for the unbelievable views of the Pacific from the high slopes of the Santa Lucias.
- **Arroyo Seco Road,** for the chance to see "the Grand Canyon of Monterey County" from the Gorge Trail.
- **The San Antonio Valley route,** with visits to Mission San Antonio, the Hacienda, the upper San Antonio Valley, and the Indians Station area.

Back Road Closures

- Fort Hunter Liggett: For military road closures, call (831) 386–2503 or (831) 386–2310.
- Los Padres National Forest: For seasonal closures of Forest Service roads, call the King City office at (831) 385–5434, or check www.fs.fed.us.
- Big Sur Station: Stop by on Highway 1 in Big Sur, or call (831) 667–2315.
- Caltrans: For Highway 1 and other major roads, call (800) 427–7623. There's an office at Big Sur Station.

Back Roads from Highway 1

Palo Colorado Road

START: Highway 1 (120 feet), 11 miles south of the Carmel River, 5.4 miles north of the Little Sur River.

DESTINATION: 10.4 miles to Bottchers Gap (2,050 feet).

ROAD CONDITION: Partly paved, partly gravel. Winding, mostly single-lane road. Local traffic is sometimes heavy. The road makes a relatively steady ascent of about 1,940 feet overall.

AMENITIES: Bottchers Gap Campground.

SURROUNDING JURISDICTION: Private property until Mill Creek, which is part of the Monterey Peninsula Regional Park District. Bottchers Gap lies just within Los Padres National Forest.

Although heavily logged in the late nineteenth century, Palo Colorado Canyon today is thickly wooded with redwoods. A lot of people live along the lower part of this road; be slow and cautious on the narrow, blind turns. At 2.2 miles the road leaves Palo Colorado Creek to climb southeast over a minor saddle. Descending slightly to Rocky Creek in Las Piedras Canyon, it quickly crosses to the south bank and climbs to Long Ridge. There follows another minor descent into the Bixby Creek drainage, crossing Turner Creek (a tributary) at 5.6 miles. The final rise to Bottchers Gap follows Mill Creek's ravine, another tributary of Bixby Creek. The Monterey Peninsula Regional Park district owns the Mill Creek Redwood Preserve, but it isn't yet open to the public; contact (831) 622–0598 for updates.

Perched on a saddle above the heavily forested upper canyon of the Little Sur River, Bottchers Gap presents some great views eastward to the Ventana Double Cone, and south to Pico Blanco. You can see Santa Lucia firs in the distance. There's a small Forest Service campground and a trailhead with links to the Ventana Wilderness. Bottchers Gap is the end of the road for motorists, unless you have reservations at the Pico Blanco Boy Scout Camp, in which case scouters can drive through the gate and 3.6 miles down several steep, tight turns to the camp in the redwoods alongside the Little Sur River, 1,250 feet below Bottchers Gap.

Old Coast Road

START: Highway 1 (260 feet) on the north side of Bixby Bridge.

DESTINATION: 10.4 miles to Highway 1 (92 feet) opposite the Andrew Molera State Park entrance.

ROAD CONDITION: Unpaved, winding, mostly single-lane road, with substantial rise and fall. Watch for cattle. Not suitable for two-wheel-drive vehicles in wet weather. There's an overall elevation gain of about 2,900 feet, and a loss of about 3,080 feet.

AMENITIES: None.

SURROUNDING JURISDICTION: Private property mostly. There's some Forest Service land at the northern end, and state park land at the southern end.

Part of the original wagon road to Big Sur built during the 1880s, the Old County Road (as it's known to locals) provides a quiet inland route between Bixby Canyon and the Big Sur Valley. From the northern anchorage of Bixby Bridge, it climbs up and then down the scrubby north wall of Bixby Canyon. Road builders took the road inland to avoid the deep canyon of Bixby Creek. Crossing the creek on a low bridge nearly a mile upstream from its mouth, the Old County Road starts the long ascent of Sierra Creek's redwood-shaded ravine to the 1,175-foot grassy saddle between Sierra Hill and Bixby Mountain. Signs on the fences and a cattle grate in the road remind you that you're in the midst of the El Sur Ranch.

Next begins a 1.8-mile descent to the valley of the Little Sur River, in which you lose more than 1,040 feet of elevation and enjoy some terrific hairpin turns with views westward to Highway 1. At the bottom you enter a thick redwood forest, crossing first the main stream of the Little Sur, and then the South Fork. You'll pass a ranch house and some large, logged stumps. The second large climb of the journey curves up the south ridge and back into the sun. At 6.5 miles (3.9 from the south end of the road), you pass the trailhead of the Little Sur Trail, with parking room on both shoulders. You top out at 942 feet before dropping to Highway 1, enjoying wide views of the Pacific Ocean, Point Sur, and the Big Sur River Valley.

Nacimiento-Fergusson Road

START: Highway 1 (195 feet), 4.2 miles south of Lucia and 8.8 miles north of Gorda.

DESTINATION: 25.5 miles to Milpitas Road (1,000 feet) on Fort Hunter Liggett.

Drivers enjoy grand views of Highway 1 from the paved Nacimiento-Fergusson Road, which rises steeply from the coast to the crest of the Santa Lucias.

ROAD CONDITION: Paved, winding, often steep, mostly single-lane road. There's an overall gain in elevation of about 2,585 feet within the first 7.1 miles, followed by a loss of 1,585 feet.

AMENITIES: Kirk Creek Campground at the western end. Nacimiento and Ponderosa Campgrounds lie along the road. The Hacienda is near the eastern end.

SURROUNDING JURISDICTION: Forest Service for the first 16 miles (west side). Fort Hunter Liggett on the eastern end. (No bicycles on Fort Hunter Liggett.) Before entering Fort Hunter Liggett, all visitors need to present photo identification at sentry box, and drivers also need to show proof of car registration and insurance. For military road closures, call (831) 386–2503 or (831) 386–2310.

This is the only paved road crossing the Santa Lucia Range from the Big Sur coast. Not only is it a fascinating drive, but few landscapes in North America can match the pure spectacle of the steep western slope and Pacific Ocean from this high road. The direction of choice is from east to west (Fort Hunter Liggett to Highway 1), mainly for the thrill of the descent to the Pacific. However, since most motorists drive west to east (Highway 1 to the interior), I describe it in that direction.

The road wastes no time before launching into a steady climb, passing the Mill Creek trailhead at 0.8 mile, whipping back and forth up the steep ridges, gaining ever more surrealistic views of the Pacific, Highway 1, and Mill Creek Canyon. Ocean and sky fill the eye with intense blue on a sunny day, but the sight of white fogbanks walling up the canyon on a summer afternoon is even more beautiful. Skirting precipitous hillsides, ducking in and out of wooded ravines, the road tops out at Nacimiento Summit in just over 7 miles. In a land where ridgetops provide the most level ground, it's not surprising to find a four-way junction here, with the dirt Cone Peak Road heading north, and the dirt South Coast Ridge Road heading south (see below).

Continuing east on the paved road, you begin the descent into the dry interior mountains, sharper and more rugged than the coastal gradients. Keeping to the shady north-facing slope, you'll pass a ranger station before lurching downward into a steep descent, soon joining with the Nacimiento River. This small stream cuts a delightful linear oasis through sear surrounding mountainsides. At 12.5 and 13.6 miles, respectively, you'll pass the shady Nacimiento and Ponderosa Campgrounds, then come to a stop at the remote sentry post that marks the boundary between Los Padres National Forest and Fort Hunter Liggett at 16 miles.

If your papers are in order, you may continue into the base, driving through an increasingly gentle landscape of woodland, oak savanna, and grassland.

Strikingly broad, flat, and empty, Stony Valley was once home to a large Salinan population, and contains many domestic and sacred sites. Ignore the side roads and continue over a range of small hills to an unmarked junction. Turn sharply right (east), and curve down to a bridge across the San Antonio River. There is also a ford here for vehicles (such as tanks and military transports) too heavy for the bridge. It's an old ford. The banks are said to be haunted by the ghost of a nineteenth-century pioneer woman, swept away with her wagon and decapitated while trying to cross during high water.

After crossing the bridge, make a sharp right at the first junction. Less than a mile ahead, the Nacimiento-Fergusson Road ends at the paved, two-lane Milpitas Road. To exit Fort Hunter Liggett, turn right (south). To go to Mission San Antonio and the Hacienda, turn left (north).

Cone Peak Road

START: Nacimiento Summit (2,780 feet) on Nacimiento-Fergusson Road, 7.1 miles east of Highway 1.

DESTINATION: 6.4 miles to road's end (4,120 feet).

ROAD CONDITION: Unpaved, winding, single-lane road. There's an overall climb of about 1,340 feet from Nacimiento Summit. The Forest Service usually closes this road in winter.

AMENITIES: Redwood Springs Camp.

SURROUNDING JURISDICTION: Forest Service. Motorized dirt bikes are not allowed.

Big Sur's second highest road hangs on the eastern side of the Coast Ridge, with spectacular views eastward. If you want a good view of the famous western slope—the steepest coastal gradient in the continental United States—you can take an easy walk from the Vicente Flat trailhead (located 3.6 miles from Nacimiento Summit), or the more demanding trudge from the Cone Peak trailhead (5.1 miles from Nacimiento Summit).

At 5,155 feet above sea level, Cone Peak has long been celebrated for its biological oddities. It's a good place to get a close look at high-country birds, Santa Lucia firs, and a ponderosa pine forest. While collecting Santa Lucia fir seeds in October 1856, a botanist named A. F. Beardsley enjoyed the kind of camping experience that the Ventana is always ready to serve up to the ill prepared (minus the grizzly): "We passed the most horrible night that ever fell to my lot to experience," he wrote. "The impenetrable darkness of the night, the howl of the tempest, the crashing of falling rocks, together with the severity of the cold rain, almost snow, made the night truly awful. We saw a large grizzly bear just before dark . . . which added nothing to the enjoyments of the night."

START: Nacimiento Summit (2,780 feet) on Nacimiento-Fergusson Road, 7.1 miles east of Highway 1.

DESTINATION: 6.8 miles to the top of Plaskett Ridge Road (3,400 feet), or 14.4 miles to the junction of Willow Creek Road and McKern Road (3,425 feet).

ROAD CONDITION: Unpaved, winding, single-lane, rolling road that follows the ridge.

AMENITIES: Chalk Peak, Prewitt Ridge, and Miguel Camps are on or near the road.

SURROUNDING JURISDICTION: Forest Service mostly, but Fort Hunter Liggett lies to the east of the road south of the Plaskett Ridge Road junction.

This road makes a good link for anyone who wants to make a loop by incorporating it with the Nacimiento-Fergusson Road, the Plaskett Ridge Road, or the

The unpaved South Coast Ridge Road offers spectacular views westward to the Pacific, and eastward into the San Antonio and Salinas Valleys.

Willow Creek Road. The views are monumental in all directions. At 4.5 miles from the Nacimiento Summit, the Prewitt Ridge Road (22S05) spurs west to Prewitt Camp. After the Plaskett Ridge Road (23S02) junction, the South Coast Ridge Road forms the western boundary of Fort Hunter Liggett—which means you should *not* drive down any of the roads to the east. At Willow Creek Road drivers have a further option of continuing yet another 9.4 miles south along the ridgetop McKern Road (20S05) to Lottie Potrero Camp.

Plaskett Ridge Road (23S02)

START: Highway 1 (200 feet), 9.5 miles south of Lucia and 3.4 miles north of Gorda.

DESTINATION: 6.5 miles to South Coast Ridge Road (3,400 feet).

ROAD CONDITION: Unpaved, steep, winding, single-lane road exposed to drop-offs. The overall climb is about 3,200 feet. The road is often closed in winter.

AMENITIES: None.

SURROUNDING JURISDICTION: Forest Service mostly, but it crosses private property at 4.9 miles.

With most of the climb within the first 3 miles, this is one steep road. Exciting views and drop-offs, and probably the fewest tourists of any road, might recommend it to the more adventurous four-wheeler. The property owner may close the gate to prevent further travel at 4.9 miles.

Willow Creek Road (23S01)

START: Highway 1 (240 feet), 11.4 miles south of Lucia and 0.9 mile north of Gorda.

DESTINATION: 7.6 miles to the three-way junction (3,425 feet) with South Coast Ridge Road (22S05) and McKern Road (20S05). Spur roads at the 6.1-mile mark lead to San Martins Top (1.1 miles farther) and Alder Creek Camp (1.7 miles farther).

ROAD CONDITION: Unpaved, steep, winding, single-lane road. The overall climb to McKern Road is about 3,185 feet.

AMENITIES: Sycamore Flat and Alder Creek Camps.

SURROUNDING JURISDICTION: Forest Service mostly, but it crosses private property.

Unpaved Willow Creek Road makes a steep ascent from the Pacific Ocean near Gorda to the old Los Burros Mining District.

This historic road led to the Los Burros Mining District, where the gold-mining town of Mansfield stood until it burned in 1892. Climbing steeply up Willow Creek Canyon, it reaches a private residential area at 6 miles from Highway 1. From there, Willow Creek Road continues upward and eastward to the unmarked junction of McKern Road (20S05).

At this residential enclave you'll also see two rough spur roads to the south, both more likely to require four-wheel drive than the Willow Creek Road. One spur leads southwest and *down* to San Martin Top (2,702 feet above sea level). The other leads southeast, 1.7 miles *down* to the site of the Buclimo Mine, Alder Creek Camp, and Alder Creek Botanical Area. If you're looking for mining ruins, you will be disappointed. There's nothing left of the old mining operations here, though some contemporary miners still nurse hope. Heed the NO TRESPASSING signs.

After J. Smeaton Chase rode down the Willow Creek Trail on horseback on his way to the coast in 1911, he penned a description that still fits the Willow Creek Road: "That morning's trail was the most delightful I had experienced on the trip, winding down the forested mountainside among yellow pines, oaks and madronos. The ground was all ashy rose with the fallen leaves of the last-named trees, and was like one of those wonderful old Persian rugs. . . . The fog was slowly drawing out to sea, and suddenly, as if a curtain were partly lifted, I could look beneath the sheet of dazzling cloud and see the crinkled water a thousand feet below, leaden in the shadow of the dense vapor."

McKern Road (20S05)

START: Junction of Willow Creek Road (3,425 feet), 7.6 miles east of Highway 1.

DESTINATION: 9.4 miles to Lottie Potrero Camp (2,380 feet), rolling up and down along a ridge. A dirt track in poor condition continues beyond Lottie Potrero.

ROAD CONDITION: Unpaved, steep, narrow, winding, remote, single-lane road.

AMENITIES: Lottie Potrero Camp.

SURROUNDING JURISDICTION: Forest Service to the west, Fort Hunter Liggett to the east.

This scenic extension of the Coast Ridge Road hugs the western side of the ridge around Alder Peak before moving to the crest of the ridge. Near Lion Den junction at 4.2 miles, it passes a grove of rare Sargent cypress. The 3,499-foot top of Lion Peak slips by on the west, followed in short order by the triple summit of Three Peaks on the east. When explorer Gaspar de Portolà crossed the Santa Lucias on a Native American trail in 1769, he passed near Lottie Potrero Camp from the Wagner Creek drainage on the west side to Pozo Hondo Creek on the east.

Back Roads of the Northern Santa Lucia Range

Carmel Valley Road (County Road G16) skirts the northern edge of the Santa Lucia Range, linking Highway 1 at Carmel with the Salinas Valley town of Greenfield, a distance of about 54 miles. Itself pretty and paved, the Carmel Valley Road passes Garland Ranch Regional Park, several wineries, and the equestrian-friendly village of Carmel Valley before narrowing and starting up the mild Ardilla Grade. Passing through Hastings Natural History State Reservation, it crosses the low pass above the Cahoon Grade, descending to picturesque Arroyo Seco Road, and thence to the Salinas Valley.

Leading south from this main road (G16) are three important spur roads that climb into the Santa Lucias: the Cachagua Road to Los Padres Dam, the Tassajara Road, and the Arroyo Seco Road.

Garland Ranch Regional Park

Garland Ranch is a natural preserve with miles of trails, ideal for hikers, equestrians, and hikers with dogs. (Cyclists can also use the Cooper Ranch addition, where equestrians are prohibited.) On a short stroll from the entrance, the range of local history encompasses many centuries, from the massive Rumsien grinding rock along the Buckeye Trail to the nineteenth-century Cooper-Tomasini Ranch. Amassed from several old Carmel Valley ranches, the park preserves a biological cross section reaching from the flats around the Carmel River to the 2,000-foot-high ridges that form the northern bulwark of the Santa Lucias, an array of riparian and dry-slope woodland, chaparral, and grassland. Casual strollers enjoy the Waterfall Trail during the wet season. More ambitious hikers can enjoy wide views from the longer trails. The main parking area is on Carmel Valley Road, 8.6 miles west of Highway 1. (831) 659–4488; www.mprpd.org.

Cachagua Road

START: Carmel Valley Road (630 feet), 16.2 miles east of Highway 1.

DESTINATION: 10.5 miles to Jamesburg Road, rolling up and down along a ridge.

ROAD CONDITION: Paved, narrow, winding, two-lane road.

AMENITIES: Cachagua General Store.

SURROUNDING JURISDICTION: Private property.

Climbing about 530 feet in 2.7 miles to the crest of Tularcitos Ridge, this old stage road descends quickly to the village of Cachagua, at 6 miles. The sunny site of this backwoods village (called Francis's Camp on some maps) has been occupied for thousands of years, but the present settlement dates from the 1880s. Father Junípero Serra reportedly visited and baptized his first Esselen convert here in 1775, following a persuasive display of military might by Spanish soldiers. (The name *Cachuagua* may be a corruption of the original Esselen village name, Xasáuan, once translated as "scratching.") Most people who turn off into Cachagua continue right on through to the nearby parking area of Los Padres Reservoir, a major trailhead for the northern Ventana Wilderness.

Cachagua's most noteworthy commercial establishment is a genuine country institution, the Cachagua General Store, surrounded by a pleasant oak woodland. Old-timers still lounge outside the front door, dogs are welcome, and service is friendly, casual, and helpful. Along with local wines and beers, snacks, and camping goods, the owners offer lunches, Monday-night dinners, and Sunday brunch. (831) 659–1857.

After reaching the Jamesburg Road, turn left to reach Carmel Valley Road, where you can loop back to where you started.

Tassajara Road

START: Junction of Carmel Valley Road and Jamesburg Road (1,590 feet), 23.8 miles east of Highway 1.

DESTINATION: 16.9 miles to Tassajara Zen Mountain Center.

ROAD CONDITION: Paved, narrow, winding, two-lane road for 3 miles to Jamesburg. Beyond, the road changes drastically: It's unpaved, narrow, and winding, climbing and falling along steep gradients and exposed to intimidating drop-offs.

AMENITIES: Cachagua General Store is near Jamesburg. The Tassajara monastery has a small store selling Tassajara-baked bread and books in summer. Tassajara is open to the public only from late April through Labor Day. The monastery offers lodging, meals, and use of the hot-springs baths only to guests with reservations.

SURROUNDING JURISDICTION: Private property for the first 6.5 miles; the Forest Service thereafter.

In the best tradition of a pilgrimage, a journey to the Tassajara monastery goes slow and bumpy, with plenty of sublime revelations along the way. The ordeal (and/or fun) begins 3 miles in, where the pavement ends at Jamesburg, a very humble congregation of dwellings. For the next 5.9 miles, the rutty Tassajara

Santa Lucia Stargazers

Five-thousand-foot Chews Ridge provides excellent sky-watching conditions. There are few large cities close by to generate smog or light pollution. To the east, south, and west, Fort Hunter Liggett, the Pacific Ocean, and the wilderness of the Santa Lucias deliver dependably dark skies, though light pollution from San Jose and the Salinas Valley does blight northern skies.

The Monterey Institute for Research (MIRA) owns and operates a 36-inch reflecting telescope at the Oliver Observing Station, just east of the Tassajara Road crest. Its staff offer tours of the facility on Sunday afternoons during the dry seasons of the year. MIRA, 200 Eighth Street, Marina, CA 93933; (831) 883–1000; www.mira.org.

Road climbs more than 3,000 feet through woodland and meadow to the top of Chews Ridge, the highest public road in Monterey County.

After Chews Ridge, Tassajara Road enters chaparral terrain extensively burned in the 1977 Marble Cone Fire, and the views open up. The vista eastward takes in the Arroyo Seco Canyon, Indians Road, and Junipero Serra Peak, while to the west you can see the forbidding jumble of peaks and canyons of the Ventana heartland. En route you'll pass three Ventana Wilderness trailheads: the Pine Ridge (10.5 miles from Carmel Valley Road at 3,320 feet), Horse Pasture (15.6 miles at 2,335 feet), and Church Creek (15.9 miles at 2,195 feet) trailheads (see chapter 5, Hiking the Trails of Big Sur).

The final 5-mile stretch into Tassajara Canyon is so steep, and the mountainsides plummet so sharply on the side, that old-time stage drivers going down to Tassajara Hot Springs used to drag logs from the back of their coaches to help with the braking. Use low gear yourself. The end of the road is Tassajara Zen Mountain Center, meditating quietly behind a traditional Japanese memorial gateway.

The monastery is closed to visitors from September through late April, when resident Zen Buddhist monks and novices work and practice daily meditation. Paying guests can stay from late April through Labor Day, when day-use guests may also use the hot-springs baths, but all need reservations. Now part of the monastery, the hot springs themselves flow from the banks and bed of Tassajara Creek, an idyllic meeting of hot (106 degrees Fahrenheit) and cold water that must have been the glory of the Esselen homeland. After it was developed as a mineral-bath resort in the 1870s, adventurous tourists arrived by Monterey Company Stage over the Tassajara Road.

Hikers may pass through the monastery property en route to Forest Service trails, but are discouraged from lingering. The picturesque, steep-sided canyon is very hot on summer days, ideal for a dip in Tassajara Creek. The short Narrows Trail heads downstream to pools and cascades popular with skinny-dippers. Longer hikes lead out of the canyon into Ventana Wilderness.

Arroyo Seco Road

START: Junction with Carmel Valley Road (710 feet), 41.5 miles east of Highway 1.

DESTINATION: 5.4 miles to the road's end (1,025 feet) in Arroyo Seco Recreation Area.

ROAD CONDITION: Paved, winding, two-lane road.

AMENITIES: Arroyo Seco Campground. The road passes some private stores before entering the Arroyo Seco Recreation Area.

Narrow Indians Road (also known as the Gorge Trail) clings to the hillside above Arroyo Seco. This hiking and mountain biking trail can be found at the end of Arroyo Seco Road.

SURROUNDING JURISDICTION: Private property mostly, but the Forest Service runs the recreation area (fee).

Arroyo Seco means "dry gulch" in Spanish. Here it refers to a stream, a canyon, a road, and the Forest Service recreation area at the end of that road. The stream was the first named, and called such because its waters sink into the gravel as they flow into the Salinas Valley. On almost any given day, there will be more water in the upper stream than the lower. The upper Arroyo Seco in the wet season is a raging river. The picturesque canyon of Arroyo Seco, sometimes called the Grand Canyon of Monterey County, cuts to 2,500 feet deep in its middle reaches, and more if you factor in the highest peaks.

The lower section is ranching country. At 4.7 miles the road enters Arroyo Seco Recreation Area, Forest Service land. On some maps this area is called "The Lakes," in reference to two small, now stagnant reservoirs dammed by local ranchers named Abbott. Passing the streamside day-use area and the campground, both popular with Salinas Valley locals, Arroyo Seco Road ends at a locked gate next to the Gorge Trail parking area and trailhead. This is the start of Indians Road, which used to carry motorists 16.6 miles up the canyon to Indians Station, just over the hump from San Antonio Valley. Locally known as the Gorge Trail, Indians Road has been closed for many years to vehicular traffic by landslides, but it's open to hikers and mountain bikers (see chapter 5, Hiking the Trails of Big Sur). An easy, 0.5-mile stroll along Indians Road from the Gorge Trail parking area is enough to give you a view down a near-vertical drop of more than 230 feet to the river.

The San Antonio Valley

San Antonio Valley Route

START: Tidball Store in old Jolon (950 feet), about 19 miles from King City on County Road G14. Prepare to drive through Fort Hunter Liggett on County Road G14, Milpitas Road, and Del Venturi Road.

DESTINATION: 22.8 miles to Santa Lucia Memorial Campground (2,075 feet) and the area known as Indians Station.

ROAD CONDITION: Wide, paved, two-lane road with two fords of the San Antonio River.

AMENITIES: The Hacienda; Santa Lucia Memorial and Escondido Campgrounds.

SURROUNDING JURISDICTION: The first 17.4 miles are Fort Hunter Liggett, and the last 5.4 miles Forest Service. Before entering Fort Hunter Liggett, all visitors need to present photo identification at sentry box, and drivers also need to show proof of car registration and insurance. For military road closures, call (831) 386–2503 or (831) 386–2310. Note that the speed limit on Fort Hunter Liggett is 10 miles per hour when passing troops and 25 mph in all other areas, unless posted otherwise.

This isn't a single road, but a route through one of the most scenic and historic valleys in California with stops at Mission San Antonio, the Hacienda, and Wagon Caves. Essentially you'll be driving from Jolon to Indians Station along County Road G14, Milpitas Road, and Del Venturi Road.

You start in tiny, historic Jolon (pronounced *ha-LONE*) at the Tidball Store. This isn't hard to find, since the old town burned in 1929, leaving but two public buildings standing. (A third prominent ruin, the adobe Dutton Hotel, was

Stately oak-and-grassland savannas line Milpitas Road through the San Antonio Valley, in Los Padres National Forest.

built by Antonio Ramirez in 1850, and served as a stage stop on El Camino Real.) The sturdy, wood-frame Tidball General Store, currently sitting idle, did a roaring business during Jolon's heyday from 1875 to 1924. Captain Thomas T. Tidball, who moved his original store from the nearby Dutton Hotel, catered to gold miners, ranchers, and travelers along the old El Camino Real.

When J. Smeaton Chase rode through town in 1911, Jolon was an important regional ranching center and supply depot for the mines and homesteads in the interior of the Santa Lucia Range. It still possessed two stores, two blacksmith shops, a dance hall, a jail, three saloons, two hotels, and two (yes, *two*) Chinatowns to serve the needs of Chinese miners. "I noted that the dialect of Jolon," Chase wrote, "is rather above than below the Western standard in amount and quality of profanity; and that days when the thermometer registers a hundred and odd degrees are pronounced by Jolonians to be agreeable."

Despite the heat and profanity, the other public building still standing proud in downtown Jolon is St. Luke's Episcopal Church. Built in 1884 of redwood

The Hacienda

On a hill overlooking Mission San Antonio, this striking hotel was built for William Randolph Hearst as a fancy ranch house. Designed in the Mission style by Julia Morgan, the Milpitas Ranch House (as it was known to Hearst) sports a long, shaded arcade and bell towers built of concrete, capped by a red tile roof. The structure was designed to house thirty ranch workers, but Hearst used it as a kind of destination for horseback rides and Californio-style fiestas. Among the many guests who stayed there were Spencer Tracy, Dick Powell, Will Rogers, Clark Gable, Herbert Hoover, Jean Harlow, Leslie Howard, and Errol Flynn. Hearst's special friend, Marion Davies, used to stay in the bell tower. Some speculate that she still haunts the place, but I myself reckon she's got better things to do.

When Hearst transferred his northern ranch lands to the military, the Hacienda became a hotel and restaurant used mainly by military personnel. It still serves that purpose, but it's open to everyone. The lunch and dinner menus in the grand dining room feature hearty American fare at economical prices. The bedrooms range from simple "cowboy" rooms without baths to the larger, better-furnished rooms in the towers. During the evenings local ranchers, military personnel, and travelers alike repair to the genial bar in the Lounge. Even if you don't stay the night, dinner at the Hacienda makes a memorable end to any day trip to the San Antonio Valley.

Many travelers come expressly for the experience of staying in a building designed by Julia Morgan for Mr. Hearst, an opportunity denied at Hearst's other local estate, La Cuesta Encantada (aka Hearst Castle). At the Hacienda you can study the architectural details at your leisure—the lamps, the filigree work, the carved doors and windows, and much more. The heroic murals that decorate the dining hall were not in Morgan's plan, but were painted in 1957 by Bill Runyan, who had been a soldier at Fort Hunter Liggett. They depict the Spanish settlement of the San Antonio Valley. A rougher-looking crew of priests, neophytes, ranchers, soldiers, and assorted tough hombres and their ladies has never graced the pages of a history book. The Hacienda, P.O. Box 115, Lockwood, CA 93932; (831) 386–2900; hacienda.newhalltele com.net.

dragged over the mountains from the coast, it was painted white and fitted with stained-glass windows shipped all the way from England. The church bell hanging outside originally graced a steam engine. Several Civil War veterans are buried in the picturesque cemetery on the hill behind the church.

Follow the signs from Jolon to the sentry gate of Fort Hunter Liggett; the gate is approximately 1.5 miles from the Tidball Store. If your papers are in order, you will be issued a pass for display on your windshield. You enter on the Milpitas Road. You are not allowed to park or walk around on the base, *except* at Mission San Antonio and in the adjacent military settlement, which includes the Hacienda, a gas station, administrative buildings, barracks, a chapel, a theater, a post exchange, a bowling alley with snack bar, and residences. Be sure to visit Mission San Antonio and the Hacienda, both of which are visible from the junction of the Milpitas and Del Venturi Roads, where this tour turns left (southwest).

At the junction of the Milpitas and Del Venturi Roads (5.1 miles from the Tidball Store), turn left (southwest) on Del Venturi Road. Almost immediately you will ford the San Antonio River on a concrete roadbed. Obviously, you don't want to do this if the river is running too high and fast, as it does sometimes after heavy rainfall. The military will try to close the road if the ford is too high, but use your own judgment. (If the Del Venturi Road is closed, you probably can use the unpaved Milpitas Road beyond Mission San Antonio; but since signs on that road warn the public away, check at the sentry gate before using it.)

After the first ford of the San Antonio River, Del Venturi Road turns north into a narrow valley bedecked with oaks. Then, just to break the monotony, you get to ford the San Antonio River a second time. On the opposite bank, the Milpitas Road (unpaved) rejoins from the right; thenceforth, the Milpitas Road *is* the paved highway.

At 17.2 miles from Jolon, the road crosses from Fort Hunter Liggett into Los Padres National Forest, where visitors are free to park and wander at will, so long as they keep the road clear. Beware of cattle and deer on the road. The upper San Antonio has a stately presence. Large oaks and spacious pastures roll in a splendid progression across the broad valley floor, while the sides rise up as chaparral-covered mountain or sandstone rock formations. Mysterious canyons and distant mountains add intrigue. The spring wildflowers are justly famous.

The first of the monolithic rocks is Wagon Caves, so called because the Harlan family, who homesteaded near Lucia on the Big Sur side of the Santa Lucias, sheltered a wagon there for their use whenever they went to town—which happened to be King City in the Salinas Valley. They started and finished their three-day round-trip journey by riding over the Santa Lucias on horseback, with pack train, along the nearby Carrizo Trail. After automobiles came into general use, the Harlans replaced their wagon with a car. This rock formation is large and complex, with many high, sheer drop-offs and mossy, slippery clefts. There are also many vernal pools in winter and early spring. If you explore, take care not only for your own safety, but also for the delicate, shallow-rooted plants that grow in and around the rocks, and for the flaky sandstone itself.

The large outcrop of sandstone rocks and boulders known as Wagon Caves is rich in San Antonio Valley history.

There are two very historic ranches in the upper San Antonio Valley, both private property, and both closed to public access.

The Avila Ranch lies on the west side, in the hills. (The unmarked, unpaved turn-off is 18.7 miles from the Tidball Store.) Before the missions were secularized, it was an outlier mule ranch for the San Antonio mission. In 1864 Vicente Avila bought it for $13 from José Maria Gil. Avila was a Salinan. He called it Rancho Salsipuedes—which means "get out if you can." The ranch is still owned by the same family, and it is private property. The historic Carrizo Trail passes close to the Salsipuedes Ranch; it is the very trail, in fact, that Vicente Avila was riding on when he stopped to visit Gil, who offered to sell the ranch to him for the contents of his pockets. To see a bit of living history, take a short walk on the Carizzo Trail. The whole footway is rough and typically requires route-finding and bushwhacking skills, but the Forest Service trailhead is clear and easy to find. Just turn left (west) onto a dirt double track 1.1 miles north of the Wagon Caves parking area. Drive down this double track about 0.9 mile to the flats by the river and park clear of the bridge, which is closed by a locked gate. (If road conditions are bad, walk the double track.) The bridge gate is emblazoned with the word, SALSIPUEDES. After crossing the bridge on foot, you will see the signposted, single-track Carizzo Trail on your right.

The *other* historic ranch of the upper San Antonio Valley is the Indians Ranch, so called because many of the displaced Mission Indians found sanctuary there after Mission San Antonio was secularized. It was therefore one of the most historical Salinan *rancherías*. The founders of the ranch—a family named Encinales—were also Salinan, and their descendants still own it. There may be some historical significance to the fact that it sits at the base of the Salinan sacred mountain, Sta'yokale. The Milpitas Road passes the unmarked Indians Ranch gate at 20.1 miles from Jolon.

More sandstone rock formations crop up as you continue your drive up the valley. The most extensive are on the western ridge, where jagged pieces of ancient seabed have been broken, uplifted, and tilted into place, like scaly armor. Where the Milpitas Road climbs up to the divide between the San Antonio Valley and the Arroyo Seco, you can park and scramble straight onto rocks. Bouldering fanatics could spend days exploring this area.

Cresting at the head of the San Antonio watershed, you make a final, short descent to the Arroyo Seco near Santa Lucia Memorial Campground, an area also known as Indians Station. During summer motorists can drive an additional 2.7 miles on unpaved Indians Road to Escondido Campground, and cyclists and hikers can go there even when the gate is closed. The idyllic enclave at Indians Station, however, is worth exploring. It occupies a bowl-shaped valley at the foot of Junipero Serra Peak, sacred to the Salinan, who know it as Sta'yokale. A handful of private cabins stand in the woods, and a rustic fishing lodge overlooks oak-shaded cascades on the Arroyo Seco. The river is pristine, though its many swimming holes are popular. Escape the summer crowds by moving farther upstream or downstream, or by coming during the off-season. Hikers can launch into Ventana Wilderness along the Arroyo Seco Trail or the Santa Lucia Trail. The latter climbs to the 5,862-foot summit of Junipero Serra Peak.

As to the scenic appeal of this place, once again the sandstone rock formations steal the show. The valley is scattered with huge rocks. One massive bluff forms a natural amphitheater, a monumental block streaked with water stains and pocked with small caves, just beyond the Santa Lucia trailhead. With the sacred peak as a backdrop, this landscape encapsulates both the mystery and the strange beauty of the interior of the Santa Lucia Range.

Back Road Camping

With the exception of Arroyo Seco Campground, back road camps in the Santa Lucias are primitive, some little more than a flat spot on a bulldozed spur. You will need to bring your own water, or the means to purify stream water. Unless otherwise stated, these camps charge no fee. Los Padres National Forest; (831) 385–5434; www.fs.fed.us.

Note that there are also developed campsites at Nacimiento and San Antonio Reservoirs (see chapter 6, More Outdoor Recreation Fun) and along Highway 1 (see chapter 3, Destinations Along Highway 1).

Alder Creek Camp
Campsites: 2
On the creek; no potable water.

Arroyo Seco Campground
Campsites: 49
A fee site with family sites and one group site near the end of Arroyo Seco Road. Potable water, showers, trailer and RV space. There's also a slightly cheaper, more primitive camping area. For reservations, call ReserveUSA at (877) 444–6777; www.reserveusa.com.

Bottchers Gap Campground
Campsites: 11
A fee site on the ridge at the end of Palo Colorado Road. No water. Some walk-in campsites.

China Camp
Campsites: 6
On Tassajara Road near Chews Ridge. No water.

Escondido Campground
Campsites: 9
On Indians Road near Indians Station. Open to vehicles only during the dry season. No water.

Lottie Potrero Camp
Campsites: Primitive
A primitive site on McKern Road.

Sandstone outcrops at Indians Station are among the most picturesque and historic formations of the Santa Lucia Mountains.

Nacimiento Campground
Campsites: 8
A fee site on Nacimiento-Fergusson Road, along the Nacimiento River. No potable water.

Ponderosa Campground
Campsites: 23
A fee site near the creek on Nacimiento-Fergusson Road. Drinking water is available.

Prewitt Ridge Campground
Campsites: 3
On Prewitt Ridge Road, near South Coast Ridge Road. No water.

Santa Lucia Memorial Park Campground
Campsites: 8
At Indians Station. No potable water.

Sycamore Flats Camp
Campsites: 4
Near Willow Creek Road. No water.

White Oaks Campground
Campsites: 7
On Tassajara Road. No water.

Chapter 5
Hiking the Trails of Big Sur

Hiking is the best way to know a rugged place like the Santa Lucia Mountains. Though its highest summit doesn't even reach 6,000 feet, the range's roller-coaster canyons, peaks, and ridges are harsher for hikers than many higher mountain ranges. The 22-mile hike along the famous Pine Ridge Trail (Hikes 14, 15, 30, 42, 43, and 45) from Big Sur Station to China Camp, for instance, has an accumulated elevation gain of more than 11,300 feet, with about 4,000 feet lost—and that's by no means the toughest 22 miles in the Santa Lucias.

If you want a gentle hike, you should generally stick to the beaches, coastal terraces, and canyon bottoms. I single out many short, easy walks elsewhere throughout this book.

In addition to steep climbs, Big Sur trails typically challenge hikers with overgrown paths, flaky trail tread on steep hillsides, scarce water, tangled blowdowns (fallen trees and branches), summer heat, and winter fords. None of these is necessarily a *bad* thing; they just go with the territory. And I haven't even mentioned ticks and poison oak—which I consider unpleasant in all firsthand encounters—or cougars and rattlesnakes, which in my book are endearing, respectable, and only marginally hazardous creatures.

Backcountry Info

Trail Maps

Point Lobos, Garrapata, Pfeiffer Big Sur, Julian Pfeiffer Burns, Limekiln, and San Simeon State Parks all publish good trail maps, as does Garland Regional Park. For Los Padres National Forest, the following three maps are popular with hikers. Keep in mind that no printed trail map shows current trail conditions.

- The Forest Service publishes a standard Los Padres National Forest map. You will need the one showing the Monterey and Santa Lucia Ranger Districts. There are no topographic lines, but townships are marked.
- The Sierra Club publishes Los Padres National Forest, Northern Section Trail Map. Again, there are no topographic lines, but townships are marked.
- The Wilderness Press publishes Big Sur and Ventana Wilderness. It has topographic lines and detailed insets of some state parks.

Current Trail Reports

- Contact the Forest Service for trail information at (831) 385-5434; www.fs.fed.us.
- Ventana Wilderness Alliance has a useful online forum, Trail Reports: www.ventanawild.org.

Permits

Hikers and backpackers do not need wilderness permits in the Ventana and Silver Peak Wilderness Areas. The Adventure Pass likewise is not required to park anywhere in the Monterey Ranger District of Los Padres National Forest.

Guided Hikes

- Big Sur Adventures: (831) 622-7777; www.tourbigsur.com.

It may be that you get lucky, and a heroic Ventana Wilderness Alliance crew of volunteers clears out a trail the week before you hike it. But by anticipating the worst, you won't be disappointed. You can also look at the bright side of a hard hike. A summer-afternoon bushwhack can evoke a Swedish-sauna kind of pleasure—with blazing sun and the whiplash of chamisal taking the place of invigorating steam heat and stinging birch switches. A backpack trip through the heart of the Ventana provokes a fuller range of emotions than mere delight. It can be tough but is usually exhilarating, the stuff of great memories and epic stories. Some of the worst trails and the best swimming holes in the U.S. national forest system can be found in the Santa Lucia backcountry. There are thousands of little glens, strange rock formations, and hidden places in the mountains accessible only to hikers willing to climb over blowdowns and to pick their ways through healthy stands of coyote brush. For old Ventana hands, the unusual beauty and fascination are worth the effort.

Backcountry Hazards

The following pointers are rudimentary, not a crash course in survival. Use your own good judgment when planning a trip. Always take local conditions and your own abilities into account. If you're new to hiking and backpacking, consult a general guide to the subject before venturing into the Santa Lucia backcountry.

Bushwhacking

Chaparral grows fast, pinching trails down to bushwhack gauntlets. If not burned or pruned back, the brush will quickly hide trails completely. In the forest hundreds of trees fall across trails every winter. Some sections of trail become virtually impenetrable after a year or two without maintenance. There are many trails clearly marked on official maps that are not obvious on the ground. The Forest Service just does not have the staff or the money to keep them all open.

State parks have smaller areas, and their trail crews generally keep popular trails clear, but downed trees are always a problem in winter. Volunteer groups certainly do their part to help. It's a huge job.

Bushwhacking is hard work and will increase the amount of hiking time required over any given distance by a factor of two or more. Backcountry hikers in the national forest should carry folding pruning saws or clippers. Every Forest Service ranger I've asked about this has welcomed hikers' help in clearing trails and cutting back branches from the trail corridor. Be sensible, though, and make sure you're clearing a trail, not blazing one. State park rangers might frown on unsupervised trail maintenance, so ask first.

Sometimes it's hard to tell the trail from the brush in the Santa Lucias. Be prepared for bushwhacking when hiking any trail in Los Padres National Forest.

Veteran hikers on Ventana trails wear long pants and carry a long-sleeved shirt for pushing through brush. They spend their rest stops picking pieces of brush from shirt collars and sleeves, boot tops, and day packs. Some plants also draw blood, a kind of Ventana baptism. Consider yourself a veteran when you first grasp why the yucca, known as Our Lord's Candle for its spectacular bloom, is also called Spanish bayonet.

Poison Oak

This beautiful but noxious shrub grows as a vine or bush, crowding trails and creekbeds all through the Santa Lucias. Touching its leaves, twigs, or berries causes severe systemic rash in most people. If you don't recognize it, have someone point it out to you before you head out to any trail. If you think you might have touched poison oak, wash the affected area with cold water. (Some people claim that dishwashing liquid helps, but I am not convinced.) If the rash breaks out, doctors can prescribe treatments for relief.

Vermin

Face flies, so called by backpackers because they buzz incessantly around hikers' heads, appear in the hot weather and are a major nuisance in the backcountry. Biting flies and mosquitoes are also pesky in summer, especially just before dusk and at dawn. Some mosquitoes may carry West Nile fever. Repellent and netting help. Ticks are especially common from spring through summer, on grasses and shrubs alongside well-worn paths, and may carry Lyme disease. After latching onto a person, they usually climb upward to the abdomen. When hiking, tuck your pant cuffs into your socks so the ticks have to climb your trousers rather than your leg, giving you more time to catch them. Stop frequently to check for ticks. If you're bitten, extract the entire body with a tweezers and save it to test for disease.

Erratic Signpostings

Bring a good map and know how to use it. Trails and junctions are often marked by trail tape (colored ribbons) tied to the brush.

High Water

There are no bridges in the Ventana and Silver Peak Wilderness Areas. Some state park creek crossings are bridged, and some not. In summer we don't need no stinkin' bridges, but with winter rains even tiny creeks can swell to torrents, and fording becomes dangerous. A stream no deeper than your ankle can knock you down. If you are inexperienced, do not risk it without veteran guidance.

Steep Trails

Dry leaves fallen on steep slope are very slippery. A walking stick helps. Be very careful on steep hillside washouts, of which there are many in the backcountry.

Rattlesnakes

This venomous snake is common throughout Big Sur, among rocks, chaparral, and tall grasses, near streams, and—in brief—just about anywhere. A rattler will warn you by shaking its tail to produce a buzzing sound. Your best defense is to let them know you're coming, so that they return the favor. Do that by walking with a stick and poking into areas ahead of you on the trail, especially around blowdowns and encroaching brush. If you hear a buzz, stop and investigate before proceeding. Immobilize, calm, and evacuate a bite victim. Never cut the wound or apply a tourniquet. Fatalities from rattlesnake bites are rare. Snakes are essential for keeping down the rodent population. Killing a rattlesnake that gives fair warning is bad policy, for it favors the propagation of snakes disinclined to give a warning rattle.

Mountain Lions

They are numerous, but shy, and many a lifelong hiker has never seen one. Although attacks are rare, mountain lions seem to be incited to attack when people bolt and run, so in the unlikely event that you meet a lion, stand your ground, shout, and make yourself look large (by opening your jacket, for instance). If attacked, fight back with all your strength. Children walking alone are at greatest risk. Refer to Bill Schneider's *Lion Sense* (Globe Pequot, 2005) for more tips.

Raccoons

When searching for food, raccoons are aggressive molesters of backpacks and tents. Store your food in a bear canister, or hang it from a tree.

Waterborne Pathogens

Don't take chances with *Giardia lamblia*, a waterborne protozoan. Drinking water infested with this parasite—and it's found virtually everywhere throughout the world these days—can give you giardiasis, a thoroughly nasty intestinal condition. Instead, be sure to carry a water filter or other means to purify water.

Heat Exhaustion

The effects of heat exhaustion are cramping, exhaustion, light-headedness, and nausea. If you get dehydrated, find shade, rest, and keep drinking. Sipping an electrolyte solution helps; make it with one teaspoon of salt and one tablespoon of sugar dissolved in a liter of water. Some commercial drinks, such as

Gatorade, also replace electrolytes. Check temperatures before you go. I like the National Oceanic and Atmospheric Administration's Web site, www.wrh .noaa.gov. For the interior of the Santa Lucias, the weather in Paso Robles is a good indicator.

Selected Hikes

Hundreds of miles of trails wind through the Santa Lucia Range. The hikes listed below are mostly day hikes or partial day hikes, with some longer loops for backpackers. For more exhaustive listings of Santa Lucia trails, see the Hiking Books section at the end of this chapter.

Distances to trailheads along Highway 1 are listed in the Highway 1 Mileage Log at the end of chapter 2, Driving Highway 1. All others are listed in chapter 4, Driving the Back Roads. Approximate elevations are given in parentheses.

The hikes range in distance from about half a mile to about 27 miles. In each entry I've listed the type of hike: loop, semi-loop, or out-and-back. Each hike is rated informally as to difficulty, from easy to very strenuous. You'll also see a listing for accumulated elevation loss and gain—a figure that summarizes elevation changes to give you a sense of how rolling the terrain will be. In these hikes elevation loss and gain ranges from "scant" to 9,243 feet.

For those seeking even more challenge, Hikes 41 through 45 give you some ideas on how to piece together trails to create long backpacking routes through Big Sur. The most strenuous of these traverses 70 miles and almost 22,000 feet of elevation change—obviously, not for novices!

Trailheads North of Big Sur

1 Cypress Grove Trail

An easy 0.8-mile loop in Point Lobos State Reserve with scant elevation change. Start and end near the information kiosk at the sea lion parking area. See map on page 40.

This trail loops through the Allan Memorial Grove, one of only two natural stands of Monterey cypresses in the world. Skirting headland cliffs, you can see Point Sur 15 miles to the south. To the north you may recognize Pinnacle Point from countless paintings and photographs. Beyond the blue backdrop of Carmel Bay, Cypress Point on the farther shore is home to the *other* natural grove of Monterey cypresses. Bent by strong sea winds, their branches grow low and crooked, like the beckoning ghost-trees of a Disney cartoon, but their shape isn't their only weird feature. As you follow the trail down granite steps into the thicker forest, notice that many of their branches, and the rocks beneath them, are covered with bright orange lichens. Spiritualists from different cultures have called this forest enchanted, even haunted.

2 Bird Rock Trail

An easy 0.8-mile semi-loop hike in Point Lobos State Reserve, with detours to China Cove and Gibson Beach. Scant elevation change. Start and end at the southern parking lot, at the end of the park road. See map on page 40.

Starting with a short climb, you'll traverse a hillside and marine terraces at a steady elevation along the edge of bluffs. The delightful views of turquoise coves, white sand beaches, wave-washed sea caves, and the forested hills and villas of the Carmel Highlands strike a Mediterranean chord. Long stairways lead down to a pocket beach at China Cove, once a smugglers' landing, and to the exquisite crescent of Gibson Beach. Birders will be mesmerized by the thousands of whirling, screaming denizens of Bird Rock.

The sea caves and white sands of China Cove appear almost tropical from the Bird Rock Trail in Point Lobos State Reserve.

Soberanes Creek–Rocky Ridge Loop

A moderately strenuous 4.4-mile loop with an accumulated elevation gain and loss of nearly 2,000 feet. Start and end at the Soberanes trailhead along Highway 1 in Garrapata State Park.

With one trail renowned for redwood forests, and the other for grand maritime views, this two-trail loop has it all. Starting from the Soberanes barn (130 feet) behind a row of cypress trees, the Soberanes Creek Trail delivers two surprises right at the start. First, there's a hillside covered in prickly pear, which is not native to Big Sur. (Perhaps a homesteader transplanted the patriarchal cactus from one of the missions, where prickly pear were grown for fruit.) Second, you enter a thick redwood forest, the front ranks stunted and pruned by ocean winds. These are a surprise only because they're so well hidden from the road. Crossing and recrossing the forest stream, you ascend sometimes on steps, sometimes with little switchbacks, sometimes delving higher into oak woodland or chaparral.

The trail through the redwoods of Soberanes Canyon in Garrapata State Park is well maintained.

At 1.5 miles you'll meet the Rocky Ridge Trail junction. If the obviously steep climb before you saps your enthusiasm, turn around here; a return trip through the redwoods is no booby prize. This back-door approach to Rocky Ridge is an arduous, poorly engineered, but well-established use trail that eschews graded switchbacks for a direct ascent of about 1,070 feet in less than a mile, but the views are nice. Once you reach the ridge (1,820 feet), the return is more reasonably graded, though still steep—but the views are even more glorious. To the north lies the canyon of Malpaso Creek; to the west, the Pacific shore, with Whale Peak and Highway 1 in miniature. The barking of distant sea lions accompanies your long descent on brushy switchbacks.

4 Jackson Camp

A strenuous 10.6-mile out-and-back hike or backpack trip with an accumulated loss and gain of elevation of about 3,440 feet. Start and end at Bottchers Gap (2,050 feet).

From Bottchers Gap, the deep, steep-walled canyon of the Little Sur River appears (in poet Robinson Jeffers's words) "a forest basin / Where two-hundred-foot redwoods look like the pile on a Turkish carpet." Walk down the unpaved road 3 miles to the river at the Pico Blanco Boy Scout Camp. This camp is private property, so stay on the track and be ready to notify any staff that you are just hiking through. Crossing the river on a footbridge (810 feet), you pass the trading post and commissary, then go up a short, steep switchback road to a signposted Forest Service junction. The left fork (east) contours through the redwood forest for 1.4 miles, dropping at the end into redwood-shaded Jackson Camp (960 feet). It's pretty, but if a scout patrol comes through, it will be crowded. No formal paths invade the upper reaches of the Little Sur's canyon, but adventurous hikers who continue upstream will find remote campsites.

5 Pico Blanco

A strenuous 11.8-mile out-and-back hike with an accumulated loss and gain of elevation of about 3,680 feet. Start and end at Bottchers Gap (2,050 feet).

The summit of Pico Blanco is private property, but this hike takes you dramatically close. From Bottchers Gap, walk down the unpaved road 3 miles to the river at the Pico Blanco Boy Scout Camp. This camp is private property, so stay on the track and be ready to notify any staff that you are just hiking through. Crossing the river on a footbridge (810 feet), you pass the trading post and commissary, then go up a short, steep switchback road to a signposted Forest Service junction. Take the right fork (southwest). Climb 1 mile up "Cardiac Hill" to Launtz Ridge (2,194 feet) for a vista over the valley of the South Fork of the Little Sur. A descent of 0.6 mile brings you to Duveneck's Hole (1,850 feet), the carcass of an early-twentieth-century hunting and fishing lodge built of hand-hewn redwood. The final outward-bound 0.5 mile of this hike climbs from the redwood gulch to more open terrain. Turn around after you have a chance to enjoy the close-up view of Pico Blanco (3,709 feet), the Esselen sacred mountain, whose limestone and marble outcrops and boulders inspired its Spanish name. An eccentric old hermit named Al Clark had his mine nearby.

Options: Backpackers could continue farther to Pico Blanco Camp, famed for its lovely swimming hole. If you're an experienced hiker—and you park a shuttle vehicle on the Old Coast Road—you could also press onward to that roadhead (12.4 miles from Bottchers Gap). Expect many deadfalls, encroaching brush, and a wet ford of the Little Sur River to slow your journey.

6 Mount Carmel

A strenuous 8-mile out-and-back hike or backpack trip with an accumulated gain and loss of elevation of about 2,770 feet. Start and end at Bottchers Gap (2,050 feet).

The Skinner Ridge Trail is a good hike on a brisk, clear day between November and April, mainly because the summer sun burns hot in the open chaparral, while the summer fog obscures the grand coastal views. The fact that most of the trailside chaparral blooms during winter also helps spruce up what might otherwise be olive-drab foliage. The path climbs first to Skinner Ridge, then descends slightly to a viewpoint (3,370 feet) at 2.1 miles, reaching the Turner Creek Trail junction at 2.3 miles. From there it begins to climb again, mounting up to Devils Peak (4,158 feet) at 3.2 miles, and finally to Carmel Peak (4,417 feet) at 4 miles. Despite the dense foliage, hikers enjoy a sporadically unfolding panorama of Mill Creek Canyon, the Pacific Ocean, the Little Sur basin, and Ventana Double Cone. By climbing on rocks above the chaparral on Carmel Peak, you might see as far as Monterey Bay and the Santa Cruz Mountains. Backpackers can stay at Apple Tree Camp (2,920 feet), 0.3 mile down the Turner Creek Trail. Expect to find water there only in the wet seasons.

7 Ventana Double Cone

A strenuous 27-mile out-and-back backpack trip with a gain and loss of elevation of about 9,243 feet. Start and end at Bottchers Gap (2,050 feet).

Of the various routes to Ventana Double Cone, this one typically has the clearest trail, in part because it's the most popular route, and in part because it mostly follows a ridge instead of a canyon bottom. Take the Skinner Ridge Trail, climbing first to Skinner Ridge, then descending slightly to a viewpoint (3,370 feet) at 2.1 miles and reaching the Turner Creek Trail junction at 2.3 miles. From there you'll begin to climb again, mounting to Devils Peak (4,158 feet) at 3.2 miles. Continue east on the Ventana Trail, making camp at Pat Spring Camp (3,740 feet), 6.4 miles from Bottchers Gap. (Water is usually available nearby from Pat Spring on the Ventana Trail.)

From this camp Ventana Double Cone is a 14-mile out-and-back trek, with an accumulated elevation gain and loss of about 4,550 feet—a strenuous day hike with some likely bushwhacking. The trail follows the ridge, rising and falling, hitting its low point of about 3,475 feet at the Puerto Suello Gap, and its high point atop the rugged granite crest of Ventana Double Cone (4,853 feet). This grand, granite subrange is emblematic of the Ventana Wilderness because it contains its namesake—the Ventana, or Window, also known as the Slot. You can see the Ventana just west from the summit. To the southeast are Ventana Cone (4,727 feet) and South Ventana Cone (4,965 feet).

Trailheads in the Big Sur River Valley

8 Headlands Trail

An easy 2.6-mile out-and-back hike with scant elevation change. Start and end at the north side of the central parking area in Andrew Molera State Park. See the map on page 46.

Starting as a single-track trail running parallel to the Big Sur River, this route delves through riparian woodland to the walk-in Trail Camp at 0.3 mile. Cross through camp on a dirt road, passing a gum tree grove and willow thicket to a bluff above the Big Sur River's lagoon. Here the trail, once again single track, mounts the bluff and strikes seaward, looping through a dwarfed, wind-shaped, wild garden of coffeeberry, sage, and poison oak. Freshened by a sea breeze and the crash of breakers, this vantage point surveys the grand arc of Molera Beach clear to Cooper Point, a thin yellow strand holding back Pfeiffer Ridge, the Big Sur Valley, and the high Coast Ridge from the restless Pacific. This is a great place to look for whales and otters, and to study the waves and currents, the whirling seabirds, and the surf-dodging gulls and waders on the sand.

9 Molera Beach

An easy 2.1-mile loop with scant elevation change. Start and end at the central parking area in Andrew Molera State Park. See map on page 46.

Begin by crossing the Big Sur River. There are plans to build a permanent bridge, but for now you cross on a two-plank footbridge during the dry season. During the wet season, the planks are removed to allow steelhead to spawn, and you have to wade. On the opposite bank the basic plan is to make a counter-clockwise loop to the beach by going out on the Beach Trail to a natural berm that backs the beach. You complete your 2.1-mile loop by returning on the

The Big Sur River flows into the ocean at Molera Beach, seen here from the Headlands Trail in Andrew Molera State Park.

Creamery Meadow Trail. Any walking that you do on the beach is extra mileage, but it is mileage well spent. Strewn with driftwood, including large logs and who knows what else might wash ashore, Molera Beach is a beachcomber's delight. Birding is rich, particularly at the mouth of the Big Sur River. It also offers plenty of seclusion, especially to those who wander south along the strand. The farther you go, the more you need to be aware of the incoming high tide, or a heavy surf can easily cover the beach up to the bluff, blocking your retreat.

10 Pfeiffer Ridge Loop

A moderate 7.4-mile loop hike with an elevation gain and loss of about 1,200 feet. Start and end at the central parking area in Andrew Molera State Park. See map on page 46.

With intimate views of a wild coast, a diverse habitat of coastal scrub, grassland, oak woodland, redwoods, beach, and rocky shore, Pfeiffer Ridge is Big Sur in miniature. No other hike offers so broad a 360-degree vista of Big Sur without making you climb at least three times its height. After you cross the Big Sur River on the plank bridge by the parking area, you'll hike a loop made of four distinct trails. Take the Creamery Meadow Trail to the beach but, instead of walking onto the sand, turn left (south) onto the Bluffs Trail. This trail follows a marine terrace above Molera Beach, a fine vantage for whale-watching. At 2.4 miles the Bluffs Trail ends at the Spring Trail, which switchbacks in 0.1 mile down to an isolated beach. Crossing a dam of driftwood logs, turn right on the beach to see the springs, with moss that hangs like living stalactites from the cliff. After this little detour, continue south on the Panorama Trail, climbing from coastal scrub into a grove of wind-stunted redwoods, before making a U-turn and topping out on Pfeiffer Ridge. Follow the Ridge Trail north, descending slowly in full sight of the Coast Ridge and the Pacific. Touching down at the Creamery Meadows Trail, return to the parking area.

11 Pfeiffer Falls–Valley View Loop

A moderate 2.2-mile semi-loop with an accumulated elevation gain and loss of about 560 feet. Start and end near the Ewoldsen Memorial Nature Center in Pfeiffer Big Sur State Park. See map on page 48.

The most popular hike in the park, the Pfeiffer Falls Trail climbs to a 60-foot waterfall in an old-growth redwood forest. You'll return a different way, with a detour to the 780-foot knoll at Valley View. From there you can look 7.2 miles down the broad bore of the Big Sur River's valley to the great rock at Point Sur. The long flanks of 3,379-foot Mount Manuel loom to the east.

12 Buzzards Roost Trail

A moderate 3-mile loop with an accumulated gain and loss of elevation of about 1,000 feet. Start and end at the trailhead on the south bank of the Big Sur River, next to the bridge that leads from the lodge toward the campground, in Pfeiffer Big Sur State Park. See map on page 48.

This beautiful trail traces a succession of biological habitats typical of a Big Sur hillside, from riparian woodland, through old-growth redwood forest and oak woodland, and on to the heavy chaparral on Pfeiffer Ridge. The ocean and mountain views from Buzzards Roost would be exceptional anywhere else, though for Big Sur they are just ordinarily exceptional. What stands out most to a naturalist is the unusual proximity of redwoods to hard chaparral, and the fun of speculating on the natural causes behind the clear lines of distinction between them and other local life zones.

13 Mount Manuel

A strenuous 8.8-mile out-and-back hike with an elevation gain and loss of about 3,350 feet. Start and end at the Oak Grove trailhead, near the large parking lot close to the softball field and picnic area in Pfeiffer Big Sur State Park (230 feet). See map on page 48.

The views en route to this summit on the Coast Ridge's Mount Manuel are stupendous, embracing much of the interior of the Ventana Wilderness and far out to sea. The trail itself is in the national forest, and you reach it by switchbacking 0.5 mile up the Oak Grove Trail from Pfeiffer Big Sur State Park's main road to the Mount Manuel Trail junction, where you turn right (east). Leaving the oak woodland behind, the path climbs steadily through grass- and chaparral-covered hillsides that drop precipitously into the Big Sur River gorge. This section can be hot going on a summer afternoon. Surmounting a side ridge at 1.8 miles, the trail turns sharply north into a wooded ravine, passing through woodland and redwoods, before emerging again in lovely chaparral. Reaching another lateral ridge at 3.1 miles, turn sharply west onto a

Rounding the back of the Coast Ridge, the Mount Manuel Trail nabs a good view of the granite heights of the Ventana Cones.

tree-shaded, north-facing slope. After attaining the main Coast Ridge at about 3.7 miles, you'll continue the rest of the way in view of the ocean. Although Mount Manuel is long and partly covered in trees and brush, the trail leads to a very satisfactory summit knoll (3,379 feet) capped by rocks and a wind-stunted oak. North of there, the trail disappears into the brush. Something to think about as you ponder the views: The Esselen believed that after death, their souls dwelled on an island beyond the horizon, and that the souls' journey passed over the Coast Ridge somewhere between Manuel Peak and Pico Blanco.

14 Sykes Hot Springs

*This strenuous 20.4-mile out-and-back route is best done as an overnighter.
The trail has an accumulated gain and loss of elevation of about 6,800 feet.
Start and end at Big Sur Station (300 feet).*

About 0.3 mile downstream from Sykes Camp (1,080 feet), these six small hot
springs on the Big Sur River are the most popular destination in the Ventana
Wilderness. Little rock dams collect water in shallow pools, where backpackers
(some buck naked for the occasion) soak in the midst of the wilderness. Add a
sizable sunbathing faction and a pervading stench of sulfur, and you've got quite
a party going. The "wilderness freeway" to Sykes is the Forest Service's Pine
Ridge Trail, a long roller-coaster hike up the Big Sur River Canyon. It's mostly
a shady trail, whose conifers and glimpses of mountain give it the flavor of mid-
Sierra forest path. Backpackers who want to make a leisurely journey can stay
along the way at Terrace Creek Camp (5.2 miles, 1,325 feet) or Barlow Flat
Camp (7.1 miles, 890 feet).

15 Coast Ridge–Terrace Creek Loop

*A strenuous 12.7-mile loop hike with an accumulated elevation gain and loss of
about 3,800 feet. Start and end at Big Sur Station (300 feet).*

A good day-hike loop is hard to find at Big Sur. To make this one work, start
with the 2-mile walk north up Post Hill on the wide shoulder of Highway 1,
not a joyous prospect, but also not an arduous one if you start early in the
morning and get it over with first. (Big Sur Bakery at Loma Mar makes a handy
breakfast stop.) At the top of Post Hill, turn left and follow the paved driveway
up toward Ventana Inn. The pavement ends near Ventana Inn, where you pass
through a gate (1,080 feet) onto the Coast Ridge Road, a long, steady, but pleasant climb with increasingly distant views of ocean, rolling hills, and the heavily
wooded Big Sur Valley. Toward the top you catch some broadside views of
4,853-foot Ventana Double Cone and its granitic ridge, including its famous
Ventana, or cleft. Topping out on the Coast Ridge at just above 2,600 feet, take
pains not to trespass on private property. Look on the left (northeast) for the
signposted junction of single-track Terrace Creek Trail, at 6.2 miles. Descend
there through thick forests of redwood, bay, oak, and madrone, keeping close
company with Terrace Creek.

Reaching the bottom at Terrace Creek Camp, turn left (west) and return on Pine Ridge Trail, whose shade will be welcome on warm afternoons. Rolling westward, the trail enjoys some rugged views down into the Big Sur Gorge and across the void to the steep Mount Manuel Trail. At about 10 miles you start a relentless descent back into Big Sur Valley, where—after walking a long half-circle around the south end of the Pfeiffer Big Sur State Park campground—you come to rest back where you started.

Trailheads Between Big Sur and Lucia

16 DeAngulo Trail

A strenuous 6.8-mile out-and-back hike with an accumulated elevation gain and loss of about 3,000 feet. Start and end at an unmarked, gated private road on Highway 1, 1 mile south of Torre Canyon.

The coastal views are spectacular, but this trail is so hard to follow that if you only want views, you're better off with a different hike. The *real* reason to hike the DeAngulo Trail is that it's an eccentric, Big Sur kind of affair—unconventional, like its namesake. Jaime DeAngulo was a local character, a highly educated, internationally acclaimed anthropologist, an authority on California Indian languages, who also dressed like a longhaired bandit, rode around Big Sur raising hell with his hard-drinking compadres, and lived like a bohemian on Partington Ridge. He willed this property for public use, so we owe this trail to him. It partly follows a private road, partly a single-track footpath, and partly a tractor cut. Overgrown in places, it's marked partly with signs, partly by ribbons, and partly by the neighbors' NO TRESPASSING signs. It ends near 3,300 feet at the Coast Ridge Road.

Once upon a time, Jaime DeAngulo took it into his head to turn this property into a dude ranch for paying guests. He called it Rancho Los Pesares—Ranch of the Sorrows. Oddly, no dudes ever showed up. "This would like to be a dude ranch," he wrote in a lengthy brochure, "but it isn't. . . . If you are looking for crooning cowboys, don't come here! Not a cowboy on the place, not a cow, not even a picturesque corral. . . . Saddle-weary and tired, you will have to sleep on the ground in a weird canyon. You won't be able to sleep. You will get the heebie-jeebies, and you'll spend the night feeding the fire." It went on in this vein. So does DeAngulo Trail. If you're looking for an easy, well-mannered trail, don't come here.

17 Partington Landing

An easy 1-mile out-and-back hike with a drop and gain of 240 feet in elevation. Start on Highway 1 at Partington Canyon, in Julia Pfeiffer Burns State Park.

This intriguing dog-hole port is linked to Highway 1 by a steep dirt track, once a wagon road but now only for foot traffic. At the bottom, Partington Creek dashes into rocky little Partington Cove, which once upon a time was a large sea cave. The roof eventually caved in, leaving this narrow, pug-nosed inlet, also known as Smugglers Cove. It's worth a little detour, but it's not the famous port. Partington Landing itself lies about 400 feet east, beyond a high ridge of granite. To get there, the trail tunnels 116 feet through the base of that ridge, emerging at another dramatic, sheer-walled channel, just deep and wide enough to ease a schooner into it. Once in, ships were moored to eyebolts in the cliffs. A wooden cargo derrick still stands at the entrance. During the late nineteenth and early twentieth centuries, thousands of tons of tanbark, lumber, and firewood cut in upper Partington Canyon were shipped out from this little port.

18 Tanbark–Tin House Loop

A moderate 6-mile loop with an accumulated elevation gain and loss of about 2,800 feet. Start and end at the large vista-point parking area between Partington and McWay Canyons, Julia Pfeiffer Burns State Park.

This excellent loop requires a 0.9-mile hike along the shoulder of Highway 1. Passing motorists pose some risk, so take care. I like to get that section over with first. The ocean side of the road offers safer walking, since the inland side has turns blinded by steep hillsides. Therefore, park at the large vista point (410 feet) and walk 0.9 mile *north* along the highway to the start of the Tanbark Trail in Partington Canyon (250 feet). The rest of the route is on state park trails. Ascend Partington Canyon by way of its south fork, following its beautiful creek through a deep and shady forest. Passing through a grove of some of the largest redwoods at Big Sur, leave the creek at 2.9 miles but continue ascending the south ridge, topping out at about 2,160 feet. After contouring to a junction with the Tin House fire road at 3.7 miles, turn left (south) for a short detour to visit the Tin House (1,820 feet). This unusual abandoned house was built during World War II of salvaged scrap from an abandoned gas station. The story goes that a man named Lathrop Brown built the house for his college classmate,

President Franklin Roosevelt. Despite the world-class coastal views, it's hard to imagine the patrician Roosevelt at home in such a remote and humble place. Return by way of the Tin House fire road, with its intriguing views across Partington Canyon, to author Henry Miller's old neighborhood on Partington Ridge. The steep dirt track drops 1,550 feet in 2 miles, meeting Highway 1 just across the road from the parking area where you started.

19 Ewoldsen Trail

A moderate 4.5-mile semi-loop with an accumulated elevation gain and loss of about 1,960 feet. Start and end at the McWay Canyon Day Use Area, Julia Pfeiffer Burns State Park.

This loop offers a very pretty, nearly complete Big Sur experience, with fine redwood forests, striking coastal views, a dashing creek, and even some handsome chaparral-covered hills. There's an interesting bird's-eye view of an enormous scar caused by a landslide that closed Highway 1.

Trailheads Between Lucia and Gorda

20 The Limekilns

An easy 1.4-mile out-and-back walk with scant elevation change. Start and end near the rangers' kiosk, Limekiln State Park.

Limestone is the prevailing bedrock hereabouts. It was quarried for cement in the late nineteenth and early twentieth centuries. The limestone was slaked on the spot before being shipped out in barrels from Rockland Landing, at the mouth of Limekiln Creek. This short path follows the old wagon road through a lovely old-growth redwood forest, crossing three wooden footbridges en route to four stone kilns squatting beneath their rusting chimneys. Around about them grows a second-growth forest.

21 Limekiln Falls

Another easy 1.4-mile out-and-back walk with scant elevation change. Start and end near the rangers' kiosk, Limekiln State Park.

In its final dash down from Cone Peak, Limekiln Creek races through a grove of redwoods.

So narrow at the mouth, so lush just upstream, Limekiln Creek and its tributaries are extraordinary. Draining the steepest coastal slope in the lower forty-eight states, it's also a stream of uncommon determination to get to the bottom as quickly as possible. Although I speculate that there must be a string of impressive waterfalls all along its 3-mile run from Cone Peak, it's hard to tell because the 100-foot wall at Limekiln Falls stops you from climbing farther up the canyon. The waterfall is spectacular in winter, but then you'll have to deal with a total of eight wet fords of Limekiln Creek—the swift west fork twice and the main branch six times.

22 Vicente Flat Trail

A very strenuous 10-mile out-and-back hike with an accumulated elevation gain and loss of about 4,500 feet. Start from Vicente Flat trailhead on Highway 1, near the Kirk Creek Campground.

Steep, long, and incredibly scenic, this classic Big Sur hike makes you work hard, but pays rewards in old-growth redwood forests and many calendar-worthy vistas. This hike is front-loaded with a heavy-caliber climb. The Forest Service trail begins with switchbacks through scrub, grassland, rocky outcrops, and shady ravine, with increasingly more profound views down and up the coast. After the trail turns inland at 2.8 miles, Cone Peak and the green expanses of Hare and Limekiln Creek Canyons will kindle yet more amazement. The path contours easily for nearly 2 miles along the north-facing Hare Canyon wall, in and out of redwood pockets, passing small Espinoza Camp (1,780 feet) at 3.3 miles, before making a moderate descent to the Vicente Flat Campground alongside Hare Creek (1,600 feet), amid the redwood forest.

23 Cone Peak Loop

A moderately strenuous 6.5-mile loop with an accumulated elevation gain and loss of about 3,580 feet. Start and end at the Cone Peak trailhead (3,730 feet) on Cone Peak Road.

Cone Peak is the easiest of Santa Lucia's grand summits to hike: The excellent 2.3-mile (one way) Cone Peak Trail climbs directly to the 5,155-foot summit from Cone Peak Road, with an elevation gain of only 1,425 feet. The hike described here incorporates that trail at the end of a longer route that loops completely around the mountain. It's worth the extra distance and work because the surrounding country is scenic, historical, and botanically unusual.

From the trailhead, walk 1.3 miles north on Cone Peak Road to the end of the road. Beyond, narrowed by slides and foliage, the old road continues as the Coast Ridge Trail, passing through the first Douglas fir forest ever to be botanically described. You can see the fire lookout tower on the top of Cone Peak—so near, and yet so far. Winding around the eastern flank of Cone Peak, the Coast Ridge Trail climbs by degree to its rightful place atop the Coast Ridge, north of Cone Peak. This section of the Coast Ridge is part of an ancient trail from the San Antonio Valley to the coast—the Quiquilit Trail of Salinan traders, also known as the Carrizo Trail to the Spanish padres, Big Sur homesteaders, and early botanists in quest of the elusive Santa Lucia fir.

The footpath up to Cone Peak passes through a forest that was recently burned and is now recovering.

Your time on the Coast Ridge is fleeting, however: Look for ribbons that mark the otherwise unsigned junction of the historic Gamboa Trail, on a spur ridge to the left (west) at 2.6 miles and 4,700 feet. This Gamboa Trail is typically overgrown. You will probably have to do a bit of bushwhacking in your 0.9-mile descent to Trail Springs Camp (3,820 feet), at the head of the south fork of Devils Canyon Creek. From there the climb up the Cone Peak Trail is kept largely free of brush in part by the natural presence of mixed forest, including Santa Lucia fir. Rapidly gaining elevation, you mount to a divide between the Devils Canyon and Limekiln Creek drainages, where the forest thins and the views open wide. The signposted spur trail to Cone Peak's summit is 0.2 mile beyond that.

The 0.4-mile (out-and-back) detour to the summit is the grand climax of this hike. The rocky summit, capped by a fire lookout, is the apex of the steepest coastal rise in the lower forty-eight states, though without knowing that fact it would be hard to guess by looking down. The vistas are vast, the topography rugged. Have lunch and sit a spell. Then complete the loop by descending the Cone Peak Trail back to the trailhead on Cone Peak Road.

Trailheads South of Gorda

24 Cruickshank Trail

A moderate 4.6-mile out-and-back hike with an elevation gain and loss of about 1,500 feet. Start at the Cruickshank trailhead (350 feet) on Highway 1.

The goal of this hike is the old Cruickshank homestead, which now serves as a Forest Service campground inside the Silver Peak Wilderness. Before it was homesteaded, it was a Salinan settlement, testament to its healthy locale. The old Cruickshank Trail climbs steeply from the highway on brushy switchbacks for 1 mile before reaching a ridge and contouring onto the southern wall of Villa Creek's canyon. From there onward it rolls more tamely through dry-slope woodlands interspersed with redwood gullies. At 2 miles it passes through the Lower Cruickshank Camp (1,300 feet), a bosky redwood glade, and shortly after intersects the Buckeye Trail. (The northbound fork of the Buckeye Trail runs 2.7 miles to Alder Creek Camp and the site of Manchester, the vanished "capital" of the Los Burros Mining District.) Beyond the Buckeye Trail junction, the Cruickshank Trail enters Upper Cruickshank Camp (1,400 feet), which occupies the old Cruickshank homestead.

William T. Cruickshank and his son, William D. Cruickshank, both worked in the gold mines around Manchester, and homesteaded here in 1883. Oddly, both men disappeared under similar mysterious circumstances—thirty years apart. The elder Cruickshank vanished in 1907 while walking westward on the trail toward the Pacific. The younger Cruickshank vanished in 1937 while walking eastward toward King City. Though healthy and strong when last seen leaving this vicinity, neither was ever seen again, dead or alive.

25 Buckeye Camp

A moderately strenuous 7.2-mile out-and-back hike with an accumulated elevation gain and loss of about 3,000 feet. Start and end at the abandoned Forest Service ranger station (350 feet) near Salmon Creek, on Highway 1.

Hovering serenely in the Silver Peak Wilderness, Buckeye Camp (2,140 feet) is spacious and comfortable, with shade and an excellent spring. It makes a good destination for large groups and for intermediate hikers who want to see some of Big Sur's most dramatic coastal views without the massive uphill slog required by so many other trails. The route is often steep—there's no getting around that—but the steep stretches are interspaced with stretches of flat ground and variations of successive ridges and ravines. The views to the south from the trail reach all the way to Piedras Blancas.

26 Spruce Creek Camp

A moderate 4.2-mile out-and-back hike with an accumulated elevation gain and loss of about 1,400 feet. Start and end at the Salmon Creek trailhead (300 feet).

Most of your climbing is right up front on this trail, doled out in switchbacks up the northern slopes of Mount Mars, in the Silver Peak Wilderness. The trail passes through a serpentine barren, then settles onto a rolling contour high above Salmon Creek. After a mile of mixed grassland and oak woodland, you'll meet the junction with the trail to Dutra Flat, then turn left for a quick descent to the wooded camp near the confluence of Spruce and Salmon Creeks (950 feet).

Trailheads Near the Carmel Valley

27 Bluff Camp

A moderate 8.2-mile out-and-back hike with an accumulated elevation gain and loss of about 1,750 feet. Start and end at Los Padres Dam trailhead (1,000 feet).

This entire walk is on land owned by the California American Water Company, proprietor of Los Padres Reservoir. From the gate at the head of the parking area, walk up the dirt road, crossing the dam spillway on a wooden bridge before mounting to the top of the dam, 1 mile from the start. The striking view of the reservoir against the backdrop of rugged, green mountains somewhat resembles a large Appalachian river as it rolls through a deep gorge. Climbing above the western shore, the road continues through dry woodland to its end, where a single-track trail takes over. Keeping straight (south) at the signed Big Pine Trail junction (1,120 feet) at 1.5 miles, you'll traverse a steep (in places almost clifflike) hillside along a contour above the narrowing reservoir. Switchback down to a ford of Danish Creek, following a rolling course up the Carmel

Los Padres Reservoir impounds the waters of the Carmel River below the heights of Miller Mountain.

River's canyon through a canopy of trees and brush to Bluff Camp (1,160 feet). Spread along both sides of the Carmel River, Bluff Camp is an idyllic spot when the river is low enough to cross. It's very popular on weekends. The trail crosses into Los Padres National Forest just upstream.

28 Danish Creek Camp

A moderate 7.4-mile out-and-back hike with an accumulated elevation gain and loss of about 2,500 feet. Start and end at Los Padres Dam trailhead (1,000 feet).

Danish Creek is the closest backpackers' camp to the Los Padres Reservoir trailhead. (Note that the local pronunciation of *Danish* is not like a resident of Denmark, but *da-NEESH*.) Walk through the California American Water Company gate and follow the dirt road across the spillway and up to the dam. The road swings west around and above the shore of the reservoir. When the road ends, a single-track trail takes over. At 1.5 miles you come to the signed

Big Pine Trail junction. Turn right (west), climbing switchbacks to a brushy ridge with extensive views over the mountains and ridges of the Carmel River backcountry. The high point on this trail is the Rattlesnake Trail junction (2,058 feet), where you take the left (west) spur 0.7 mile downhill to Danish Creek Camp, at an elevation of 1,490 feet.

Tassajara Road Trailheads

29 Anastasia Canyon

A moderate 4.2-mile out-and-back hike with an accumulated loss and gain in elevation of about 1,750 feet. Start and end at the trailhead (3,580 feet) on Tassajara Road.

This is the canyon where the bandits Anastacio Garcia and Tiburcio Vásquez supposedly came to cool their heels when the law turned up the heat down in Monterey. It's still remote. The trail starts on a ridge and drops 0.9 mile to the creek in Anastasia Canyon, at the junction of the Bear Trap Canyon Trail (2,790 feet). The left-hand fork goes downstream to private property, so take the right-hand fork, which goes upstream into Bear Trap Canyon. At the head of this side canyon, Cahoon Spring (3,575 feet) flows into a bathtub watering trough. Beyond the spring is a ridge called the Bear Trap, which is crisscrossed by a network of dirt tracks. If you want to explore the area, head to the right (south) on the ridge—*not* the left (north), which is private property. The Bear Trap takes its name from a natural salt lick that attracts hoofed animals, including deer and wild pigs. During the Spanish and Mexican eras, vaqueros used to come here to trap grizzly bears that came to hunt at the salt lick. The captured bears were shipped down to settlements in Monterey and the Salinas Valley for bear-and-bull fights.

30 Pine Valley

A moderately strenuous 9.4-mile out-and-back hike with an accumulated elevation loss and gain of about 3,750 feet. Start and end on Tassajara Road near China Camp.

This is one of the finest short, year-round backpacking destinations in the Ventana, and it receives a lot of visitors. Its sandstone boulders and cliffs, and nearby Pine Falls, are good reasons for an overnight stay, but Pine Valley is

Camping on the floor of Pine Valley can be pleasant at any time of year.

close enough for a day hike. The approach is along the Pine Ridge Trail high on an open ridge that falls steeply away into Church Creek Valley. Hiking alternately through chaparral and steep grassland hillsides dotted with woodland copses, you will enjoy fantastic views of the historical and mysterious sandstone rock outcrops (the Church Creek Formation) that loom above the Church Creek Ranch. Descending on switchbacks through chaparral, you arrive at a four-way junction in the Church Creek Divide, which separates the Arroyo Seco (and Salinas River) watershed on the east from the Carmel River watershed on the west.

Turn right (west) and follow the headwaters of the Carmel River down an easy incline through woodlands. At nearly 4 miles into your hike, the landscape broadens and flattens into Pine Valley. Tucked down behind a sandstone ridge, the floor of Pine Valley rolls smoothly along for about 1.5 miles, hovering between 3,130 and 3,270 feet in elevation. Forested with ponderosa pines, Pine Valley is a camper's paradise, with comfy logs and stones for lounging, soft shade, bird music, seasonal gardens, and good, sweet water flowing right past your front step. An affable gentleman named Jack English owns a cabin about midway through the valley. He has erected a monument there to his wife, Mary, who died in 2001. It reads: her cabin, her garden, her valley.

Option: Pine Falls is a scramble down the Carmel River from the junction of the Carmel River Trail and Bear Basin Trail, about midway through Pine Valley. Follow the creek about 0.6 mile downstream to the top of 50-foot Pine Falls. Enjoy the view, but take care if you try to make the slippery, perilous climb down to the swimming hole at the bottom.

31 The Windcaves

A moderate 5.4-mile out-and-back hike with an elevation gain and loss of about 1,560 feet. Start and end at the Church Creek trailhead on Tassajara Road.

The Windcaves are an outcrop of massive sandstone rocks known to geologists as the Church Creek Formation, and to early homesteaders as "Grindstone Canyon." The rocks and the surrounding Church Creek Valley were important to the Esselen as both a home and a spiritual place. (The most archaeologically significant caves are protected on the private Church Creek Ranch and are not open to the public.)

The Church Creek Trail passes right through the middle of an outcrop known as the Windcaves; these are on Forest Service land and are open to explore. Your approach route climbs through a narrow gulch of riparian and mixed-oak woodland, with some chaparral and meadow. You'll know you're nearing the Windcaves when the trail draws near a chaparral-covered saddle with exposed sandstone ledges tilted askew. Mounting short switchbacks to the saddle, you will find a wind-sculpted hoodoo (inevitably dubbed "Skull Rock") staring down from above the trail through eyeless sockets. (Kids enjoy climbing in one and out the other.) Ahead, there is a handsome view westward over the Church Creek Valley.

32 Horse Pasture Loop

A moderate 5-mile loop with a gain and loss in elevation of about 1,850 feet. Start and end at the Tassajara Mountain Zen Center parking area (1,570 feet). You may cross the monastery grounds, but please do not stop unless you have reservations. See map on page 243.

Walk through the monastery grounds to the Narrows Trail, and follow Tassajara Creek 0.6 mile downstream to the junction of the Tassajara Cut-Off Trail.

The Windcaves on the Church Creek Trail offer a picturesque hike from the Tassajara Road.

Turn left (north) to climb steeply out of the canyon on a south-facing wall, a beautiful, fascinating, arid landscape sparsely dotted with yucca and other tough shrubs, not to mention skittering lizards. Good views of the Narrows frame Tassajara Creek, with distant ridges along the Arroyo Seco. Hitting the Horse Trail junction (2,290 feet) high above the canyon, turn left, hiking in and out of several small gulches until you reach the Horse Pasture (2,200 feet) at 2.2 miles. With large oak trees and a memorial stone carved with KATIES GARDEN, this is a peaceful spot, a pastoral island amid a rough sea of chaparral. Complete the loop by following the trail westward over the ridge to Tassajara Road, which you follow back to the monastery gate.

33 Strawberry Camp

A strenuous 15.4-mile out-and-back hike with an accumulated elevation gain and loss of about 6,000 feet. Start and end at the Tassajara Mountain Zen Center parking area (1,570 feet). You may cross the monastery grounds, but please do not stop unless you have reservations. See map on page 243.

There's a serene, timeless quality to Strawberry Camp, an oasis-like meadow with a big oak tree surrounded by chaparral. Little Strawberry Creek dries out by early summer, one of two inconveniences that enforces the quietude. The other inconvenience is the long, hard trek to get there. Start by crossing through the monastery grounds, past Tassajara Hot Springs. After fording Tassajara Creek—typically a rock-hop by late spring—hike up the Tony Trail, climbing some 1,300 feet to the ridgetop (2,950 feet) before dropping more than 1,100 feet to Willow Creek. Unofficially maintained by monks at Tassajara, the Tony is usually a passable trail, though you may have to duck for low branches on the north side, take your bushwhacking quota on the south side, and deal with steep stretches of slipped tread on both sides. Once you're on the banks of Willow Creek, find the Marble Peak Trail on the south bank and head upstream, crossing again to the wide, duff-covered Willow Creek Camp (1,900 feet), 3.2 miles from the start.

Climbing west from this camp through thick woodlands, the Marble Peak Trail hits open chaparral at a saddle between the Willow and Zigzag Creek drainages, 4.6 miles from the start. From here onward to Strawberry, it's a dream path for Ventana veterans, rolling on a high contour through the best kind of brush (that is, *mostly* free of poison oak) and crossing two tributaries that usually flow through midsummer: Camp Creek at 5.1 miles and Shovel Handle Creek at 5.9 miles. Dropping slightly to Strawberry Valley, turn right (northwest) at the junction, and you will soon arrive at Strawberry Camp, 7.4 miles from the start. Before returning, take the 0.3-mile detour up to the low saddle just northwest of the camp for a view down into the Big Sur watershed.

Arroyo Seco Trailheads

34 The Gorge Trail to Horse Bridge

A moderate 6-mile out-and-back hike with an accumulated elevation gain and loss of about 1,250 feet. Start and end at the Gorge Trail parking area (1,000 feet) at Arroyo Seco Recreation Area.

The Gorge Trail follows the Arroyo Seco at a very respectable height above the water.

Scoff if you like at the Arroyo Seco's nickname, "the Grand Canyon of Monterey County," but it's still pretty impressive. Less than 0.5 mile from the parking area, the Gorge Trail—a dirt road also known as Indians Road—squeezes between a rocky bluff on one side and a near-vertical drop of more than 230 feet to the river on the other. At this same spot you can look up to see a point on the brim of the canyon more than 2,500 feet above the stream. Arroyo Seco is a very respectable canyon. The wide Gorge Trail rambles in and out through stony road cuts and shady ravines, often within sight and sound of cascades. At the junction of the Marble Peak Trail (1,190 feet), a single-track path switchbacks down to a handsome little suspension span, Horse Bridge (1,000 feet). Willow Creek pours into the Arroyo Seco on the western shore, where summertime waders enjoy the small beach.

A moderate 4.4-mile loop with an accumulated elevation gain and loss of about 940 feet. Start and end at the Gorge Trail parking area (1,000 feet) at Arroyo Seco Recreation Area.

The Santa Lucia Trail has historically led to Junipero Serra Peak and the San Antonio Valley, but is chronically in need of maintenance. The short, single-track section between Arroyo Seco and Santa Lucia Creek is typically kept in better repair. On the north bank of Santa Lucia Creek stands a refurbished Forest Service patrol cabin built in 1908, but no longer in use. Made of local cobblestones and adobe, the cabin served as a line shack for rangers patrolling the

The scenery along the Santa Lucia Trail is among the most pastoral inland from Big Sur.

backcountry on foot or horseback, keeping lookout for wildfires, timber thieves, illegal grazers, and poachers.

To return, walk the dirt road west to the Gorge Trail (Indians Road) and follow that double-track right (northward) back to the start.

36 Arroyo Seco to Tassajara Monastery

A strenuous 9.3-mile point-to-point hike with an accumulated elevation gain of about 3,370 feet and an accumulated loss of about 2,730 feet. Start from the Gorge Trail parking area (1,000 feet) at Arroyo Seco Recreation Area, and end at Tassajara Mountain Zen Center parking area (1,570 feet). You may cross the monastery grounds, but please do not stop unless you have reservations.

You don't have to be a guest at the Tassajara monastery to hike this trail, but if you do have reservations, there's no finer way to arrive than afoot. This route is a pilgrim's dream: lonely, lovely, laborious, spiritually cleansing, and free of bandits. The rise and fall for the first 5 miles is minimal: Just follow the Gorge Trail to Horse Bridge and continue 2 miles up the Marble Mountain Trail by the side of shady Willow Creek. The gradient then steepens steadily to the Tony Trail junction (1,790 feet), which signals that the time has come to start paying your dues.

The Tony Trail makes a steep climb to 2,950 feet on a south-facing slope through heavy chaparral, a 1.2-mile slog burdened with pricking, pungent chamisal, slipped tread, and switchbacks, but blessed with increasingly dramatic downcanyon prospects of the Arroyo Seco watershed. Reaching the top of the ridge, you descend into the canyon of Tassajara Creek through thick woodlands of oak, bay, buckeye, and madrone. After crossing the creek at the bottom, you'll enter the grounds of the Tassajara monastery. If you don't have reservations for a hot-springs bath, a cool dunk along the Narrows Trail will rejuvenate you.

37 Indians Road

A strenuous 16.6-mile point-to-point hike with an accumulated elevation gain of nearly 4,500 feet and a loss of about 3,400 feet. Start at Gorge Trail parking area (1,000 feet) at Arroyo Seco Recreation Area; you'll end at Indians Station.

Completed in 1939, this remarkable roadway winds up through Los Padres National Forest to elevations more than 1,500 feet higher than the Arroyo Seco River. Landslides closed the road to vehicles many years go, and it's uncertain if the Forest Service will reopen it. This is a boon for hikers and mountain bikers: The scenery is dramatic, the encroachment of brush is minimal, and it can also be linked with other trails to make a loop. Water is available in many streams that it crosses during wet seasons, as well as year-round usually at Jackhammer Spring (7.3 miles) and below the crossing of Hanging Valley Creek (9.6 miles). Camping is prohibited in Hanging Valley.

Chaparral predominates along most of Indians Road, interspersed with dry slope and riparian woodlands. After passing the junction to Horse Bridge, the road climbs for the next 5 miles, a steady gain of about 1,700 feet. For the next 5 miles beyond that, it rolls along between 2,700 and 2,900 feet, with long views west into the Ventana Wilderness and down into the Arroyo Seco Canyon. At about 12.5 miles it begins descending to Indians Station.

Trailheads Near the San Antonio Valley

38 Arroyo Seco Trail to the Coast Ridge

A strenuous 9.4-mile out-and-back hike with 2,760 feet of elevation gained and lost. Start and end at the fishing club (2,080 feet) at Indians Station.

Of all the trails that climb to the Coast Ridge from the east, this is one of the shortest and most scenic. Staying close to the Arroyo Seco stream, the trail climbs steadily through a rocky canyon and mixed forest to a break on the higher slopes, where the trees step back and the chaparral takes over. Views open up downcanyon to Junipero Serra Peak and the great rock outcrops that ring the basin around Indians Station. Switchbacks carry the trail to the top of the Coast Ridge (4,420 feet), at a point about 3 miles north of Cone Peak. Backpackers can stay at Forks Camp at 2 miles or Madrone Camp at 2.5 miles.

39 Junipero Serra Peak (Sta'yokale)

A strenuous 12-mile out-and-back hike with an elevation gain and loss of about 4,000 feet. Start and end at Indians Station (2,100 feet).

The highest summit of the Santa Lucia Range rises to 5,862 feet in lonesome splendor at the head of the San Antonio Valley. Labeled Santa Lucia Peak on old maps, it was known as Sta'yokale (and also Pimkolam) to the Salinan people, who revered it as the birthplace of human life after great floods inundated the world. The mountain is listed on the Sacred Lands Inventory of the California Native American Heritage Commission, and hikers are urged to be aware of its central role in Salinan heritage.

The ascent is very steep and direct. From Indians Station the route follows an old jeep road east to an initially broad, precipitous ravine—the very ravine, in fact, that flows down to the Indians Ranch. The trail climbs switchbacks up this ravine, transferring to a spur ridge at 3.4 miles. At 4.9 miles it reaches the summit ridge and passes to the north side, where snow may pile up in winter. It finishes by climbing through Coulter and sugar pine forests to the twin-peaked summit. An abandoned watch tower stands on top. Wander around the summit area enjoying all the views, which reach from the Sierra Nevada in the east to the Pacific Ocean in the west. Pinyon Peak (5,264 feet) and Bear Mountain (4,771 feet) rise in the eastern foreground.

40 Escondido Campground to the Arroyo Seco

In the dry season when Indians Road is open to Escondido Campground, this is an easy 1.6-mile out-and-back hike with an elevation loss and gain of about 475 feet. Start and end at Escondido Campground. In the wet season, when Indians Road is closed to vehicles at Indians Station and must be walked, it's a moderate 7.3-mile out-and-back hike with an accumulated elevation gain and loss of about 1,400 feet. Start and end at Indians Station.

The trail from the wooded bench of Escondido Campground (2,175 feet) is a straightforward descent on the single-track Lost Valley Trail to the Arroyo Seco River (1,700 feet). The shaded rocks beside the river are a bucolic setting for a picnic or bit of sunbathing on a hot afternoon. The Lost Valley Trail continues on the opposite bank, but is maintained and traveled far less frequently than this initial section.

Long Backpack Routes

Many interesting backpack loops appear on maps but are much less obvious on the ground because of poorly maintained trails. Hikes 41, 42, and 43 are three examples of interesting but problematic routes that are very likely to require some skills in route finding and creek crossing, and a great deal of bushwhacking. These trips are recommended only to experienced backpackers up for an adventure.

To improve your odds of avoiding a long bushwhack, you can try to incorporate trails and dirt roads that are better maintained. Routes that are typically more dependable follow state park trails, the Pine Ridge Trail, Coast Ridge Road, Cone Peak Road, Tassajara Road, and Indians Road. Hikes 44 and 45 are hopefully designed to avoid a lot of bushwhacking, but of course there are no guarantees.

41 Arroyo Seco–Lost Valley Loop

This 17-mile loop starts at Indians Station. Ascend the Arroyo Seco Trail to the Coast Ridge Trail; then hike north to the Lost Valley Trail, east to Escondido Campground, and south on Indians Road back to your start. About 6,600 feet in elevation is gained and lost. You will have to ford the Arroyo Seco.

42 Carmel River Loops

The idea here is to make a loop incorporating the Carmel River and Miller Canyon Trails, connecting at China Camp. This will be a 23-mile loop if you start at China Camp, or a 27-mile loop if you start at Los Padres Reservoir. Either way, you'll encounter scores of stream crossings, plenty of likely bushwhacking and poison oak, and an elevation gain and loss greater than 6,800 feet.

43 Northern Ventana Loop

This 50-mile loop around the northern Ventana starts at Big Sur Station and has an elevation gain and loss of about 19,600 feet. The route incorporates the Pine Ridge Trail to Church Creek Divide, where it turns west into Pine Valley; thus far your trail is likely to be clear. The link from Pine Valley to Bottchers Gap via the Carmel River, Puerto Suello, Ventana, and Skinner Ridge Trails is likely to feature a good deal of poison oak, stream crossing, and bushwhacking. From Bottchers Gap back to Big Sur Station, you will probably encounter a weak link between Launz Ridge and Mount Manuel.

44 Coast Ridge Route

Clear hiking is quite likely on this 38-mile point-to-point hike from the start of the Coast Ridge Road (near Ventana Inn) to Kirk Creek Campground. The route follows the Coast Ridge Road, Coast Ridge Trail, Cone Peak Road, and Vicente Flat Trail. From north to south there's an accumulated elevation gain of about 9,450 feet, and a loss of about 13,700 feet. Avoid trespassing on private property along the Coast Ridge Road. Backpackers on the Coast Ridge will need to hike down side trails to camp and find water at Terrace Creek Trail, Cold Springs Camp, Upper Bee Camp, or Cook Springs Camp, which will increase distance.

45 Grand Ventana Loop

Here's a formidable 70-mile loop through the central Santa Lucias that starts and ends at Indians Station or along Tassajara Road (China Camp). The circuit is traced by the Arroyo Seco Trail, Coast Ridge Trail and Road, Terrace Creek Trail, Pine Ridge Trail to China Camp, Tassajara Road to the Tassajara Zen Mountain Center, the Tony Trail to Willow Creek, the Marble Peak Trail to Horse Bridge, and Indians Road back to Indians Station. Probably the Arroyo Seco and Tony Trails will present the most bushwhacking, but generally this should be a very passable loop that gains and loses about 22,000 feet in elevation, overall. If you don't mind lengthening it a bit, you could also start and end at Big Sur Station, Arroyo Seco Recreation Area, or the end of Cone Peak Road.

California Coastal Trail

A work in progress, the California Coastal Trail (CCT) is designed to eventually connect Oregon with Mexico. Much of the Big Sur trail section does not yet exist, meaning that Coastwalkers will have to walk long stretches along the shoulder of Highway 1. The route swings inland to follow the Old Coast Road, the Coast Ridge Road, and the Cruikshank and Buckeye Trails. A trail easement is planned through the long coastal strip of San Simeon State Park, but completion is many years away. www.californiacoastaltrail.info.

Creek Hiking

Some of the oldest trails in the Santa Lucias are creekbeds. Native Americans employed them as paths. Gaspar de Portolà followed the Pozo Hondo, Nacimiento, and other streams. Streambeds still make manageable "trails" during certain times of year, mainly because they cut a clearer passage through the brush and poison oak than many trails do.

Opportunities for creek hiking abound in the Santa Lucias. In his poem "Oh, Lovely Rock," Robinson Jeffers describes being moved to metaphysical rapture by the sight of a cliff in the "pathless gorge" of Ventana Creek.

Creek hiking is a decathlon event: It involves swimming, bouldering, and other climbing skills, as well as hiking. You will encounter shaky rocks, logjams, and precarious dams made of tangled branches and rocks. Creek hiking requires more common sense and outdoor experience on your part than does trail hiking, because it entails all the same risks . . . combined with the chance of drowning. If you get injured in a remote creekbed, you have no reason to expect anyone to find you for a long, long time.

If you hike the more remote streams and creeks, be sure you're experienced, and travel with experienced companions. Keep close watch on one another. You may need a rope, and you must know how to use it. Of foremost importance is knowing when a stream is low enough to travel safely (which is a matter of experience and sense, not book learning). Give some thought to your gear. You will need creek shoes, though cheap canvas shoes are adequate for short creek hikes. On a longer trip you'll need a good dry bag, the kind that kayakers use for storing food, dry clothes, first-aid kit, map, camera, and anything else that needs to remain dry. Be considerate of the natural world, too. If a tangle of tree limbs impedes your passage up a creek, turn around instead of dismantling or cutting them. For the sake of the fish, turtles, amphibians, and other wildlife, don't muddy the creeks, restack rocks, or cave in banks.

Some stream sections close to civilization are excellent for beginners. Thousands of people every summer explore the Gorge Trail in Pfeiffer Big Sur State Park, the sections of the Big Sur next to the resorts at Big Sur Center, and the pools at Arroyo Seco Recreation Area. Tassajara Creek along the Narrows Trail is another famous hiking stream.

More challenging are the pools along the Arroyos Seco near Indians Station. Another popular, but challenging creek scramble is the 2.8-mile stretch to Horse Bridge from the day-use area at the Arroyo Seco Recreation Area (you can also use the Gorge Trail to get there). Heading upstream, you will pass two main tributaries: Rocky Creek and Santa Lucia Creek. The narrow gorge and cascades of the lower Arroyo Seco prevent a safe passage until the water volume drops, well into summer in most years. A less popular but still "known" scramble is Roosevelt Creek, which intersects Indians Road near Indians Station, and which leads to a narrow slot canyon noted for its hanging ferns. Many hike the Little Sur River above Jackson Camp, Salmon Creek near Highway 1, and the Big Sur River near Sykes Camp.

The Grand Prix of Santa Lucia creek-hiking trips is the Arroyo Seco, a wilderness route. Don't even consider doing this one until the water slackens to a lackadaisical flow, usually by the end of summer in a typical year. Check the river flow with rangers before you go, but be ready to call off the trip if you arrive to find the water deeper or faster than you expected. Another point to consider: Even when the air temperature is balmy, the stream temperature will be fifty-seven to sixty degrees Fahrenheit. The stream distance from Indians Station down to Horse Bridge is 11 miles, and entails wading or swimming through pools and climbing down cascades. You can cut 3.3 miles off the route by starting on the trail below Escondido Campground. The largest tributaries that you meet along the way are Roosevelt, Lost Valley, and Willow Creeks. Some do this as an overnighter, and some push through in one grueling day. You will encounter many slippery rock slopes along the way, so you really need to anticipate that it may take much longer than you think.

Hiking Books

Elliot, Analise. *Hiking and Backpacking Big Sur.* Berkeley, Calif.: Wilderness Press, 2005. This is the more up-to-date and user-friendly successor to Schaffer's book. It also covers the Silver Peak Wilderness.

Schaffer, Jeffrey. *Hiking the Big Sur Country: The Ventana Wilderness.* Berkeley, Calif.: Wilderness Press, 1988. Out of print but still available in many stores, Schaffer's close observation of landmarks is still helpful when route-finding on overgrown trails.

Ventana Chapter, Sierra Club. *Trail Guide to Los Padres National Forest, Northern Section, Ventana Wilderness and Silver Peak Wilderness.* P.O. Box 5667, Carmel, CA 93921. Compact and succinct, easy to carry along, this book comes with a large, folding map.

Chapter 6
More Outdoor Recreation Fun

This chapter is about recreation at Big Sur *other* than hiking (for which you should see the chapter 5, Hiking the Trails of Big Sur). All sport is risky, and conditions at Big Sur typically increase the risk of most recreational activities. If you are a beginner in a sport, you'd be wise to get your experience elsewhere, or at least to hire an experienced, professional guide. In listing recreational activities, below, this book is not guaranteeing your safety. This book cannot and does not attempt to address the range and depth of hazards that you might encounter in the streams or the ocean around Big Sur. It is your responsibility to know your skill level and experience, to make your own decisions about risks, and to research any vendor or guide that you are willing to trust and to hire.

Stream Fun

The old swimming hole is the highlight of many a Big Sur summer vacation. The early-twentieth-century traveler J. Smeaton Chase really caught the special essence of a Santa Lucia swimming hole, this one on the Nacimiento River:

"The water was crystal clear, and perfect in temperature. White sand formed the bottom; one side was fringed with small cottonwoods, and the other, where the water was deepest, was walled directly by the dark, perpendicular rock, from the crevices of which waved fringes of delicate fern. The moon was nearly full, but it was not yet an hour past sunset, and the day hovered on that quiet borderland where one can hardly tell shadows from thoughts. A pale flicker of moonlight caught the ridges of water that flowed about me as I swam slowly to and fro, and once a water-snake slipped noiselessly away before me, the little black head rippling the water into lines of pallid silver. After the heat and thirst of the day I felt half inclined to sleep in that delicious pool."

Swimming, splashing, or just soaking in a Big Sur stream (sensible of the dangers inherent in any water play, of course) is safer than entering the rough, cold ocean along the Big Sur coast. There are few conditions in life more idyllic than drifting on an inner tube through the redwoods on a hot summer's afternoon. The inner tube is probably the most perfect of vessels on Santa Lucia streams because it's as light as it is buoyant, and handy for portaging over the rocky stretches between pools. Wear creek shoes to protect your feet. The lower Big Sur River and Arroyo Seco are the most popular streams, but there are many opportunities to find your own private swimming hole in the Santa Lucias.

River Paddling

During high-water season paddlers enjoy exploring the lagoon of the lower Carmel River. The Big Sur River also attracts paddlers, who put in at the cen-

Organized Sporting Events

- **Big Sur International Marathon:** Racing along Highway 1 from Big Sur to Carmel, this is one of the world's most spectacular marathon courses. Other events include a 21-mile power walk, 5K run, 9-mile walk, 10.6-mile walk, and marathon relay. Held in April. P.O. Box 222620, Carmel, CA 93922-2620; (831) 625–6226; www.bsim.org.
- **Big Sur River Run:** Local charities benefit from a 10K foot race and 5K walk among the redwoods along the Big Sur River. Held in October. (831) 624–4112; www.bigsurriverrun.org.
- **Wildflower Triathlon Festival:** The world's second largest triathlon event pits more than 6,000 athletes in swimming, biking, and running competition on the south shore of Lake San Antonio. Spectators meanwhile enjoy food booths, entertainment, and a sports expo. Held in May. (831) 373–0678; www.tricalifornia.com.

tral parking area of Andrew Molera State Park. Being a smaller river, the Big Sur's depth is less predictable than the Carmel's, sometimes disappointing kayakers who hope to paddle the 1-mile journey to its mouth, and instead end up having to drag their craft over low spots. Check the water level with a ranger before making the drive down: (831) 667–2315.

Cycling

Experienced riders can find challenges worthy of a lifetime goal. Highway 1 is, of course, one of the world's classic rides. The steep dirt roads and trails of Los Padres National Forest will test the mettle of even the strongest mountain biker. Big Sur is less accommodating to novice cyclists, but there are some options. Young families, mindful of traffic, might enjoy cycling around the extensive campground roads in Pfeiffer Big Sur State Park, San Simeon State Park, San Antonio Reservoir, and Nacimiento Reservoir.

Cyclists need to note a few important restrictions on their sport:

- Designated wilderness areas (Ventana and Silver Peak) are closed to all cycling.
- Fort Hunter Liggett is closed to all cycling.
- The Coast Ridge Road between Ventana Inn and Cone Peak Road is closed to cycling.
- State park trails are typically closed to bikes, unless explicitly stated otherwise. This leaves mainly public roadways and Forest Service trails that are outside wilderness areas. Stay on designated roads and trails, keep your speed under control, and *always* anticipate that you may meet pedestrians, equestrians, and vehicles. Respect private property, and avoid gouging ruts through muddy roads.

Road Touring

A good road for leisurely family riding is the 5.2-mile one-way trip along paved Milpitas Road from Wagon Caves to Indians Station, all on Forest Service land. It is paved, pretty, and seldom crowded with vehicular traffic, except for the rush of local traffic to the Indians Station water holes on hot weekends. There is a 740-foot climb to the divide between San Antonio Creek and Arroyo Seco, and a drop of 200 feet to Indians Station. Of course, you will then have to do all that in reverse.

The Carmel Valley Road (G16), Cachagua Road, and Arroyo Seco Road are popular cycling corridors (see chapter 4, Driving the Back Roads). Some of the two-lane country roads around Lakes Nacimiento and San Antonio provide excellent riding, though boating and winery traffic increases on weekends.

Cycling down the Big Sur coast on Highway 1 is a dream ride for many bicyclists, but the great views also come with a narrow bike lane and risky vehicular traffic.

There's a good 50-mile circuit around Lake San Antonio, for instance, on Country Highways G14, G19, and G18; starting and ending from the visitor center at San Antonio Reservoir's south shore, the loop racks up an accumulated elevation gain and loss of about 4,100 feet.

A much more demanding paved-road tour is the Nacimiento-Fergusson Road between Highway 1 and the gate of Fort Hunter Liggett (again, see chapter 4, Driving the Back Roads). You have to be in very strong condition to scale these gradients, but the views are out of this world.

The classic road tour of Big Sur is a ride along Highway 1 (see chapter 2, Driving Highway 1). Traffic is the greatest risk. The shoulders are narrow. Cyclists are sometimes clipped by the mirrors on passing vehicles. The southbound route is recommended because prevailing winds blow southward, and because you are on the ocean side of the road, and therefore able to enjoy the best views without having to cross the median. Windblown sand is sometimes a nuisance. Despite the drawbacks, the payback in thrilling vistas keeps this high on the list of serious cyclists' to-do lists. You might consider starting the ride in Salinas and ending in San Luis Obispo, where you can catch a train back to Salinas. Bike-in campsites along Highway 1 encourage you to linger.

Mountain Biking

Beginners should look to Garland Ranch Regional Park, Andrew Molera State Park, and the San Antonio Reservoir. Most rides around Big Sur are very challenging because of the severe uphill gradients and the need for control on the downhill runs. See chapter 4, Driving the Back Roads, for a description of the network of steep Forest Service roads that connect with Highway 1.

Garrapata State Park

Bikes are permitted only on the Rocky Ridge Trail, a very steep climb indeed.

Old Coast Road

Ridden in whole or part, this 10.4-mile unpaved road between Bixby Bridge and Andrew Molera State Park offers steep gradients, redwood forests, and spectacular views. You could even make an 18.8-mile loop, with Highway 1 as the missing link.

Andrew Molera State Park

Mountain bikes are restricted to the Pfeiffer Ridge Trail and a loop formed by the Beach and Creamery Meadow Trails, which is mostly level. Bring a lock if you want to explore Molera Beach.

Bike-In Campsites

Cyclists along Highway 1 can, like anyone else, make use of all campgrounds, but the following sites are geared for bike-in or hike-in visitors. (For a fuller description of campground facilities, see chapter 3, Destinations Along Highway 1.)

- **Andrew Molera State Park** allows cyclists to use the walk-in site, but they must push their bikes 0.3 mile along the trail from the central parking area.
- **Pfeiffer Big Sur State Park** has some bike-in sites in redwoods near the campground entrance.
- **Kirk Creek Campground** has a hiker-biker area on the north end.
- **Plaskett Creek Campground** has a hiker-biker area.
- **San Simeon State Park** has bike-in sites in the San Simeon Creek Campground, though the Washburn Campground might be nicer because it's more remote.

Hang Gliding

Pacific Valley is a designated hang-glider landing zone. The launch area is about 3,300 feet up on the ridge above Pacific Valley, at the head of Wild Cattle Creek, near the Prewitt Ridge Campsite, accessible via the South Coast Ridge Road and Prewitt Ridge Road (see chapter 4, Driving the Back Roads) in Los Padres National Forest. Hang gliders must register at the Pacific Valley Station.

Cone Peak Road

This high, unpaved road from Nacimiento Summit to the shoulder of Cone Peak is the most moderate of any of the roads along the Coast Ridge. A 12.8-mile round trip, it offers fine views to the east.

South Coast Ridge Road

You can set your own distance and difficulty by choosing a section of the South Coast Ridge Road anywhere from Nacimiento Summit clear down to Lottie Potrero Campground. One-way distances from Nacimiento Summit are 6.8 miles to Plaskett Ridge Road, 14.4 miles to Willow Creek Road, and 23.8 miles to Lottie Potrero on the McKern Road. The ridge is a roller coaster with killer views.

Garland Ranch Regional Park

Two sections of this park are open for mountain bikes. The Cooper Ranch section offers some flat riding and is accessible from the main park entrance. Horses are restricted from the Cooper Ranch area. The Kahn Ranch area is more rugged, with ridge views over Carmel Valley. Riders need permits to ride on the Kahn Ranch; these are available (free, with maps) from the Garland Ranch park entrance. To get to the Kahn Ranch, you must transport your bike by vehicle up Hitchcock Road to the staging area. Cycling is not permitted on Hitchcock Road. Bikes are not permitted in other parts of the park.

Indians Road

This is an adventure, running 16.6 miles one way between the Arroyo Seco Recreation Area and Indians Station—but there's no reason you need to do it all to have a good ride. The unpaved road is closed by slides to vehicular traffic.

At Indians Station you have an additional 5.2 miles of the paved Milpitas Road on Forest Service land to Wagon Caves, but you may not ride beyond the gate of Fort Hunter Liggett.

Lake San Antonio

With 26 miles of trail open to mountain bikes (and shared with hikers), the Lake San Antonio Recreation Area, South Shore, offers something for novices and more advanced riders. The 8.1-mile Long Valley Loop provides an overview of the recreation area and incorporates an advanced section along the Harris Creek arm of the lake, with steep gradients between the shore and the higher ridge.

Horseback Riding

The Carmel and San Antonio Valleys have been active equestrian areas since mission days, and horses have served long and honorably on many old Santa Lucia ranches. If you have your own horse, Garland Ranch Regional Park offers many miles of excellent public trails. On the north shore of Lake San Antonio, the Los Robles Equestrian Trail winds 11 miles through oak woodland and savanna within sight of the lake.

With an extensive network of interesting trails, Garland Ranch Regional Park is a favorite destination for equestrians.

In Big Sur itself you can rent mounts at Molera Stables, in Andrew Molera State Park. Wranglers offer guided tours of various length and difficulty, including private excursions. Walk-ins and beginners are welcome. (831) 625–5486 or (800) 942–5486; www.molerahorsebacktours.com.

Reservoir Sports

Two large reservoirs on the southeast edge of the Santa Lucias provide a wide array of recreational activities, including waterskiing, Jet Skiing, windsurfing, and boating of all kinds. Many visitors come to fish, camp, hike, mountain bike, ride horses, or swim, but with full-service marinas, lodging, stores, restaurants, and even houseboats available, not all vacationers are here for strictly outdoor recreation.

At an elevation of about 900 feet, Lake San Antonio has 60 miles of shoreline. The North Shore offers camping along 4 miles of lakeshore. The South Shore is more developed, with a visitor center, trails, marina, and other amenities. Monterey County Parks Department charges a modest entry fee. Lake San

Lake San Antonio can be very quiet in the cooler months, but summer brings crowds of boaters, water-skiers, swimmers, and other reservoir-sport devotees.

Antonio Resort, (800) 310–2313 or (805) 472–2313 outside California; www.lake sanantonioresort.com.

Nearby Lake Nacimiento is roughly as long as Lake San Antonio but has 165 miles of shoreline—a testament to the narrower and more twisted canyon of the Nacimiento River. The rugged topography and extensive forests make Lake Nacimiento an unusually attractive reservoir. There is a day-use area just north of the dam, but most amenities, including the marina, campgrounds, store, and lodging, are on the south shore. Entrance fees are higher than at Lake San Antonio. (800) 323–3839 or (805) 238–3256; www.nacimiento resort.com.

Hunting and Fishing

Hunting

Los Padres National Forest allows hunting for mule deer, rabbit, wild turkey, quail, dove, band-tailed pigeon, and chukar, but it's probably best known among hunters for wild pigs. These big, bad-tempered, omnivorous, sharp-tusked animals are not native, and they cause great destruction to fields, fences, and private property.

Because of the danger of lead poisoning to condors and other scavengers, hunters must bury or pack out any gut piles or other carcass parts shot with lead. Hunters must possess a valid California Department of Fish and Game hunting license and the appropriate tags. Consult the California Department of Fish and Game for information on hunting seasons, regulations, and hunting licenses.

Target shooting is also popular on Forest Service lands. Rangers request that you use paper targets and bullets that do not leave lead residue, and that you clean up when you finish. Consult the Monterey District office for regulations.

Fort Hunter Liggett opens up to 130,000 acres to hunters on weekends and on federal holidays, except Christmas. In addition to your California hunting license and tags, hunters need a special permit from the base itself. Game species include wild pigs, tule elk, deer, coyote, bobcat, jackrabbit, cottontail, tree squirrel, dove, quail, pigeon, turkey, duck, and goose. You must apply for a Fort Hunter Liggett hunting permit by mail, but applications are available online at www.liggett.army.mil.

Fishing

It's no surprise that Big Sur offers ocean and shore fishing, but the interior mountains also have a number of cold-water fly-fishing streams and several warm-water ponds and reservoirs. All anglers sixteen years and older need a California state fishing license. The California Department of Fish and Game regulates fishing. In an effort to preserve threatened and endangered species, its restrictions on any particular fishery change not only seasonally, but from year to year as well. Before planning any fishing trip, always consult its Web site for the latest information.

Lakes San Antonio and Nacimiento are known for catfish, large- and small-mouth bass, striped bass, bluegill, red ear, and crappie. Both reservoirs rent boats of all kinds and sizes.

Fort Hunter Liggett allows the public to fish for bass, bluegill, and catfish in ten ponds and reservoirs scattered across the base. Anglers require a state fishing license and a permit from Fort Hunter Liggett, which must be arranged in advance.

Catch-and-release fly fishing with barbless hooks prevails over much of Big Sur's inland streams. Anglers catch trout on the Big Sur River above the gorge, the Little Sur River above Pico Blanco Boy Scout Camp, the Carmel River above the Los Padres Reservoir, and the Nacimiento River alongside the Nacimiento-Fergusson Road west of the Fort Hunter Liggett gate. Steelhead trout are endangered and heavily regulated, but can be found in Garrapata Creek, Rocky Creek, Bixby Creek, the Little Sur River, the Big Sur River, Partington Creek, Anderson Creek, Hot Springs Creek, Vicente Creek, Big Creek, Limekiln Creek, Salmon Creek, and others. The Arroyo Seco is historically good habitat for trout and black bass, but the stock needs to recover.

You can charter sportfishing boats in Monterey and San Simeon. Ocean salmon season runs May through August north of Point Sur, and from May through September farther south. Coho and steelhead are protected at sea. The California Department of Fish and Game bans or restricts fishing in designated waters off Big Sur, San Simeon, and Piedras Blancas, so check its Web site. Sea For Yourself kayak tours in Cambria offers kayak fishing trips for rockfish, kelp bass, bottomfish, halibut, and lingcod. (805) 927–1787; kayakcambria.com.

Taking abalone is not permitted at any time in the Big Sur area. Anglers cast for surfperch and rockfish from beaches all along the coast south of Malpaso Creek, and from bluffs at Garrapata State Park and Jade Cove.

The pier at Hearst Memorial State Beach is one place where you can fish without a license (though a license is required if you fish from the beach below). The adjacent San Simeon Landing store sells bait, tackle, groceries, and California fishing licenses. It also rents rods and reels, and arranges charters for sportfishing boats that go out from spring through fall, weather permitting. (805) 927–4676.

You don't need a license to fish the pier at William Randolph Hearst Memorial State Beach.

Hunting and Fishing Contacts

- **California Department of Fish and Game:** www.dfg.ca.gov.
- **Fort Hunter Liggett:** To learn which training areas and reservoirs are open to hunting and fishing, call the recorded information line at (831) 386–3310, or check the Web site www.liggett.army.mil.
- **Monterey District Office, Los Padres National Forest:** 406 South Mildred, King City, CA 93930; (831) 385–5434; www.fs.fed.us.

Ocean Recreation

Big Sur has a long, cliff-bound coastline, exposed to the full force of the sea, and with few protected coves. Strong currents, big waves, cold water temperatures (usually in the low fifties), and unforgiving rocks make it risky for any recreation. This does not prevent experienced surfers, kayakers, scuba divers, and others from enjoying the water, but the ones who do so safely are either highly experienced and well informed about local conditions—or under the direct guidance of a responsible party who is. If you're new at your sport, get your experience in safer, warmer waters. If you are not in prime condition, don't tempt these waters. Even when walking along the shore, be wary of incoming tides and rogue waves.

If you are determined to wade or swim during your stay at Big Sur, the peninsula of San Simeon Point *usually* breaks some of the chilly ocean swells at Hearst Memorial State Beach. If you like warmer waters, however, the beaches of *Southern* California below Point Conception will be more to your liking.

Winter and spring generally have the strongest winds and swells, while summer can be very foggy. Winds generally blow from north to south. Winds and waves typically grow stronger in the afternoon. Of interest to boaters, divers, surfers, and windsurfers, the National Data Buoy Center updates a real-time map of Northern California buoys, showing air and water temperature; size, direction, and period of swells; and wind speed and direction. The Cape San Martin and Monterey Bay buoys will give the most information for Big Sur: www.facs.scripps.edu.

Kayaking

Big Sur is a rough, exposed, cold-water coast, not suited for greenhorns. Experienced kayakers consider it a supreme challenge and venture out only with the proper equipment and current information from dependable, expert sources. Winter weather is unpredictable and can be brutal. Summer fogs can be very thick. September through November are considered the best months to be on the water.

Big Sur's wild grandeur is, of course, its big draw, and kayaking provides the best way to explore its remote coves and beaches, sea caves, hidden tide pools, and coastal islets. Paddlers also enjoy spectacular perspectives of the front of the Santa Lucia Range unknown to drivers on Highway 1. They also enjoy close-up views of kelp forests, otters, basking sea lions, and even whales.

Good put-in and take-out points are few and far between. Highly experienced kayakers, of course, have a wider choice of accessible beaches and coves. Carmel Bay is a popular launch site. Another is Whalers Cove in Point Lobos State Reserve, where launchings are strictly regulated. If you plan to launch there on a weekend, you need reservations (www.pt-lobos.parks.state.ca.us). If you bring your kayak on a trailer, you need to park it at the Rat Hill boat parking area. The reserve's Web site also lists current regulations.

Molera Beach is one of the best launch sites on Big Sur's north coast, but you need to portage your kayak about a mile from the central parking area. Mill Creek and San Simeon Cove are the preferred put-in points on the central Big

Sur coast. Mill Creek gives access to the slight indentation of coastline between Lopez Point and Cape San Martin that kayakers know (somewhat optimistically) as Lucia Bay.

San Simeon Cove, blocked from most northern swells by San Simeon Point, typically offers the calmest coastal paddling in the vicinity. Sea For Yourself Kayak Tours rents kayaks on the Hearst Memorial State Beach. Leffingwell Landing and Moonstone Beach are also popular launch sites.

Kayakers can find the calmest waters of all at Lakes Nacimiento and San Antonio. Both reservoirs rent kayaks.

Kayaking Outfitters

- **Big Sur Kayak Adventures (Pacific Coast Kayak Adventures):** This company concentrates on northern Big Sur, from Carmel Bay to Mill Creek, with half-day, full-day, and custom trips. Day trips put ashore for lunch and exploration. Beginners are encouraged. (888) 524–4787 or (831) 883–9289; www.bigsurkayakadventures.net/.
- **Sea For Yourself Kayak Tours:** This Cambria-based outfitter and store offers short tours for beginners and intermediate paddlers off Moonstone Beach, Leffingwell Landing, and San Simeon Cove, where staff rent kayaks on the beach. They also offer advanced and custom trips elsewhere on the southern Big Sur coast. 604 Main Street, Suite D, Cambria, CA 93428; (805) 927–1787; www.kayakcambria.com.

Diving

Point Lobos State Reserve is one of the top diving areas of the continental United States. One of the richest marine habitats in California, it's known for its 70-foot-high kelp forests, colorful seascapes, playful otters and seals, and array of protected fish that include lingcod, cabezone, and rockfish. Whales sometimes swim past. The underwater topography is varied with coves and pinnacles. Scuba diving and snorkeling are restricted to Whalers Cove and Bluefish Cove, and divers must enter and exit the water only at the ramp at the Whalers Cove parking lot. Fishing, collecting, and disturbing marine life are strictly forbidden in this reserve. All divers must register upon entering the reserve, and since numbers are restricted, reservations are recommended. For regulations, underwater maps, and dive sites at Point Lobos State Reserve, check out this Web site: www.pt-lobos.parks.state.ca.us. Another site that provides some subjective and more current reviews of diving at Point Lobos is www.shorediving.com.

Experienced divers also trek to Carmel Bay, in large part because of the great submarine canyon that comes close to Monastery Beach. Diving enthusiasts trade observations at www.shorediving.com. You can find specifics by clicking on the links for "Monastery Beach North" or "Monastery Beach South"; if you prefer to enter the bay just north of the Carmel River, click on "Carmel River North."

The underwater preserve at Julia Pfeiffer Burns State Park reaches between Partington Point and McWay Creek. The steep drop-off of the Partington Submarine Canyon brings great variety to its animal and plant life. Caves and coves invite exploration. Partington Cove is the usual entry and exit spot. Divers need special-use permits to enter the water, obtained from Big Sur Station; contact (831) 667–2315. The buddy system is in force. Bring your dive card to prove competency.

Jade Cove is a popular diving site mainly among jade collectors. It's also a tough place to dive. The cove is about 40 feet deep, and the swells roll in and out with powerful currents. Winter weather is very rough, but in summer the kelp grows thick enough to obscure vision.

The mouth of Big Creek also offers rich and interesting diving. Before heading down, prospective divers must apply for permission and file a dive plan with the UC Santa Cruz diving safety officer; contact (831) 459–4286.

Outfitters also lead diving adventures to seldom seen (and even uncharted) offshore sites, including sea mounts and fantastic submarine rock formations. For more information, contact Adventure Sports Unlimited of Santa Cruz (831–458–3648) or Truth Aquatics of Santa Barbara (805–962–1127).

Surfing

Big Sur is closer to the hard-core surfing world of Northern California than it is to the "beach-boy" surfing culture of warm-water Southern California. The local surfing community is small, and they like it that way.

Big Sur's ocean is rough and cold, and surfers wear wet suits. This is also great white shark territory. The Northern California coast is likewise noted for its big waves, of which Mavericks on the San Mateo Coast (north of Monterey Bay) is the most famous. Closer to Big Sur, the surf breaks off Ghost Tree on the Monterey Peninsula have recently attracted attention internationally for surfers who have successfully ridden some of this spot's 65-foot, beautifully curved waves. Ghost Tree will not develop the status of Mavericks, however, because personal watercraft (which are necessary for big-wave surfing) have been banned from this part of the Monterey Bay National Marine Sanctuary, effectively putting a stop to big-wave surfing in Monterey County—at least on a formalized, international level.

Local surfers continue to chase more modest waves from a relatively small handful of shore locations. September is the optimum month. Willow Creek is the most popular of Big Sur's surfing spots. Many nonsurfers enjoy parking at Los Padres National Forest picnic area just to watch the action. The north end

Two surfers return from the breakers off Willow Creek, the most popular surfboarding spot on the southern Big Sur coast.

of Molera Beach is considered one of the better places, though it requires a 1-mile walk from the central parking lot of Andrew Molera State Park. On the south end, San Carpoforo Beach attracts increasing numbers of surfers. You can also see surfers test the waves at Pfeiffer, Kirk Creek, Mill Creek, and Sand Dollar Beaches.

Windsurfing and Kiteboarding

The San Simeon coast is world famous for windsurfing and kiteboarding. The best beaches are in the undeveloped, fenced, northern section of San Simeon State Park, north of old San Simeon. Rangers intend to keep the fences in place while they draw up long-term use plans, but they are tolerant of traditional public use. To avoid further restrictions, it is important for beach users not to trample foliage, damage property, or disturb bird or animal life, including elephant seals.

Most beaches are known by word of mouth among the fraternity of windsurfers and kiteboarders. The most famous is Arroyo Laguna, which probably has the best conditions for windsurfing. From spring through October, winds blow parallel to the shore, offering flat-water cruising or wave sailing, depending on conditions. The winds begin to rise in late morning, and blow strongest in the midafternoon. Park in the wide, unpaved lot next to the Arroyo Laguna Bridge. Veteran windsurfers traditionally hop the gate. The state has hopes to install a turnstile gate.

Chapter 7
Big Sur Nature

Big Sur is biologically remarkable because it's odd. There's no other place like it. In part this is a function of the area's spectacular range of elevations. This is a place where sea otters lolling in their kelp beds can watch snow falling on peaks not 3 miles distant; where hikers can toil all morning up a steep mountain slope rampant with sagebrush, and still hear sea lions barking in the fog below.

Big Sur's uniqueness is also geographic. Sitting where the dry Mediterranean climate of Southern California meets the cooler, wetter climate of Northern California, Big Sur is a place where yuccas grow near redwoods, and where condors can roost and steelhead spawn at the top and the bottom of the same tall tree.

Take advantage of the many nature walks and programs offered by the state parks, the Big Sur Land Trust, and other Central Coast organizations. The Junior Ranger programs at Pfeiffer Big Sur and San Simeon State Parks offer many nature activities aimed specifically at kids. The Pelican Network Web site posts current information on organized nature hikes and activities: www.pelican network.net. The Ventana Wilderness Alliance site is another trove of local natural history information: www.ventanawild.org.

Geology

The Formation of the Santa Lucia Range

The Santa Lucia Range is compact but exceptionally rugged. The view from Highway 1 does not do these mountains justice. To glimpse them at their most rugged, drive to the Post Ranch Inn for a sight of the granitic Ventana Cones. Even better, drive the Nacimiento-Fergusson Road up to the Coast Ridge, from which you can look east to a seemingly chaotic jumble of plunging, steep-sided, sun-blasted canyons, peaks, and ridges. Nearby Cone Peak, which rises from the sea to 5,155 feet in 3 miles, is the steepest coastal gradient in the United States outside Alaska.

The steep drop of the Santa Lucias continues under the Pacific. Two submarine canyons plunge to depths of 3,000 feet just off the Big Sur coast: the Sur Submarine Canyon south of Point Sur, and the Partington Submarine Canyon, near Grimes Canyon. The colossal Monterey Submarine Canyon begins in Monterey Bay, immediately north of the Big Sur region. A spur canyon reaches into Carmel Bay.

The Santa Lucia Range is young, though it was built of ancient rocks carried there by the geological conveyor belt of plate tectonics, or continental drift. Starting about 130 million years ago, the Farallon Plate began sliding eastward beneath the North American Plate, pushing up the Coast Ranges to form a string of islands off the coast of North America, which was then defined by the Sierra Nevada. Other pieces of land, including seamounts, islands, and buckled seafloors, rode in from the west on the Farallon Plate, crashing into the "islands" and adding more pieces of land.

After the Farallon Plate had completely disappeared beneath the North American Plate about twenty-nine million years ago, the North American Plate found itself in direct contact with the Pacific Plate. The contact zone between these two plates was and is the San Andreas Fault, which lies east of the Big Sur area, beyond the Salinas River. Unlike the Farallon Plate, which slammed into the mainland head-on, the Pacific Plate makes more of a glancing blow as it moves inexorably in a northwest direction at an average speed of 1.5 inches per year. Over the millennia this slow-motion sideswipe collision has carried in yet other blocks of rock from remote locations far to the south, creating a hodgepodge of exotic rocks from near and far. (Some of these rocks contained gold, which sparked a minor gold rush to the Santa Lucias in the 1870s.) The northwest pull along the San Andreas Fault has also skewed the entire Big Sur region along a northwest–southeast alignment. If you look at the map, you will see that the coastline, the main ridges, the prevailing courses of most of the river valleys (including the Salinas, Carmel, Big Sur, Nacimiento, and San Antonio Rivers), and the San Andreas Fault itself are aligned mainly along a northwest–southeast axis.

Seen from the Coast Ridge Road, the Ventana Double Cone (right) and Kandlbinder Peak (left) stand at the granite heart of the northwestern Ventana Wilderness.

Starting about five million years ago, pressures from this tectonic collision began to lift the Santa Lucia Range upward. As the mountains rose, the streams ran faster and cut deeper, steep-sided canyons, following the path of least resistance. The easiest route for many streams was to cut straight through broken rock in zones of stress caused by tectonic movement. Consequently, many stream channels follow minor earthquake faults in the Big Sur region. The coastline itself largely demarks the major Sur-Nacimiento Fault.

A particularly interesting tour of Santa Lucia geology is to hike or bike along Indians Road (aka the Gorge Trail), which traverses the eastern wall of the so-called Grand Canyon of Monterey County, the Arroyo Seco. At heights of more than 1,000 vertical feet above the river, the track provides intimate views of a Santa Lucia cross section cut by the river, as well as countless road cuts ideal for checking out geological formations.

Much of the sand deposited on seafloors in ancient millennia crops up today in spectacular sandstone rock formations of the interior mountains. Carved by

Natural History Museums

There are small natural history collections at Pfeiffer Big Sur State Park (the Ernst Ewoldsen Memorial Nature Center), Garland Ranch Regional Park, and the Lake San Antonio Visitor Center, above the South Shore. The best public collection of birds, mammals, and other fauna from Monterey County, however, is found at the Pacific Grove Natural History Museum. The Museum of Natural History in Morro Bay is strong on Central Coast ecology, though the emphasis is (naturally) on Morro Bay.

- **Pacific Grove Museum of Natural History:** 165 Forest Avenue, Pacific Grove, CA 93950; (831) 648–5716; www.pgmuseum.org.
- **Museum of Natural History:** Morro Bay State Park, State Park Road, Morro Bay, CA 93442; (805) 772–2694; www.slostateparks.com.

wind and rain into fantastic shapes, caves, and even arches, some of the best outcrops accessible to the public are found along the Arroyo Seco and San Antonio Rivers, Church Creek, the presently inaccessible Reliz Rocks, and the upper Carmel River in Pine Valley. Between Lakes Nacimiento and San Antonio, a small BLM property on Tierra Redonda Mountain protects some unusual sandstone formations in addition to some extremely rare inland sand dunes.

A Short Geology Tour of Highway 1

A drive along Highway 1 is a good introduction to local geology, since so much of Big Sur's complex and fascinating geology can be read in its coastal cliffs, outcrops, and road cuts.

The coastline itself is defined by the dynamics of continental drift. Running parallel to the Big Sur coastline, the Sur-Nacimiento Fault divides the Salinan Block from the Franciscan Complex. To the east of the fault line, the Salinan Block consists largely of granitic and metamorphic rock, a mass of land that is thought to have been detached and carried north from the southern Sierra Nevada by movement of the Pacific Plate. To the west of the fault line lies the Franciscan Complex, remnants of ancient seafloor carried into the continent by the Farallon Plate, leveraged into their present (but temporary!) position by the Pacific Plate.

In two places along the Big Sur coast, the Sur-Nacimiento Fault lies west of the shoreline, under the ocean. In these spots the shoreline consists largely of the granitic rock characteristic of the Salinan Block. More resistant to erosion than the more brittle Franciscan rocks, granite has been so celebrated by seascape painters and by writers such as Robinson Jeffers that visitors to Big Sur can be excused for thinking that granite is a hallmark stone of this rugged coast. The longest section of granite shoreline stretches from the Monterey Peninsula down to near Point Sur, and includes Carmel Beach, Point Lobos, and Garrapata State Park. A shorter stretch of granite shoreline fronts Julia Pfeiffer Burns State Park, where Partington Cove serves as an easily accessible example.

Marble, limestone, and schist are also characteristic stone of the Salinan Block. The largest mass of limestone and marble on the California coast is Pico Blanco, readily visible from Highway 1 near Point Sur and Andrew Molera State Park. At 3,709 feet above sea level, this beautiful mountain is privately owned and currently locked in a court battle over quarrying rights.

Since the Sur-Nacimiento Fault lies inland for most of the coast, Franciscan Complex rocks make up most of the Big Sur shoreline. Crumbly, unstable, and prone to slides, these rocks are a curse to road builders, but they sure do make a fine, wild-looking landscape. Most of the monumental sea-carved cliffs, islets, and sea stacks so characteristic of Big Sur are part of the Franciscan Complex. Some are layered sedimentary rocks, formed on the seafloor by layers of mud, shellfish, sand, or other debris hardening into mudstone, limestone, sandstone, and so forth. Road cuts and coastal bluffs expose these layered sedimentary faces, typically bent by plate tectonics into diagonal planes. One spectacularly twisted example is the sedimentary bluff on the north side of Pfeiffer Beach.

Other Franciscan rocks are remnants of undersea volcanism, raised to the surface by plate tectonics. Massy Point Sur is a supreme example. Millennia ago it was an island, but sea currents sweeping through the gap deposited sediments, forming the enormous sandbar that today connects it to the mainland. (Geologists call this flat, sandy, natural landfill a tombolo.)

Yet other Franciscan Complex rocks were heated and compressed so greatly by tectonic pressures that they transformed into metamorphic rocks, such as serpentine and blue schist. Serpentine, California's state mineral, decomposes into soil that is toxic to most plants, save for a few specially evolved species. Where you find serpentine soil, therefore, you find areas largely devoid of vegetation, known to scientists as serpentine barrens. You can glimpse a serpentine barren from Highway 1 just south of Salmon Creek, on the eastern (uphill) side. A brief jaunt up the Salmon Creek Trail gives you a closer look. You can also see serpentine (some with asbestos) at Jade Cove.

Among the obvious signs of the Santa Lucia Mountains' five-million-year-old uplift are marine terraces, remnants of ancient wave-cut shorelines now raised far above the sea. Marine terraces are visible on coastal hillsides, but the biggest were used by road builders as a route for Highway 1. The largest marine terraces on the Big Sur coast—adjacent to Point Sur, in Pacific Valley, and south of Ragged Point—are easily noticed because the cliffs recede and the road straightens and levels out.

Coastal and offshore faults increase the odds of tsunami strikes along the Big Sur coast. Historical records of large seismic events are scant, but several have been recorded along more populated coastal areas south of Big Sur over the past 200 years. Chumash oral tradition tells of huge, devastating waves on the Santa Barbara coast. Spanish clerks at the mission chronicled a wave higher than 50 feet rolling up the Santa Barbara Channel in 1812. Residents of Morro Bay recorded unusually large waves in 1868, 1878, and 1909. Modest but potentially destructive tsunamis of 5 to 9 feet hit the San Luis Obispo and Monterey coasts after the 1946 Aleutian Island Earthquake, the 1960 Chilean Earthquake, and the 1964 Alaskan Earthquake. Geologists estimate that seismic waves of up to 40 feet (the height depending on the tide) hit the Central Coast on average every 500 years. Drivers along Highway 1 may take some comfort in knowing that the roadbed is considerably higher than 40 feet above sea level for most of the route.

Rockhounding Big Sur

Rock collectors are allowed to pick up samples for personal collections from the national forest. (Jade has special rules, see below.) Rockhounding is also permitted on state park beaches, unless otherwise posted, but is limited to fifteen pounds per person per day. Collectors should respect private property and the natural world, and practice the code of ethics espoused by the American Federation of Mineralogical Societies. Among their many sensible directives is to collect only in reasonable quantities.

Monterey County is known to collectors for fossil leaves, bivalves, gastropods, and crabs. Some have been found in road cuts along County Road G16 between Carmel Valley and Greenfield. Sandstone cliffs on Tierra Redonda Mountain, between Lakes San Antonio and Nacimiento, are rich in marine fossils. Known as the Vaqueros Formation, they contain a wealth of mollusks, echinoids, sand-filled worm tubes, foraminifers, fish bones, and turritellas. Please note that the small, public part of Tierra Redonda Mountain is preserved by the BLM for research, not collecting, and that all the surrounding land is private property.

Moonstone Beach in Cambria is named for a translucent, milky-colored agate (chalcedony) that beachcombers find on the shoreline. (You should be aware that this local "moonstone" is *not* the orthoclase gemstone more widely known as moonstone.) Tumbled by the surf, the best and largest pieces wash ashore after heavy winter storms.

Although the Salinan preferred making arrowheads and spear points from obsidian imported from elsewhere in California, they also knapped local chert to make projectile points. Chert is a hard sedimentary rock found in colors of red, green, and gray. Archaeologists have rediscovered ancient chert quarries at

Cooper Point, in the San Antonio Valley, and at Point Piedras Blancas.

You can see some nice samples of mica in the road cuts along the north end of Indians Road (aka the Gorge Trail). A rare mineral called geikielite is found in Santa Lucia marble deposits. Another rare mineral, a reddish variety of penninite called kämmererite, was commercially mined in the Santa Lucias west of King City, along with chromite and uvarovite, a garnet. The Plaskett Creek drainage has produced some stibnite. Cinnabar ore was heavily mined around San Simeon on what is now Hearst property. Rock hounds have found gem-quality rhodonite in Limekiln Creek and in coastal strands south to Jade Cove. Also along Limekiln Creek, pale lavender axinite crystals occur with epidote and quartz in serpentine.

California's state mineral, serpentine, occurs throughout the Franciscan Complex. You can find good specimens along the coast between Gorda and Pacific Valley and most easily at Jade Cove, where chrysotile serpentinite is infused with asbestos.

Jade Cove

Of all the minerals found in Monterey County, the most renowned is the type of jade known as nephrite. Valued since ancient times for its extreme hardness and beauty by the Chinese, Aztecs, and others, jade is too hard to carve, and

The cold blue waters of Jade Cove wash up the best pieces of California jade after big winter storms.

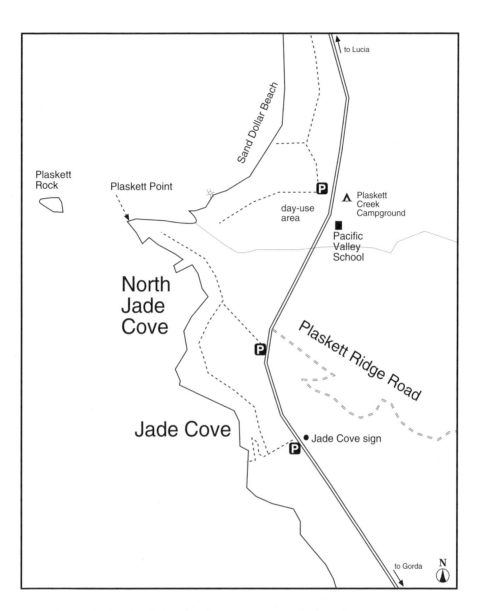

must be worked and polished by abrasion. You can find nephrite in stream grav-
els between Point Sur and Cambria, but it is concentrated between Plaskett and
Willow Creeks, with the epicenter at Jade Cove, north of Gorda. Monterey
jade comes in many colors, ranging from pure white (very rare) to red, blue,
emerald green, and black, but the most common color is grayish green. Most
collectible specimens are pebbles rolled by the sea, but there are some massive
rocks and veins of jade in bedrock at Jade Cove. When searching among the
rocks, watch the sea and beware of getting trapped by the incoming tide. The

Forest Service restricts collecting to pieces found below mean high-tide level, and to quantities that a collector can carry unaided.

The shortest path to Jade Cove starts from a turnout on Highway 1 near the Jade Cove sign, about 0.5 mile south of Pacific Valley School and 3 miles north of Gorda. Cross the fence at the stile and walk 0.2 mile to the bluff, where a rough path descends to the shore, partly on steps. If instead you walk north along the bluff, you will find other use trails to Jade Cove and North Jade Cove, most of them extremely steep and treacherous, though the use trail at the promontory dividing the two coves isn't too bad. You can find low-grade pieces of jade in the sand and gravel between the boulders, but gem-quality pieces favor the lucky or the diligent. Some good pieces wash ashore in heavy surf after winter storms. Divers who collect from the floor of Jade Cove are hampered by heavy surf in winter and spring, and by thick kelp forests in summer. Rock hounds can also find good specimens of serpentinite, slick and greasy, some with fibrous veins of asbestos (chrysotile serpentine).

The Pacific Grove Natural History Museum displays a massive nephrite boulder from Jade Cove. Gorda sponsors an annual jade festival in October, when jade dealers from near and far gather at nearby Pacific Valley School to trade and celebrate with food, music, and crafts. (831) 659–3857; www.sur coast.com.

Rockhounding Contacts

- **Carmel Valley Gem and Mineral Society:** P.O. Box 5847, Carmel, CA 93921; www.cvgms.org.
- **Monterey Bay Mineral Society:** P.O. Box 12, Salinas, CA 93901.
- **Santa Lucia Rockhounds:** P. O. Box 1672, Paso Robles, CA 93447.

Big Sur Habitats

The Santa Lucia Range is famous among botanists because it holds such a great diversity of plant habitats within a relatively small area. Big Sur sits in a transitional zone between Northern and Southern California, so that many southern species (like the yucca) reach their northernmost range in the Santa Lucias, while northern species (such as the redwood) reach their southernmost range. Many Big Sur plants are endemic: They grow here and nowhere else.

The botanical uniqueness of the Santa Lucias attracted international attention early in California's history. Unbeknownst to each other, two British botanists both arrived in California in 1831 and took up winter quarters in Monterey. Botanical lore claims that David Douglas and Thomas Coulter (from whom we get the names of two Santa Lucia trees, the Douglas fir and the Coulter pine) met there and struck up a friendship, setting out together to hunt,

Wildflower Tours

You can find wildflowers anywhere at Big Sur, depending on the season, but the trails and back roads provide the most leisurely opportunities for close observation. Accessible only to hikers, mountain bikers, and equestrians, Indians Road from Arroyo Seco (where it is also known as the Gorge Trail) is excellent for chaparral and riparian flowers in spring. The Nacimiento-Fergusson Road offers a succession of woodland, grassland, riparian, and chaparral displays, all from a paved surface.

The San Antonio Valley serves up probably the most celebrated wildflower displays in the Santa Lucia Range. The approach route from Mission San Antonio along Del Venturi Road is very beautiful, but stopping is prohibited on Fort Hunter Liggett. Beyond the northern gate of Fort Hunter Liggett, the road enters Los Padres National Forest and changes name to Milpitas Road. The 5.25-mile stretch from the military gate to Santa Lucia Memorial Park Campground passes stately oak savanna, chaparral, oak woodland, grassland, mixed-evergreen forest, vernal pools (in winter and spring), and riparian habitats, all blooming profusely through the springtime months with a rich variety of wildflowers. Since this is Forest Service land, you may park on the shoulder at will, or get out of the car altogether and explore on foot. At Indians Station the pavement ends; during the wet season a Forest Service gate blocks further vehicular travel on Indians Road. From late spring through fall, the Forest Service usually opens the gate, letting vehicles drive another 2.75 miles up unpaved Indians Road to Escondido Campground, passing a cornucopia of chaparral and woodland wildflowers.

Wildflower enthusiasts should plan to visit the Pacific Grove Museum of Natural History in April for the annual three-day wildflower exhibition. With more than 600 varieties from the Central Coast on display, it's the largest wildflower show in California. (831) 648-5716; www.pgmuseum.org.

The Monterey Bay Chapter of the California Native Plant Society, which helps sponsor the show, also offers wildflower walks and field trips to different parts of Monterey County. (831) 373-4341; www.cnps.org.

fish, and botanize in the Santa Lucia Mountains. The result is that botanical historians sometimes credit Douglas with the "discovery" of the Santa Lucia fir, and sometimes Coulter. Regardless, their descriptions of this "new" species stirred up so much lasting interest among botanists that the resulting spate of major botanical expeditions to the Santa Lucias ran right on into the twentieth century. Among other well-known botanists who have explored the range were Alice Eastwood, who collected for the California Academy of Sciences in 1897, and Willis Jepson, whose 1901 expedition for the University of California helped lay groundwork for his *Jepson Manual*, now considered the greatest authority of California botany.

As pristine as the Santa Lucias are, Big Sur still hosts a great many "weeds," plants imported from elsewhere that now thrive, displacing native species. Among the most invasive are wild oats, pampas grass, mustard, yellow star thistle, French broom, cape ivy, and—most shockingly!—ice plant, that exotic weed that has become a fraudulent icon of the California coast.

Habitat concerns more than botany. Animals, like plants, depend on special conditions for life. In the Santa Lucias such conditions can change dramatically within a very short distance. Elevation and soil type make big differences. So does climate, such as exposure to fog, wind, and sunlight. Anyone who crosses the Coast Ridge, for instance, can see how much drier the interior of the range is than the western slope, which is exposed to the foggy, moderating maritime climate.

Another interesting pattern is determined by the angle of the sun. North-facing slopes receive less direct sunlight and are consequently shadier, moister, and more heavily wooded. South-facing slopes in the very same canyon catch more direct sunlight, are too dry to support trees, and consequently tend to be covered in drought-resistant grass or chaparral. Whether a trail is on a north-facing slope or a south-facing slope should be a matter of great interest to any hiker.

Deep Ocean

The tremendous and abrupt range of ocean depths offshore from Big Sur permits a great variety of marine life to thrive relatively close to shore. Just north of Big Sur, Monterey Canyon plunges to depths of 12,000 feet within 60 miles of the shore of Monterey Bay, a natural gateway that allows deep-sea creatures and ocean birds to approach shore without leaving their native habitat. At the other end of the spectrum, the Davidson Seamount rises more than 7,000 feet above the surrounding ocean depths, about 60 miles southwest of Point Sur. Although its summit still lies some 3,700 feet below the surface, this dead volcano supports colonies of plants and animals that thrive in shallower depths. These in turn attract fish and flocks of birds that feed upon them.

Established in recognition of its extraordinary richness of marine life, the Monterey Bay National Marine Sanctuary protects the ocean out to an average distance of about 30 miles from shore, along a coastline that stretches 276 miles from Marin County to Cambria. The sanctuary is home to the nation's largest kelp forests, thirty-three marine mammal species, nearly a hundred seabird species, and more than 340 species of fish. Among the remarkable creatures that you can see on boat tours from Monterey or Morro Bay are blue whales, humpback whales, fin whales, orcas, dolphins, seals, sea lions, sea turtles, jellyfish, and many varieties of pelagic birds.

Rocky Shore

Because so much of Big Sur's rocky shore is inaccessible from the highway, intertidal life is pristine. Tide pools protected from the full force of the sea are relatively uncommon, however. More common are animals and plants that inhabit exposed rocks and beaches of boulders or cobbles. Creatures designed to survive the rough waves on exposed rocks include mussels, barnacles, limpets, chitons, and sea stars. Sea palms, algae in the likeness of foot-high palm trees, are commonly seen on exposed rocks bobbing about in the rough surf. Coastal strands made up of cobblestones provide homes for sea stars, brittle stars, and crabs of all kinds, including porcelain crabs, purple shore crabs, pebble crabs, and large red rock crabs. Protected tide pools can support many of these creatures, plus anemones, sea slugs, octopuses, sponges, worms, tunicates, sea stars, sea urchins, and a wider assortment of crustaceans, mollusks, and seaweeds.

Protected by sheer cliffs or private property, Big Sur's best tide pools are accessible by boat or kayak, and consequently must be left to adventurers to discover on their own. (If you approach a private shoreline by boat, you have no legal right to trespass above the mean high-tide line.) Intertidal areas that are readily accessible by foot from Highway 1 for the most part consist of rock fields or exposed rocks. These can be rich in certain types of life, but protected tide pools that are favored by most recreational tide poolers are few and far between.

Coastal Scrub

The typical habitat along most of Highway 1, coastal scrub is dominated by wind-pruned shrubs including California sagebrush, lizardtail, ceanothus, low coyote brush, blackberry, and yellow bush lupine. The steeper slopes slightly inland are covered with coyote brush or buckwheat, sagebrush, monkey flower, and poison oak. Songbirds nest in the brush, which also shelters lizards, snakes, brush rabbits, rodents, and bobcats.

Chaparral

The most dynamic of Big Sur's terrestrial habitats, chaparral is a forest in miniature of evergreen shrubs growing in extensive, low, often impenetrable thickets. Although common in California, chaparral is a rare habitat worldwide, occurring only in Mediterranean climates, which the Santa Lucia Range manifests in its long, dry summers and mild, wet winters. Roughly half the area of the Santa Lucias is covered with chaparral, which is visible along Highway 1, mostly on the higher slopes. For a closer look, take just about any Santa Lucia back road that climbs above the canyon bottoms and redwood forests.

Big Sur Tide Pools

For clams, sun stars, and well-equipped marine biologists, Big Sur's tide pools are fantastic. For casual visitors who view tide pooling as a recreational activity, however—and especially for families with children—Pacific Grove, Carmel, the San Simeon coast, and Cambria offer much more extensive, varied, protected, readily accessible, and easily explored tide pools than *anywhere* along the Big Sur coast.

Intertidal life is extremely fragile. Collecting or disturbing any kind of intertidal life is strictly forbidden by law. Observe tide pool life as unobtrusively as possible. Always be mindful of rising tides and sneaker waves. Do not cross private land to get to tide pools.

- **Middle Beach:** Midway between Monastery Beach and the mouth of the Carmel River, you can find a small area of protected pools amid an outcrop of granite boulders.
- **Point Lobos:** There are popular, protected tide pools near Weston Beach.
- **Malpaso Creek:** Look for exposed rocks. You can get there from a trail on Yankee Point Drive.
- **Garrapata State Park:** Protected by bluffs, the granite shoreline has plenty of exposed rocks and rough surge channels to explore from above, but they are dangerously exposed to a rough sea. An easier path goes to rocks and pools at Garrapata Beach.
- **Point Sur:** The rocky coast between Point Sur and False Sur ranks high among Big Sur tide pool areas, but it's closed to public access, except for those who approach by boat and stay below the mean high-tide line.
- **Molera Point:** Good tide pools on private property just north of the state park boundary are accessible only by boat.
- **Pfeiffer Beach:** Expect exposed rocks and rock fields.
- **Esalen:** A stairway leads to a cobble beach with exposed rocks at the mouth of Hot Springs Creek.
- **Limekiln State Park:** You'll find a cobble beach and exposed rocks here.
- **Kirk Creek Campground:** A short path leads down to exposed rocks and rock fields.
- **Mill Creek:** Look for rock fields.
- **Willow Creek:** There are more rock fields here, along with exposed rocks.
- **Sand Dollar Beach:** The south end of the beach has some exposed rocks.
- **Jade Cove:** Boulder fields are here for exploring.
- **Ragged Point Inn:** A steep stairway leads to exposed rocks.
- **Arroyo de la Cruz:** The long, rocky shoreline south of the creek is now part of San Simeon State Park.

(Continued)

Visitors at Esalen Institute enjoy access to a rocky tide pool just north of Hot Springs Creek.

- **Hearst Memorial State Beach:** The 1.3-mile trail to San Simeon Point follows a bluff with access to some protected tide pool areas.
- **Cambria:** The semi-protected tide pools all along Moonstone Beach are extensive and very popular. The Leffingwell Day-Use Area provides ready access to cobbled shoreline and exposed rocks.

Chaparral plants are specially adapted to withstand harsh summer droughts. Veteran backcountry hikers know some of these adaptations intimately. Thick, tough, waxy, leathery, or needlelike leaves scratch and puncture clothes and skin, and the stiff branches grow so tangled and thick that even the most masochistic bushwhacker cannot navigate through. These same defenses provide ideal protection for small birds, mammals, and reptiles fleeing from larger predators. Trails hacked through chaparral must be regularly maintained, or they disappear under new growth.

After about twenty-five to fifty years of growth, many chaparral shrubs reach maturity and begin to die back, creating a dry and combustible biomass of deadwood that nature cleans out periodically by a very efficient means: fire. Ignited by lightning or human carelessness, a chaparral fire burns intensely hot and is virtually unstoppable. The Santa Lucias have hosted some enormous wildfires. Many animals die in these conflagrations, but others survive by sheltering in deep burrows or by fleeing. While clearing out deadwood, wildfire releases nutrients in the form of ash and inspires the germination of new seeds, thus restarting the cycle in the life of a chaparral forest. Many chaparral plants have evolved to resprout from root crowns after the tops are burned.

Grasslands and Oak Savanna

Green in winter and spring, tawny yellow in summer and fall, Big Sur's grasslands are yet another hallmark California landscape. Where the pastures are interspersed with oak trees, the landscape is known as oak savanna. San Antonio Valley is a prime example of an oak savanna, but the Santa Lucias are rich with these ecosystems, especially on the east side and the coastal ridges. Even in the midst of heavy brush cover, the mountains are dotted with thousands of little meadows such as Horse Pasture and Strawberry Camp, delightful isles in the midst of a hot chaparral sea, rank with grasses and shaded by great old oaks. Many areas along the coast, including parts of Pacific Valley and the Hearst Ranch, were once covered with coastal scrub and chaparral but have been transformed into grassland by burning, and are maintained as such by grazing cattle. (Cattle were banned from Pacific Valley in 2005, so it will be interesting to

Recent Wildfires

Although Native Americans and ranchers cleared chaparral in the Santa Lucias with fire, the Forest Service suppressed the practice in the twentieth century, allowing brush to build to dangerous levels. Several large fires toward the end of that century caused the Forest Service to reconsider the policy, but the issue is complicated by a rugged terrain and the extreme interest of local property owners.

Fire	Year	Consequences
Buckeye Fire	1970	60,000 acres burned around Buckeye Creek
Molera Fire	1972	4,300 acres burned in Andrew Molera State Park; rains on denuded slopes caused mudslides at Big Sur Center that winter
Marble Cone Fire	1977	178,000 acres burned in Ventana Wilderness, the second largest wildfire in California history
Rat Creek Fire	1985	60,000 acres burned around McWay Creek
Gorda Fire	1985	20,000 acres burned around Gorda

observe how the foliage on this marine terrace will change over the coming years.)

Most of the grasses are exotic weeds, such as wild oats, but many native plants still survive in grassland pockets throughout the Santa Lucias. Arroyo de la Cruz, for instance, harbors 520 plant species, the greatest diversity of vegetation of any place in San Luis Obispo County (although the creek east of Highway 1 flows through Hearst property and is closed to the public without special permission).

Streamside Woodlands and Redwood Forest

Streamside (or riparian) habitats of the Santa Lucias are remarkably different from the chaparral, woodland, savanna, and grassland habitats that thrive immediately adjacent. Riparian habitats may embrace springs, small marshes, redwood forests, and mixed woodlands of bay laurel, oak, tanbark oak, alder, willow, and other broad-leaved trees. A cool pool of water at the bottom of a canyon, banked by ferns and home to newts, crayfish, and pond turtles, may lie only a stone's throw from a sunbaked hillside choked with brush. Although most riparian habitats of the Santa Lucias are long, narrow, and sinuous, the lower Big Sur River drains a broad coastal valley for several miles. Big yellow banana slugs are among the most colorful residents of moist woodlands along riparian corridors. Other inhabitants include raccoons, bobcats, foxes, deer, skunks, owls, and steelhead trout. Winter hikers sometimes find hibernating ladybugs that swarm in masses on streamside trees and bushes.

Many Santa Lucia streams are intermittent. In winter even minor streams run so high and fast that experienced hikers find them dangerous to ford, and periodic floods wreak havoc along the lower Big Sur River. In summer most inland streams run at a trickle or dry up, and the Big Sur River itself, second in size only to the Carmel River, lulls along so peacefully that vacationers set chairs down in the current and settle in for a snooze.

White Redwoods

Albino redwood trees are extremely uncommon. Since they cannot manufacture chlorophyll, most die as sprouts. Only rarely is one able to survive by taking sugars from host trees that share its root system. Big Sur's most legendary albino redwood reportedly lives in the remote canyon of Doolans Hole Creek. No trails go there, and very few people have ever seen it. Big Sur's second known albino redwood, however, is very easy to find. It grows right beside the entrance kiosk at Fernwood Campground in Big Sur Center.

At the height of summer, the larger streams of the Ventana's interior, such as Tassajara Creek near the Narrows, can be shady, cool oases in the midst of a wilderness of sun-blasted chaparral.

Redwood forests are a distinctive riparian habitat at Big Sur. They grow in canyons that are close enough to the ocean to receive abundant winter rain and summer fog. Redwoods are able to survive most forest fires, even when nearly gutted by the flames. Most redwood groves contain perfectly healthy trees with blackened hollows and even tunnels burned clear through them. Shallow roots make them vulnerable to strong winds, so redwood forests do not thrive directly exposed to the sea, but take shelter beyond the first bend or two of coastal canyons. Even there, the front ranks of trees are often picturesquely deformed by wind, cropped and streamlined into unusual shapes. Though beautiful and well proportioned, the redwoods of Big Sur are not as big or tall as the specimens farther north on the California coast. Big Sur marks the southern limit of this ancient tree's range. The last natural grove grows just south of Redwood Gulch in the Southern Redwood Botanical Area, though you may see one or two scrawny survivors south of there.

Dry-Slope Woodlands and Forest

Other trees of the Santa Lucia Range do not require the moist confines of a stream channel to thrive, but are adapted to live on drier slopes. The Monterey pine is quite common as a landscape plant, but grows naturally in only five groves around the Monterey Peninsula, Cambria (including San Simeon State Park), and the Carmel Highlands. Point Lobos Ranch hosts a pristine grove of Monterey pine, as well as the rare Gowen cypress. Coniferous forests hug the coast at Point Lobos, one of only two places where Monterey cypress grows naturally. Broad-leaved woodlands of oak, laurel, madrone, buckeye, and hardwoods grow on higher hillsides, mostly on north-facing slopes. Here also is found the huge Shreve's oak, a hybrid of the coast live oak and interior live oak. At yet higher altitudes, these hardwoods mix with Douglas fir, Santa Lucia fir, sugar pine, ponderosa, Coulter pine, Sargent cypress, and other evergreens.

The Santa Lucia fir is Big Sur's most celebrated endemic. It grows naturally in a range roughly 56 miles north to south, 12 miles west to east, and nowhere else. The padres at Mission San Antonio knew the tree and used its resin to make incense for church services. Mission expeditions to gather the resin from groves on Cone Peak followed the old Salinan trail that led to Quiquilit village. It was to this trail (known to the Spanish as the Carrizo Trail) that the padres directed British botanists David Douglas and Thomas Coulter to their first and fateful meeting with the Santa Lucia fir. If you want to see these firs without a long walk, drive to the end of Cone Peak Road.

Stricken Woodlands

First reported in 1995, the funguslike pathogen *Phytophthora ramorum* has killed thousands of tanbark oaks throughout California. Other trees, including redwoods, madrones, and bay laurels, carry the pathogen, but so far appear to be unharmed. Known as sudden oak death syndrome, the devastation is obvious in Big Sur's mixed woodlands. Although biologists are searching for solutions, the Forest Service and state parks meanwhile ask hikers to clean the mud from their boots and bike tires after tracking through infected woodlands to avoid spreading it farther. An epidemic of pine pitch cancer disease is also devastating woodlands of Monterey pine.

The Forest Service has established three special botanical areas to protect rare and endangered plants in the upland forest and woodland of the Santa Lucia Mountains. The 2,787-acre Cone Peak Gradient Research Natural Area (RNA) safeguards the unique sequence of plants that grow on the steep rise from near sea level to Cone Peak. Alder Creek Botanical Area and Lion Den Springs Botanical Area protect forests in two headwater drainages in the Silver Peak Wilderness. All three are approachable on back roads.

Habitat Contacts
- **California Native Plant Society (CNPS):** 2707 K Street, Suite 1, Sacramento, CA 95816-5113; (916) 447-2677; www.cnps.org.
- **Monterey Bay Chapter CNPS:** (831) 373-4341; www.mbay.net.
- **San Luis Obispo Chapter CNPS:** www.cnps-slo.org.

Wildlife-Watching
Terrestrial Wildlife
You don't have to search hard to see squirrels and deer in Big Sur country; raccoons, too, make regular appearances in almost any campground. Streamside hikers routinely encounter banana slugs and newts, small but dependable hike stoppers. The Santa Lucia Range is also a good place to *listen* for wildlife: for hooting owls and drilling woodpeckers in the oak woodlands; for chiding scrub jays, and the haunting bay of sea lions in the fog; for whining cicadas in the summer heat, and the lonesome night choruses of coyotes. Night drivers along Highway 1 in January are sometimes surprised by the extent and volume of the croaking frogs. (So loud a racket do these amphibians make that Richard Brautigan's alter ego in the novel *Confederate General from Big Sur* procured an alligator to cull his pond.)

One indigenous beast that you will not see is the grizzly bear. They have been extinct in the Santa Lucias probably since the late 1800s, though they were once commonly sighted at Tassajara Hot Springs, Pine Valley, the San Antonio Valley, and elsewhere. (In John Steinbeck's novel *East of Eden*, one character remarks that the last grizzly killed in Monterey County was shot near Pleyto, a settlement now under the waters of San Antonio Reservoir.) Because grizzlies hunted black bears, the latter historically shunned the grizzlies' range. Since the grizzlies' demise in the Santa Lucia Range, however, the smaller and less aggressive black bear has begun to colonize it. In recent years some have even wandered into Carmel and Salinas, but thus far black bears remain rare enough that Ventana backpackers, when storing their food for the night, should concern themselves more with rodents and raccoons than with bears.

Wild turkeys are non-native but common in the Santa Lucias. Another new-comer is the feral pig, active mostly at dawn and dusk. Although a favorite game of hunters in Los Padres National Forest and Fort Hunter Liggett, feral pigs are destructive, causing great damage to meadows and hillsides by rooting for food with their tusks. Those tusks can be dangerous, too. Never corner or crowd a pig. So many wild pigs cross Highway 1 just south of the Carmel River Bridge that the state has erected PIG CROSSING signs. Collisions between cars and pigs have been harmful to both.

After depletion by nineteenth-century fur trappers, beavers have expanded their range along the San Antonio River downstream from the reservoir.

Elk and antelope were resident in the grasslands east of the Santa Lucias when the Spanish arrived, but were soon killed off. Today a herd of tule elk resides in the San Antonio Valley on Fort Hunter Liggett. Elk-watching is dif-ficult on the base, because visitors are not allowed to stop along the roadside. Though elk numbers are still smaller on the west side of the Santa Lucias, a more convenient spot for watching elk is along Highway 1 between San Car-poforo Creek and Hearst Castle, and especially around Arroyo de la Cruz. Stop only in turnouts where you can pull completely off the highway.

The many wild streams along the Big Sur coast are habitat for steelhead trout, a member of the salmon family. Hatched in freshwater pools, they soon migrate to the ocean to mature, returning to spawn at the end of a three-year cycle. After laying or fertilizing some 1,500 pinkish eggs, steelhead do not rou-tinely die, but swim back down to the sea. Steelhead require clean, free-flowing, year-round streams, with riffles and vegetation that hangs over the water to help hide them from predators. The many west-side streams that sup-port steelhead include the Big and Little Sur Rivers. Ranger-led tours during summer seek out steelhead runs in Molera, Pfeiffer Big Sur, and other state parks. On the east side of the Santa Lucias, steelhead still spawn in the Arroyo Seco and Lost Valley Creek, reaching the Pacific by way of the Salinas River. Another endangered fish, the tidewater goby, lives in salt water in the Santa Rosa Creek Preserve at the south end of Moonstone Beach.

Richard Brautigan called the Santa Lucias a "thousand year old flop-house for mountain lions." Though reclusive and seldom seen, they are plentiful. A century ago ranchers used to shoot great numbers of them every year. Hikers are cautioned never to run from mountain lions, because running triggers a predatory instinct in the lion to chase you as prey. Instead, boldly stand your ground, wave your arms, shout and make an aggressive display, and, if attacked, fight back. That said, mountain lion attacks are rare, and many a lifelong hiker has never seen one.

Bobcats are more commonly seen, typically in grassy areas near woodland. Among the places they frequent are the San Antonio Valley, marine terraces

Marvels of the Rodent and Shrimp World

Biologists enjoy a double windfall at San Simeon State Park. Although most passersby detect nothing special about the landscape along the San Simeon Nature Trail just east of Washburn Campground, biologists note it as one of the few places in California where vernal pools and mima mounds occur together. A natural feature rapidly disappearing from the California landscape, a vernal pool is an intermittent puddle that fills in the rainy season, and dries out in late spring and summer. At San Simeon they form in hardpan on high ground, and are home to a unique species of shrimp.

Mima mounds are more mysterious in origin, but scientists believe that gophers or other rodents build them for their burrows when the surrounding ground is too hard for digging. Ranging in size from a few inches to many feet, a mima mound might be the work of centuries, the rodent equivalent of Holland's network of dikes and polders.

near Point Lobos and Missionary Beach, and the aptly named Bobcat Trail in Andrew Molera State Park.

Pacific Grove is justifiably more famous for its butterfly trees, but Big Sur also hosts wintering colonies of monarch butterflies, which congregate and roost typically on Monterey pines and eucalyptus trees from midfall through spring, laying eggs on available milkweed. These insects migrate for hundreds of miles during their lifetimes, a migration cycle that ultimately reaches from Canada to Mexico, though no individual makes the whole journey. A complete migration cycle takes many generations, the instinct to push onward being passed genetically from one to the next. New flocks of butterflies arrive every winter on the Central Coast, covering selected trees with thousands of fluttering orange wings, an amazing sight. Four areas to find butterfly trees in winter are the eucalyptus grove just west of the campground in Andrew Molera State Park, the Esalen Institute, the Monterey pines of San Simeon Natural Preserve, and the eucalyptus grove next to Sebastian's Store in San Simeon.

Marine Mammals

Otters

Almost exterminated by nineteenth-century pelt hunters, the southern sea otter was thought extinct until 1938, when an observer spotted a group near the newly opened Bixby Bridge. The state established the Otter Game Refuge in 1941 to accommodate them. Since then their numbers have greatly rebounded. You can see them floating and frolicking among kelp beds in semi-protected coves from many observation points along Highway 1. Their seemingly playful ways and interesting habits always attract and hold an audience. Bring binoculars and look for them from rocks and bluffs at Rocky Point, Sand Dollar Beach, Jade Cove, and Point Lobos, Garrapata, Andrew Molera, Julia Pfeiffer Burns, and San Simeon State Parks.

Otters live about twenty years. Males grow to about eighty-five pounds and almost 6 feet in length, including a foot-long tail. Females are smaller. An otter is born floating atop the sea in kelp beds and lives its entire life in the sea. The kelp provides some protection from sharks, but otters sometimes swim in the open ocean. When an otter sleeps, it entangles itself in the kelp to keep from drifting. To generate heat, the otter must eat about 15 percent of its body weight daily, a considerable volume of abalone, sea urchins, crabs, scallops, and other shellfish, which it gathers from rocks under the sea at depths of up to 300 feet and carries to the surface along with a rock. Then, lying on its back in the kelp with the shell cradled on its abdomen, the otter raises the rock in its forepaws and hammers the shell until it breaks open. Otters are tool-using animals.

The impact of otters on the fishing industry is a complex matter of give and take. Fishermen have blamed otters for the decline of abalone. That's partly true, because otters eat abalone. On the other hand, otters also keep sea urchins in check and thereby contribute to the growth of kelp beds, which the urchins would otherwise deplete. Kelp beds in turn provide sanctuaries for young fish populations, a boon for fishermen.

Otter Contact

- **Friends of the Otters:** 125 Ocean View Boulevard, Suite 204, Pacific Grove, CA 93950; (831) 373–2747; www.seaotters.org.

Sea Lions and Seals

Sea lions and seals are members of the same family, the pinnipeds.

Two sea lion species are frequently sighted on offshore rocks along the Big Sur coast: the California sea lion and the Steller's sea lion. Both eat fish and squid, and in turn are eaten by great white sharks, although they are far from simply helpless prey. Sea lions are far more dexterous swimmers than sharks, and if not taken by surprise can often evade them.

California sea lions are black and well known to humans as the so-called trained seal (though only the females are selected for this training). Males can weigh up to 700 pounds and grow to 10 feet in length. California sea lions "bark" as a territorial warning to other males, a sound that inspired the name *Point Lobos*, Spanish for "point of the wolves." Steller's sea lions are less common and larger, the males reaching up to 13 feet and 2,200 pounds. They are most easily distinguished by their yellowish brown color. Dominant males from both species try to form harems and defend them vigorously against other males. In both species, however, the smaller, promiscuous female has no loyalty to her mate and changes harems at will.

Harbor seals are smaller than sea lions, tipping the scale at about 300 pounds. Their round, doglike heads are often sighted bobbing in the surf. Individuals can range in fur color from black to white. To feed, they dive to depths approaching 1,000 feet and can remain submerged for more than 20 minutes.

The largest of all California pinnipeds is the northern elephant seal. This hulking beast can weigh up to 5,000 pounds and reach lengths of 16 feet. Females are smaller, averaging about 2,000 pounds and 11 feet in length. The elephant seal is named for the fleshy, bulbous, foot-long protuberance that hangs from the male's snout. Employed as a flail in territorial battles, the snout is also thought to amplify the seal's belchlike roars.

Blubber hunters nearly drove the northern elephant seal to extinction in the nineteenth century. A large individual could be rendered down into several barrels of high-quality lamp oil. After the species was reduced to a small rookery of about a hundred seals on Guadalupe Island, Mexico, it began a recovery, slow at first, but accelerating over the twentieth century. After establishing rookeries on many California islands, elephant seals began to colonize the mainland in the 1970s. Establishing a new beachhead near Piedras Blancas in 1990, they have returned in greater numbers with every passing year. Thousands now cover the beaches between San Simeon and Piedras Blancas from winter to spring. More recently elephant seals have hauled out at Moonstone Beach in Cambria, and at Gorda and Cape San Martin on the Big Sur shoreline. When colonizing new areas, they are not afraid to haul out on beaches where humans, and even dogs, are present. There is as yet no telling when the rookeries will reach their limits.

The largest rookery on the Big Sur coast remains the 2.3-mile stretch of beach starting 11 miles north of Cambria and ending just south of the Piedras Blancas Lighthouse. Visitors are permitted to stop and view the elephant seals. Similar to the "bear jams" encountered on Yellowstone's roads, Highway 1 along here sometimes experiences "elephant seal jams" when parking areas fill up and traffic slows to a crawl. Worse, curious people trample the foliage and climb down to the beach, oblivious to the dangers posed by surprisingly fast elephant seals, and even more oblivious to the stress that they cause the beasts in return. Please observe elephant seals from a safe distance atop the bluff. Use binoculars or a telephoto lens for a closer look. Restrain all dogs. Docents are often on hand to answer questions.

Life in the elephant seal rookeries reaches its dramatic peak from December to March. Cows give birth and nurse their pups. Bulls fight gargantuan battles for territory and mates. Beach masters breed with harems of ten to one

Elephant Seal Seasons

Males spend eight months of their year at sea, and females about ten months, though individuals can haul out at any time of year. Winter is the most exciting time to view elephant seals, and early fall the quietest.

April–May: Females and juveniles return to molt.

June–August: Males return to molt and rest.

September–November: Juveniles and subadults haul out. Mock battles.

November: Bulls begin arriving toward end of month.

December: Bulls continue arriving. Females begin arriving, birthing.

January: Females continue arriving. Birthing and mating.

February: Climax of mating season. Adults begin to depart to sea.

March: Last adults depart to sea. Pups teach themselves to swim.

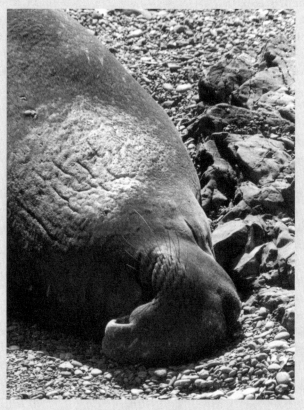

The elephant seal takes its name from the fleshy protuberance below its snout, though it serves more as a club than a trunk.

hundred cows. By late spring the beach drama subsides as the animals go to sea to eat and build up their blubber reserves. Their journeys take them as far as Alaska in quest of squid and fish, requiring dives to depths of more than 3,000 feet and submersion for more than 45 minutes. This is an astounding feat, amounting in some cases to a migration of 6,000 miles per year. (No wonder they laze in the sun when they get the chance!)

In summer individuals and small groups haul out to rest and molt, at which time they appear ragged and sickly, though they're perfectly healthy. Young males hone their fighting skills in mock battles, slamming their chests together and belching out extended roars, a scene somewhat reminiscent of a high school locker room after football practice. Most of the time, however, they just lie there, basking in the sun.

By late November the rookery begins to fill up again. Mature males return to stake out territory and determine dominance. Pregnant females arrive to give birth to pups that were sired the previous spring. Pups grow rapidly on their mothers' fat-rich milk. About the time the pups are weaned, mating begins anew. Since only one out of every twenty-five males ever gets to mate, numerous frustrated stags loiter on the periphery, or haul out on remote rocks and beaches. Some are not content to hang back, but challenge the beach master, whereupon a fierce battle ensues. Starting with verbal intimidation, they progress to flailing snouts. If this doesn't settle matters, they escalate mayhem, crashing their great bulks together, slashing with their tusks, and biting until—bloodied and roaring—one drives the other into the sea.

Pinniped Contacts

- **Friends of the Elephant Seal:** P.O. Box 490, Cambria, CA 93428; (805) 924–1628. The Web site is excellent: www.elephantseal.org.
- **Friends of the Elephant Seal Visitor Center:** Suite 3B, Plaza del Cavalier, 250 San Simeon Avenue, San Simeon, CA 93452.

Dolphins and Whales

Year-round whale-watching boat tours from Monterey or Morro Bay have recorded an impressive array of whale species off the Monterey and San Luis Obispo coasts, including dolphins, porpoises, blue whales, orcas, fin whales, beaked whales, gray whales, and humpback whales. Gray whales are the star attraction of winter and spring trips, while summer and fall trips search mainly for humpback and blue whales. Dolphins and porpoises live offshore all year round, and excursion boats report that schools numbering up to 1,000 mammals are sometimes seen.

Whale-watchers do not need a boat to catch a glimpse of cetaceans at Big Sur, however. Observers on marine terraces and coastal bluffs routinely see dolphins swimming just beyond the surf line. California gray whales also swim very close to shore, and are therefore the prime target of land-based whale-watching.

A baleen whale that grows to about 50 feet in length, the California gray whale is the state's "official" marine mammal. They look gray because their black skin supports a growth of white barnacles. They summer in Arctic seas, filling up on vast quantities of plankton. Their wintering harbors in the Gulf of California require an annual migration of 5,000 miles southward in fall, and a comparable northbound distance in spring—at about 10,000 miles, the longest migration of any mammal. The southbound migration passes Big Sur from mid-December to January. Because they swim closest to shore while southbound, winter is absolutely the best time for whale-watching on the California coast. Although food is scarce in balmy Mexican waters, whales are adapted to live off their blubber reserves while they mate. Females pregnant from the previous year bear and nurse their calves. By March and April the whales are migrating north to their Arctic feeding grounds, though farther out at sea on this leg of the journey.

California gray whales apparently use the coastline to guide their journeys. Observers sometimes claim to spot them standing on their tails, a type of behavior known as spying out, which biologists think allows whales to see the coast to get their bearings. They often travel in pods of up to fifteen whales, at average speeds of about 3 to 5 miles per hour. Fortunate viewers can see them breach, when they build up speeds to about 30 mph and leap from the water, clearing about two-thirds of their bodies before falling back with a spectacular splash. Some biologists speculate that breaching might be a way to loosen barnacles from their hides. Others suggest that they do it for fun.

Good onshore whale-watching spots include any high cliffs along Highway 1. You can also spot whales in winter from lower bluffs, such as those above Sand Dollar Beach, around Carmel Bay, and around San Simeon. The bench overlooking the cove on the Overlook Trail in Julia Pfeiffer Burns State Park is an inspiring spot. Point Lobos, San Simeon Point, and Point Piedras Blancas all harbored whaling stations in the mid–nineteenth century and are still good whale-spotting points. (The Whalers Cabin at Point Lobos State Reserve preserves many reminders of the trade.) Three restaurants that provide good vantage are Rocky Point Restaurant, Sierra Mar, and the deck of Lucia Lodge. And then there's the classic Whale Watcher Café in Gorda, where even the menus proclaim, "The gods do not deduct from man's allotted time the hours spent whale watching."

Dolphin and Whale Contacts

- **American Cetacean Society, Monterey Bay Chapter:** P.O. Box HE, Pacific Grove, CA 93950; www.starrsites.com.

- **Chris's Whale Watching Tours:** 48 Old Fisherman's Wharf 1, Monterey, CA 93940; (831) 375–5951; www.chriswhalewatching.com.
- **Monterey Bay National Marine Sanctuary:** Check the Web site for wildlife: http://montereybay.noaa.gov/visitor/whalewatching/welcome .html.
- **Monterey Bay Whale Watch:** 84 Old Fisherman's Wharf, Monterey, CA 93940; (831) 375–4658; www.gowhales.com.
- **Monterey Whale Watching Cruises:** 96 Old Fisherman's Wharf 1, Monterey, CA 93940; (831) 372–2203; www.montereywhalewatching .com.
- **Randy's Whale Watching:** 66 Old Fisherman's Wharf, Monterey, CA 93940; (831) 372–7440.

Birding Big Sur

Owing to its great diversity of habitats, Big Sur lies within one of the richest birding areas in California. The nerve center for bird studies is the Big Sur Ornithology Lab (BSOL), founded in 1992 by the Ventana Wilderness Society and housed in the outbuildings of the Molera Ranch in Andrew Molera State Park. The BSOL sponsors programs to reintroduce eagles and condors to Big Sur skies, but staff and volunteers keep vital statistics for all local bird species and maintain an ambitious banding program. They are active in education, sponsor a nature camp for kids, and organize an annual twenty-four-hour bird census in spring, the Bird-A-Thon. (831) 373–1000; www.ventanaws.org.

The Monterey Peninsula and Morro Coast chapters of the National Audubon Society organize the Christmas Bird Count, as part of the annual national bird census. Volunteers are always needed. Both groups also offer an extensive program of birding field trips. Check local birding Web sites for the latest sightings and field trips. Los Padres National Forest and some state parks publish local bird checklists.

Birding the Ocean

Groups of birders interested in pelagic species can charter boats from the Monterey and Morro Bay harbors. Individuals may prefer to sign up for preorganized pelagic birding trips. Check the Web sites of local Audubon Society chapters for oceangoing field trips, or contact Monterey Bay Whale Watch, 84 Fisherman's Wharf, Monterey, CA 93940; (831) 375–4658; www.monterey seabirds.com.

Among the pelagic species that you might see off the Central Coast are common murres (year-round); sooty shearwaters (April through October); storm petrels (mainly in summer and fall); jaegers (August through October); phalaropes (mainly in spring and fall); tufted puffins (fall); Sabine's gulls (April

Birders scope out the lagoon at Carmel River State Beach.

through May and August through October); pigeon guillemots (March through September); Cassin's auklets (fall and winter); rhinoceros auklets (fall and winter); Laysan albatrosses (January through February); and blackfooted albatrosses (February through midsummer).

Birding Highway 1

Note that fog frequently obscures coastal views in morning and late afternoon during summer. The best time for shore viewing is at early morning on clear, fogless days, with the sunrise at your back. Birding can be good anywhere along this coast. Here are just a few suggestions.

Carmel River State Beach

The south side of this park is accessible to walkers from public-access trailheads on Ribera Road and at Monastery Beach; please respect the private driveways. The mouth of the Carmel River offers diverse birding terrain: one of the Central Coast's largest marshes, a beach, dunes, granite tide pools, a brackish lagoon, and a clean bay protected as the Carmel Bay Ecological Reserve. The Carmel River breaks through to the sea only during high-flow periods in winter. In drier seasons it's halted by a sandbar, backing up at the mouth into a brackish lagoon and marsh. The vicinity is excellent for waders and marine birds year-round, shorebirds and waterfowl in winter, spring songbirds, summer cliff swallows, and fall and winter migrants. Virginia rails nest in the marsh. Rare vagrants, including pelagic species blown close to shore, are sometimes sighted. Wilson's warblers use the Carmel River for rest and food during their fall migration to Central America.

Point Lobos State Reserve

With more than 150 bird species recorded, Point Lobos is particularly rich in seabirds. Birders from May through July sometimes spot migrating black-footed albatrosses from the rocky points. Take the Bird Rock Trail to see an offshore rocky nesting ground for gulls and some 2,000 Brandt's cormorants. Woods along interior trails host songbirds in spring. Look for black oyster-catchers and black turnstones on rocky shores.

Rocky Point

In summer look for black swifts among the rocks just south of the restaurant. The garden grounds sometimes host rufous, Allen's, and Anna's hummingbirds.

Garrapata State Beach

Beach terraces provide good views down to rocky shores, a likely spot for black oystercatchers. Interesting sightings among the grasslands, scrub, and chaparral of the Rocky Ridge Trail might include Costa's hummingbirds and black-chinned sparrows in summer. Look for condors above the ridge.

Castle Rock

Common murres nest on this rocky islet. You can observe with binoculars from turnouts just north of Bixby Canyon Bridge.

Hurricane Point

From a turnout on this high bluff, you can scope out numerous seabirds (including a colony of common murres on the offshore rocks), black oyster-catchers, and peregrine falcons.

Little Sur River

Although private land surrounds Highway 1 here, you can park in a roadside pullout and zero in on the shore and lagoon with a spotting scope or binoculars. Look for western and least sandpipers, roosting gulls, and pelicans.

Point Sur

Highway 1 enters a broad marine terrace here, flat grasslands that are rich in hawks and falcons, especially in winter. With private land on both sides of the highway, you are restricted to pullouts, unless you take a guided tour of the light station on Point Sur itself. From that great rock you have a fine view down on seabirds and shorebirds, including shearwaters and snowy plovers. Vagrant species are not unusual.

Andrew Molera State Park

Home of the Big Sur Ornithology Lab and blessed with riparian, coastal, dune, scrub, redwood forest, grassland, oak woodland, and chaparral habitats, this park has nearly 200 species on its bird list. Among the common sightings are chickadees, kinglets, white-crowned sparrows, wrentits, California thrashers, willits, lazuli buntings, woodpeckers, cliff swallows, purple martins, Wilson's warblers, Swainson's and hermit thrushes, and rufous hummingbirds. Raptors and seabirds are resident year-round.

When the footbridge across the Big Sur River is dismantled during winter, coast-bound birders will have to either wade the stream or stick to the Head-lands Trail. This latter may well be the most diverse birding hike in the park, as it follows the north bank of the stream through riparian habitat, grassland, coastal scrub, and even a non-native but historical eucalyptus grove that attracts orioles and yellow-rumped warblers in winter. As you approach the river's mouth, the trail cuts through an area known to birders as the Headlands Patch—the willowy shore of a brackish lagoon that plays host to swifts, egrets, herons, purple martins, and waterfowl. From there the trail climbs to Molera Point, justly famous among local birders for its bird's-eye view over a cornu-copia of habitats: beach, lagoon, rocky coast, ocean, and scrub. Look for wan-dering tattlers, black turnstones, and black oystercatchers on the rocks. Offshore sightings of brants, cormorants, pelicans, grebes, loons, and surf scot-ers are common.

In seasons when the footbridge is in place, birders have easy access to Creamery Meadows, Molera Beach, marine terraces, and the coastal scrub of Pfeiffer Ridge. Other trails follow both banks of the Big Sur River upstream through riparian woodlands, home to owls, American dippers, belted kingfish-ers, great blue herons, hummingbirds, swallows, warblers, and vireos. Birders who explore the steep East Molera Trail will be treated to chaparral species, including perhaps a burrowing owl. Look for condors above the ridgeline.

Pfeiffer Big Sur State Park

In winter condors often perch in redwoods here, commonly in the convenient snag immediately outside the main Big Sur Lodge building. (There is a condor display case outside the building.) The park offers riparian woodlands, chaparral, and oak woodland habitats. Look for yellow warblers along the Big Sur River. Listen for western screech-owls and northern saw-whet owls when camping here.

Pfeiffer Beach

This is a good place for shorebirds.

Julia Pfeiffer Burns State Park

You can see black swifts, black cormorants, brown pelicans, and black oyster-catchers from the McWay Falls overlook. Spotted owls and marbled murrelets may live among the redwoods. The trail to Partington Landing provides coastal access for spotting marine birds.

Lucia

There's an expansive view over the ocean and coast here. Watch for condors in the sky above the ridges.

Limekiln State Park

With luck, you might see a spotted owl or marbled murrelet among the redwoods.

Pacific Valley

The large marine terrace hosts many raptors, especially in winter. From the bluffs above Sand Dollar Beach and Jade Cove, you might see black oyster-catchers, pelicans, and snowy plovers. Look for condors above the ridge.

Ragged Point Inn

The high cliffs behind the inn provide expansive (and comfortable) views up and down the rocky coast, sweeping from the mountains to the sea.

San Simeon State Park

The broad marine terraces are prime habitat for raptors, particularly numerous in winter. Snowy plovers nest on the beach. Many species of shorebird use the seasonal wetlands behind the beach. On the high ground around Washburn Campground, look for hawks, vultures, kestrels, western bluebirds, western meadowlarks, and great horned owls. With brush, pristine beach, grassland, and marsh, Arroyo de la Cruz is particularly rich in natural habitats that attract a great variety of bird life.

Birding the Back Roads

Bottchers Gap

With ready access to redwoods, mixed-evergreen forests, and chaparral, look for ash-throated flycatchers, wrentits, black-chinned sparrows, spotted owls, and winter wrens. In summer you can find Cassin's and warbling vireos and black-throated gray warblers; in winter, wrens.

Nacimiento-Fergusson Road

As you climb into the Santa Lucias, you will pass through grassland, riparian habitats with ready access to redwood forests, chaparral, and oak woodland. Look for black-chinned and rufous-crowned sparrows, purple martins, mountain quails, and western tanagers. After the crest, on your descent into the Nacimiento River drainage, you might see mountain quail, Cassin's vireos, black-throated gray warblers, and yellow warblers.

Cone Peak

From the top of the Nacimiento-Fergusson Road, this road leads north to the foot of Cone Peak, a good route to find high-elevation birds. The road ends at an elevation of about 3,650 feet. Mountain chickadees, mountain quails, western tanagers, red-breasted nuthatches, canyon wrens, blue-gray gnatcatchers, yellow-rumped warblers, and purple martins are some of the unusual species common here. Even Clark's nutcrackers have spent winters here. A trail leads to the summit of 5,155-foot Cone Peak, an excellent vantage point to search for condors.

Carmel Valley Road

Look for woodland and chaparral birds, and keep an ear cocked at dusk for great horned, screech-, northern pygmy, and even spotted owls. Common poor-wills live in adjacent chaparral. Garland Ranch Regional Park is a good choice for black-shouldered kites, acorn woodpeckers, red-shouldered hawks, and (non-native, but charismatic) wild turkeys. Violet-green swallows and great horned owls breed there. Paloma Creek, on the east side of the Cahoon Grade divide, offers good riparian habitat for summer migrants, including Lawrence's goldfinches and rare yellow-breasted chats. Rufous-crowned sparrows, Swainson's thrushes, blue-gray gnatcatchers, Bullock's orioles, and phainopeplas occur regularly.

Tassajara Road

At nearly 4,900 feet above sea level, Chews Ridge is the highest point reached by road in Monterey County. Condors have been known to roost here. Chaparral and woodland provide habitat for pygmy nuthatches, purple martins, dusky flycatchers, and ferruginous owls. Just south of Chews Ridge, the high, partly wooded area around China Camp hosts summer visitors such as the dusky flycatcher, Lawrence's goldfinch, western tanager, and black-headed grosbeak. It's a good place to spot owls.

Tassajara Hot Springs

The riparian corridor in this deep canyon is bordered by chaparral and wood-land wilderness, and easily reached by the Narrows Trail from the monastery. Look for golden eagles, common poor-wills, and black-chinned sparrows.

Arroyo Seco Road

Birding from the road, you can search the coastal scrub and oak savannas for such songbirds as rock and canyon wrens, black-chinned hummingbirds, an occasional Cassin's kingbird, and even a greater roadrunner.

San Antonio Valley

An extensive oak savanna makes the San Antonio Valley one of the best places to see western meadowlarks, western bluebirds, yellow-billed magpies, acorn and Nuttall's woodpeckers, and the largest breeding population of Bullock's ori-oles in the region. Stopping on Fort Hunter Liggett is prohibited, but if you drive beyond the northern end of the military reservation via Del Venturi Road to Milpitas Road, you are free to park at roadside and roam about on Los Padres National Forest land. Golden eagles are fairly easy to spot in this open range, while unusual riparian birds such as green herons thrive along the San Antonio River. Some waterfowl species, including wood ducks and cinnamon teal, winter in the valley. Prairie falcons like the dry, open county.

Lake San Antonio

With more than a hundred species of birds listed, this large reservoir in the lower San Antonio Valley hosts a variety of waterfowl, including rare blue-winged teal and Eurasian widgeons. Redheads, American widgeons, cinnamon and green-winged teal, American white pelicans, northern shovelers, canvas-backs, ring-necked ducks, lesser scaups, ospreys, western and Clark's grebes, and common mergansers spend winters on the lake. The population of raptors soars from December to mid-March, and the lake is known for the largest pop-ulation of eagles in Central California. The Monterey County parks depart-ment offers Eagle Watch Tours in winter aboard the 56-foot tour boat *Eagle One*; phone (888) 588–2267 for reservations. Golden eagles eat rodents and other small mammals, while the rarer bald eagle prefers a diet of fish.

California Condors

Slouching on a snag, its head and neck devoid of feathers, spreading its 9-foot wingspan in the sun, the condor is an imposing bird. When gliding down to dine on a carcass, it uses its commanding size, amplified by hissing and flushing its head a startling shade of red, to frighten away ravens, turkey vultures, and other scavengers. Largest of the North American land birds, California condors mate for life and can live up to seventy years.

California condors once ranged over western North America. They were killed in great numbers as vermin, and crowded out by civilization. Museum collectors also did their share to decimate numbers. Most specimens of the California condor in museums around the world were collected in the Santa Lucia Mountains of Monterey County. The last wild condor at Big Sur was seen in 1980. With the species on the verge of extinction in 1985, when scientists counted only nine of the great vultures living in the Transverse Ranges of Ventura and Santa Barbara Counties, the U.S. Fish and Wildlife Service captured all survivors and sent them to a captive breeding program at the Los Angeles Zoo. To raise the fledglings in confinement, handlers had to train them to shun humans and power lines in preparation for their return to the wild.

Many young condors have since been reintroduced to remote parts of their old range. The Ventana Wilderness Alliance reintroduced condors to Monterey County in 1997. Today you can see condors at Big Sur again. They fly up to 150 miles per day over the Santa Lucias in search of food, riding thermals above ridgelines, roosting in redwood snags, and even feasting upon dead sea lions on isolated beaches. They do not build nests, but use small caves on cliff faces or in large trees for shelters. Birders should know, however, that released individuals are not "countable" under the American Birding Association policy. If you want a California condor on your life list, you will need to wait until a new generation actually hatches and is raised by birds in the wild.

Lake Nacimiento

Bald eagles reportedly fish the reservoir. Prairie falcons live on Tierra Redonda Mountain, which rises above the north shore near the middle of the lake.

Birding Contacts

- **Big Sur Ornithology Lab:** Ventana Wilderness Society, Andrew Molera State Park, Big Sur; (831) 455–9514; www.ventanaws.org.
- **Monterey Peninsula Audubon Society:** www.montereyaudubon.org.

- **Morro Coast Audubon Society:** P.O. Box 1507; Morro Bay, CA 93443; http://morrocoastaudubon.org.
- **Ventana Wilderness Society:** 19045 Portola Drive, Suite F-1, Salinas, CA 93908; (831) 455–9514; www.ventanaws.org.

Nature Reserves

To some extent all parks are nature reserves, but Big Sur also has many public and private nature preserves without a recreational mandate. Some are open only by permit or for special tours. Consult the Web sites for tour schedules.

Federal Lands

In 2002 the Trust for Public Land helped buy the historic 1,226-acre Brazil Ranch and transfer it to Los Padres National Forest, preserving a beautiful stretch of coast and hills south of Bixby Bridge. Once owned by Alan Funt, the host of the original *Candid Camera* television show, the property now hosts the Brazil Ranch Environmental Center, a venue for conservation education programs. The Forest Service has not yet developed long-range plans for the property. (805) 625–3564; http://bigsurenvironmentalinstitute.org.

State Lands

The state owns some undeveloped parklands along the Big Sur coast. Located just south of Esalen Institute, John Little State Reserve has no public access. The recently acquired Point Lobos Ranch, covering some 1,300 acres about 2 miles south of the Carmel River Bridge, is presently undeveloped, as are several miles of San Luis Obispo County's north coast, recently transferred from the Hearst Corporation to San Simeon State Park.

The University of California owns and operates two large research stations in the region. The 2,329-acre Hastings Natural History Reservation sits on a tributary drainage of the Carmel River and is reserved for researchers, program participants, and occasional conservation groups. www.hastingsreserve.org or www.nrs.ucop.edu.

The 3,911-acre Landels-Hill Big Creek Reserve extends from offshore kelp beds to ponderosa forests on the high ridge above Big Creek and Devils Canyon, and contains some hot springs. Maintained for researchers, the reserve sponsors an annual open house in May, when the general public can come to explore. www.redshift.com or www.nrs.ucop.edu.

Monterey County Lands

In addition to public parks and San Antonio Reservoir, the Monterey Peninsula Regional Park District (MPRPD) administers several limited-access natural preserves. To obtain permits and check for group hikes, contact the MPRPD office at 60 Garden Court, Suite 325, Monterey, CA 93940-5341; (831) 659-4488; www.mprpd.org.

After The Nature Conservancy and the Big Sur Land Trust obtained the deed to the 10,000-acre Palo Corona Ranch (known to locals as the old Fish Ranch), they transferred some 4,300 acres to Monterey County for the new Palo Corona Regional Park. Starting just south of the Carmel River Bridge, Palo Corona Regional Park climbs from near sea level to more than 3,000 feet in elevation, embracing a swath of coastal terrace, woodlands, mountains, and stream basins that are home to eagles, redwoods, and Monterey pine forests. The California Department of Fish and Game administers the remaining acreage of the old ranch as a nature preserve, allowing public access only by permit. A 1.3-mile trail climbs 850 feet to Inspiration Point. For information and a permit, contact (831) 649–2870; www.mprpd.org.

Now part of Garland Regional Park, the 1,116-acre Kahn Ranch offers hiking, biking, and equestrian use. Trails are open to hikers who enter through Garland Ranch. Anyone who wants to enter from Hitchcock Road needs a permit; www.mprpd.org.

The Mill Creek Redwood Preserve occupies a 1,100-acre ranch once owned by Charles Bixby. Embracing part of Bixby Creek and its tributaries, including Beartrap Canyon and Mill Creek near the upper Palo Colorado Road, the preserve is best known for a forest of old-growth redwoods. The county plans to control public access with permits, and to allow only twenty-five visitors per day. For updates, contact (831) 622–0598; www.mprpd.org.

The centerpiece of the 1-mile-square Joshua Creek Ecological Preserve is a forest of old-growth redwoods along a tributary of Garrapata Creek. The California State Department of Fish and Game manages the property and allows access only by permit. (831) 649–2870; www.mprpd.org.

Two small parcels closed to the public, except by permit, are the 5.4-acre Thomas Open Space, an open pasture in Carmel Valley, and the 5-acre Laidlaw-Apte Pine Forest Preserve in the Carmel Highlands. For more information on both, visit www.mprpd.org.

Private Land Trusts

The Nature Conservancy, California Coastal Conservancy, and other agencies work to preserve open space at Big Sur by buying development rights to large ranches and forming conservation easements, or by acquiring the land outright for transfer to public parkland. The Trust for Public Land, for instance, recently facilitated the transfer of the historic 1,226-acre Brazil Ranch to the Forest Service, preserving a beautiful stretch of coast and hills south of Bixby

Bridge. The Big Sur Land Trust (BSLT) bought development rights to the El Sur Ranch, which will remain private, undeveloped rangeland.

The BSLT has been instrumental in acquiring many lands now administered by government agencies, such as Point Lobos Ranch State Park and the 10,000-acre Palo Corona Regional Ranch, but it also retains some properties as reserves. The 860-acre Glen Deven Ranch, on a ridge above Palo Colorado Road, is open to BSLT members on scheduled tours. The group has also arranged conservation easements on part of the 360-acre Smith Ranch, south of Bixby Bridge, and on the 3,000-acre Gamboa Ranch.

The 1,100-acre Mittledorf Preserve is the flagship of BSLT properties. Spread along the eastern boundary of the Palo Corona Ranch, it preserves grassland tracts, oak woodland, and redwood forest, including what's claimed to be the largest and oldest individual redwood in Monterey County. With miles of hiking trails, the preserve is open for tours by members, who also may reserve overnight use at a stone lodge on the property. Nonmembers can sign up for designated tours. Every July, an Environmental Day Camp at Mittledorf Preserve exposes children to the study of Ohlone culture and history; local plants, animals, and birds; wilderness survival; map and compass orientation; and watershed ecology. For more information, contact the Big Sur Land Trust at P. O. Box 221864, Carmel, CA 93922; (831) 625–5523; www.bigsurlandtrust .org.

Natural History Publications

The online journal of the Ventana Wilderness Alliance, the *Double Cone Register*, contains many excellent articles, current and archival, on the natural history of Big Sur: www.ventanawild.org.

Alt, David, and Donald W. Hyndman. *Roadside Geology of Northern and Central California*. Missoula, Mont.: Mountain Press Publishing Company, 2000.

Brown, Vinson, David Allan, and James Stark. *Rocks and Minerals of California*. Happy Camp, Calif.: Naturegraph Publishers, 1987.

Henson, Paul, and Donald J. Usner. *The Natural History of Big Sur*. Berkeley and Los Angeles: University of California Press, 1993. If you are buying only one volume on Big Sur, this is it.

Jameson, E. W., Jr., and Hans J. Peeters. *California Mammals*. Berkeley: University of California Press, 1988.

Mission San Antonio de Padua Herbs: Medicinal Herbs of Early Days. Available at Mission San Antonio, this illustrated, undated monograph (with a forward by Val Heinsen) is based on Father Zephyrin Englehardt's 1929 publication, which compiled Father Doroteo Ambris's studies of Salinan medicinal lore.

Parr, Ivan. *Southern California Chaparral*. P.O. Box 20823, Castro Valley, CA 94546: Suisun Bay Publishing, 2006.

————*Northern California Tidepools: A Guide to Intertidal Plants and Animals from Oregon to the Central Coast*. P.O. Box 20823, Castro Valley, CA 94546: Suisun Bay Publishing, 2002.

Roberson, D. *Monterey Birds*. Carmel, Calif.: Monterey Peninsula Audubon Society, 1985.

Schoenherr, Allan A. *A Natural History of California*. Berkeley and Los Angeles: University of California Press, 1992.

Snyderman, Marty. *California Marine Life*. Port Hueneme, Calif.: Marcor Publishing, 1988.

Wobber, Don. *Jade Beneath the Sea: A Diving Adventure*. Pacific Grove, Calif.: The Boxwood Press, 1975.

Chapter 8
Big Sur History

The chief historical sites of the region might be Hearst Castle, the Point Sur Light Station, and Mission San Antonio, but the broader historical tapestry of Big Sur is much richer and more subtle. The mountains and coastlands harbor many old settlements, homesteads, and Native American sites that have all but vanished into the underbrush, requiring some effort, and perhaps some conjuring with your imagination, to appreciate.

Because history here is so localized and elusive, history buffs should seek out guided hikes and programs offered by the state parks and other organizations. The Junior Ranger programs at Pfeiffer Big Sur and San Simeon State Parks offer historical activities just for kids. The Ventana Wilderness Alliance's online journal, the *Double Cone Register*, contains an archival trove of historical articles about Big Sur: www.ventanawild.org. The Pelican Network Web site also offers extensive, current information on organized activities with a historical bent: www.pelicannetwork.net.

History Contacts

• **Big Sur Historical Society:** P.O. Box 176, Big Sur, CA 93920.

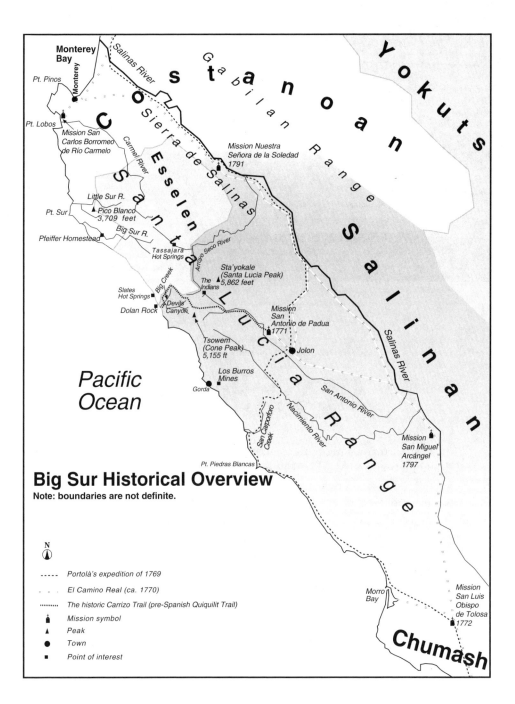

Monterey
Bay

Pt. Pinos

Monterey

Salinas River

Gabilan

Costanoan

Yokuts

Pt. Lobos

Mission San
Carlos Borromeo
de Río Carmelo

Carmel River

Sierra de Salinas

Gabilan Range

Mission Nuestra
Señora de la Soledad
1791

Santa Esselen

Little Sur R.

Pt. Sur

Pico Blanco
3,709 feet

Big Sur R.

Pfeiffer Homestead

Tassajara
Hot Springs

Arroyo Seco River

Sta'yokale
(Santa Lucia Peak)
5,862 feet

Salinan

Slates
Hot Springs

Big Creek

The
Indians

Dolan Rock

Devils
Canyon

Mission
San
Antonio de Padua
1771

Salinas River

Pacific
Ocean

Tsowem
(Cone Peak)
5,155 ft

Los Burros
Mines

Jolon

Santa Lucia Range

Gorda

San Carpoforo Creek

Nacimiento River

San Antonio River

Pt. Piedras Blancas

Mission
San Miguel
Arcángel
1797

Big Sur Historical Overview

Note: boundaries are not definite.

N

----- Portolà's expedition of 1769

. . . El Camino Real (ca. 1770)

.... The historic Carrizo Trail (pre-Spanish Quiquilit Trail)

⚑ Mission symbol

▲ Peak

● Town

■ Point of interest

Morro
Bay

Mission
San Luis
Obispo
de Tolosa
1772

Chumash

- **Monterey County Historical Society:** Boronda Adobe, 333 Boronda Road, P.O. Box 3576, Salinas, CA 93912; (831) 757–8085; www.mchs museum.com.
- **Monterey Public Library; History Room:** 625 Pacific Street, Monterey, CA 93940; (831) 646–3932; www.monterey.org.
- **San Antonio Valley Historical Association:** Londak Route, Box 20, King City, CA 93930.

The Original Inhabitants

Before the Spanish arrived, thousands of people lived as hunters and gatherers throughout the Big Sur region. We know little about them because their traditional ways of life disappeared so quickly. Based on language and other cultural characteristics, the Native Americans of Big Sur are commonly divided into three distinct peoples: the Costanoan, Esselen, and Salinan. The Costanoan, also known as the Ohlone, lived from San Francisco Bay down to the Big Sur, including the lower Carmel, Salinas, and Big Sur Valleys. South of them and embracing the rest of the Big Sur region dwelled the Esselen and the Salinan peoples. The Salinan and Esselen spoke versions of the Hokan language, the oldest of California's language families. The Costanoan spoke a Penutian language, which suggests that they were more recent arrivals from the Central Valley. Some anthropologists believe that the Costanoan might have displaced the Esselen, driving them from the lowlands deeper into the Santa Lucia Mountains. Although warfare was rare, the three peoples did not maintain friendly relations among themselves. They lived by hunting and gathering edible plants and seafood, and all maintained semi-permanent villages but traveled seasonally to follow shifting food supplies.

The Santa Lucias preserve one of the richest groupings of pre-Spanish archaeological sites in California. Sprawling Fort Hunter Liggett alone harbors more than 600 known sites of ancient villages, shrines, burial sites, and pictographs, all of which are restricted from public access by the military. Although this book does not specify locations of fragile sites, alert travelers might discover some elsewhere in the Santa Lucias. If you should find any historical artifact, do not remove or damage it, or advertise it to someone who will.

To the Salinan, Esselen, and southern Costanoan, Big Sur and the Santa Lucias provided a fortress, a homeland, a cornucopia of edible plants and shellfish, a hunting ground, and a spiritual sanctuary. The Salinan (and probably the Esselen) believed that it was their place of origin. Salinan accounts told of an ancient flood that covered the world except for the sacred peak Sta'yokale, today better known as Santa Lucia Peak and Junipero Serra Peak. The highest point in the Santa Lucias, Sta'yokale was the spot from which Eagle drove back the floodwaters and breathed life into human beings. The Rumsien (Costanoan) and Esselen had similar origin stories based on Pico Blanco.

The Esselen were the smallest tribal group in California, numbering probably between 500 and 1,000 people. Their homeland was the most rugged part of the Santa Lucia Range, comprising the upper Carmel and Big Sur River drainages and the highlands around Ventana Double Cone, but also such salubrious places as Tassajara Hot Springs, Sykes Hot Springs, the hot springs at Esalen, and Pine Valley. Their coastal territory may have reached from near Nepenthe south to Dolan Rock, a prominent sea stack clearly visible for miles along Highway 1, but all of these boundaries are disputed. Villages were separated by high ridges and deep canyons, and probably provided a leaner, more isolated existence than the Salinan and Costanoan enjoyed in their larger, richer territories. The Esselen left behind intriguing pictographs on rocks walls in Church Creek Valley—elongated white handprints. Located on private property, they are inaccessible to the public. www.bigsurcalifornia.org.

The Salinan were a far more numerous and far-flung people than the Esselen, embracing the remainder of the coast at least to San Carpoforo Creek, and perhaps as far south as Morro Bay. All the land eastward to the middle and upper Salinas Valley was Salinan. In daily life, however, Salinan people identified their homelands as smaller territories or districts, each one a grouping of several villages under a common chief, each speaking a distinctive dialect. They maintained good relations with the Yokuts to the east, trading shells and other goods for fish, hides, and obsidian. From the Chumash to the south, they imported wooden bowls and steatite, a soapstone that could be carved into kitchen utensils and smoking pipes.

Even now, much of the Santa Lucia Range is so far removed from modern development that an insightful traveler can glean a hint of how the old Salinan world thrived. By recognizing some of the native California plants and animals of the Santa Lucias, and their uses, you can begin to see landscapes not merely as wilderness, or even as forests or grasslands, but as storehouses of an amazing variety of life-sustaining foods and useful plants. The San Antonio Valley, for instance, is not simply a stately oak savanna or superb grazing allotment (which is how the Mexican and American ranchers saw it), but a land rich in flowing water, grass, game, seeds, nutritious acorns, fibers, flat ground, wood, birds, and handy kitchen rocks—in short, a land of plenty, providing everything you need for life if you know where to look and how to use it. The many bedrock mortars where Salinan women ground seeds, pine nuts, and acorns to make their staples of mush and meal cakes confirm this. Archaeologists estimate that about 3,000 Salinan were living in the San Antonio Valley when the Spanish arrived, making it the largest population center in the interior of the Santa Lucia Mountains.

With water, wood, flat ground, rock, and a great variety of game, acorns, and other foods, the San Antonio Valley was a major population center for the Salinan people in the Santa Lucia Mountains.

Other, less populous, farther-flung Salinan districts had their own distinctive cultural characteristics and dialects. Consider the residents of the rugged coastal districts of Quiquilit and Lamaca, for instance. They enjoyed diets rich in seafood, a luxury for their cousins in the San Antonio Valley. Local abundances of various commodities in different districts gave rise to trade, by which shells, dried seafood, salt grass, shell beads (used as tender), and other goods were carried eastward over the mountains in exchange for acorns, minerals and pigments, deer and antelope hides, and more. Through trade, the cultural links between Salinan districts were reinforced, and local economies and standards of living enriched. Many of the old village sites of Lamaca later became homesteads, and one at Kirk Creek is now a Forest Service campground.

Ancient Trails

Early travelers in California reported that some Native paths were worn quite deep, and that routes were marked with stacked rocks, pictographs, and other objects (including, in one instance, a dead skunk). Some of these ancient paths are still in use today in the Santa Lucia Range. The exact tread has changed, of course. Destinations have shifted; switchbacks have been built. But basic routes still follow many of the same passes, ridges, creeks, and slopes chosen by Native Salinan mountaineers.

Anyone who hikes the Santa Lucia backcountry today quickly realizes the logic behind these routings. They tended (where possible) to run along south-facing ridges above the chaparral line or, if the terrain was overgrown and otherwise impassable, along creekbeds. (Like other California Indians, the Salinan periodically burned chaparral to encourage grass and game and to facilitate travel.) The preference for high ground in part avoided bushwhacking, but also provided a lookout for grizzly bears. Motorists can see a good example of just such a high, open, south-facing route when they drive the Nacimiento-Fergusson Road, itself derived from an ancient Salinan path known to the Spanish as the Nacimiento Trail.

The longest section of ancient trail still used as a footpath today follows the ancient Quiquilit Trail, which led up the San Antonio Valley to Wagon Cave, where it turned west into the mountains. Climbing to a point near Cone Peak, it jogged north along the ridge and descended to the coast through the Big Creek watershed. Later used by soldiers and incense collectors from Mission San Antonio, it became known as the Carrizo Trail. Early botany expeditions followed this path; gold miners and homesteaders packed their goods to and from the coast along it. Several official trails through Los Padres National Forest today still trace the route of the old Quiquilit Trail. These include parts of the present-day Carrizo, Coast Ridge, North Coast Ridge, and Bee Trails. The current Gamboa Trail is another old spur. (To find the Carrizo trailhead, see chapter 4, Driving the Back Roads.)

When John Peabody Harrington, an ethnologist working for the University of California, came to the Santa Lucias in 1932 to learn what he could of Salinan culture, Tito Encinales and two other Salinan guides led him to the coast along the Carrizo Trail, relating place-names and village sites of the Quiquilit district en route. According to his guides, for instance, the site of Lower Bee Camp was once the premier deer-hunting camp of the district, known as Tr'a ktén.

The Ventana Wilderness Alliance has proposed resurrecting some of the historic trails of the Santa Lucia Range, among them the Lamaca Trail, which Portolà apparently followed to the San Antonio Valley.

The complexities of Salinan culture developed over a long period of time. Archaeologists have excavated sites dating back at least 6,400 years. By dating artifacts, they have discovered that the Salinan experienced a kind of economic and cultural renaissance in the fourth century B.C., launching a long era of modest but sustained prosperity. The slow catalyst of this growth was an arduous millennium of discovery and experiment, by which the Salinan built a huge working bank of knowledge of the Santa Lucias' natural resources. Their greatest wealth was this hard-won knowledge—the habits of local game; the seasonal availability of different acorns, seeds, pine nuts, roots, berries, and fish; the properties of medicinal herbs; which plants and shellfish were toxic and which were edible; and which stones made the best projectile points, which woods the best bows, which grasses the best baskets, and much more. As they expanded their diet and territory, crafted more sophisticated tools and utensils, extended trade, and studied the seasons and local phenomena, they came to know the Santa Lucias with an intimacy that no one since has matched.

Spurred by increased efficiency in their gathering and stockpiling of food, populations grew and cultivated new patterns of life, customs, cultures, and leisure. The social center for village men was the sweat lodge, but everyone enjoyed music, dance, games, gambling, sports, and storytelling. Medicine men healed with herbs and magic and organized the yearly cycle of celebrations and rituals. Using natural pigments of white (made from ground seashells), black (from charcoal), and red (from hematite), they painted colorful pictographs on rocks and cave walls. Their most sacred place, the Painted Cave, contains a large collection of pictographs possibly associated with the observance of the winter solstice. (Located on Fort Hunter Liggett, the Painted Cave is closely protected by the military and strictly off-limits to the public.)

Intimate with the natural world, resilient in their ability to adapt to its seasonal abundance and scarcity, the Salinan's dynamic culture thrived for centuries until the Spanish arrived and tipped the balance. For more information, contact the Salinan Tribe of Monterey and San Luis Obispo Counties, P.O. Box 708, King City, CA 93930-0708.

Hispanic Influences
The Spanish

In search of ports for Spain's Manila galleons, the sea captain Sebastián Vizcaíno dropped anchor in Monterey Bay in 1602, after several exhausting months of tacking up the California coast. Vizcaíno was so delighted to see the harbor and gentle shorelines of Monterey Bay that he described it in the most flattering terms. Many historians since have scoffed at his enthusiasm, especially in light of Portolà's later failure to recognize Monterey Bay based on

Vizcaíno's description. But neither Portolà nor the grudging historians of later years were looking at it from the point of view of a sailor who had just completed a long sea passage up the treacherous, craggy coastline of Big Sur. Monterey may indeed be wanting as a harbor, but compared with Big Sur it is a glorious haven.

Big Sur therefore looms large in the background of that glowing report that the Spanish governors of Mexico reread 167 years after Vizcaíno's visit. Fearful of Russian encroachment, they dispatched an expedition of priests, soldiers, artisans, farmers, and neophytes (Native Americans newly converted to Catholicism) with a mandate to found the first colonies in Alta California, at San Diego and Monterey. Led by the soldier Gaspar de Portolà and Franciscan priest Father Junípero Serra, the Sacred Expedition (as it was known) set out in 1769 with three ships and two land contingents. (Among the soldiers accompanying Portolà were three whose families would eventually help settle Big Sur: Alvarado, Boronda, and Soberanes.) Shipwreck, scurvy, starvation, and desertion shrunk their numbers by half, but they managed to gain a precarious foothold at San Diego, where Father Serra founded California's first mission.

From there a half-starved regiment of soldiers led by Portolà pushed north in quest of the second goal, the fabulous Monterey Bay. The coastline was their guide, but when they arrived at the intimidating mountains beyond the canyon of San Carpoforo Creek—the southern end of Big Sur—they were forced to turn inland to cross the Santa Lucias. Portolà probably followed an existing trail through the Salinan district of Lamaca, for he recorded passing through several villages, where he received a warm welcome and traded beads for much-needed food. (This old path through the Santa Lucias is one of the very few stretches of Portolà's route that is wilder today than it was in 1769.) Crossing the crest, the Spaniards descended by way of the Pozo Hondo (a creek) to the Nacimiento River near the sandstone bluffs known as the Palisades. (Pozo Hondo and the Palisades today lie within Fort Hunter Liggett and are off-limits to the public.) Crossing to the San Antonio Valley—which impressed him greatly as a land of rich potential, for both souls and agriculture—Portolà next descended the Salinas River to Monterey Bay, which he failed to recognize. He wandered north to San Francisco Bay before realizing his error. Returning to the right spot, he planted two crosses—one at Monterey Bay and one on Carmel Bay on a knoll above Middle Beach—before returning to meet Father Serra in San Diego.

Father Serra and Portolà founded Monterey in 1770. It was designed as a complete Spanish colonial city of mission (church), presidio (fortress), and pueblo (town). The following year Father Serra moved his mission 4 miles south to the Carmel River, naming it San Carlos Borromeo de Río Carmelo. The location had more fresh water and was more heavily populated with potential converts than Monterey. Later that same year (1771), acting on Portolà's earlier recommendation, Father Serra journeyed to the San Antonio Valley and there founded California's third mission, San Antonio de Padua.

Although the Spanish built three more missions ringing the Santa Lucias—at San Luis Obispo (1772), Soledad (1791), and San Miguel (1797)—the Carmel and San Antonio missions were the two most significant to Big Sur's history. The Carmel mission drew most of its converts from the Esselen and southern Costanoan peoples, while the Salinan of the northern Santa Lucias gravitated mostly to Mission San Antonio.

The mission system has been both romanticized and vilified. There's no room here to do justice to either view. The Franciscans intended to turn the Native peoples of California into Catholic subjects of New Spain, much as they had done with some success to the native peoples of Mexico. They did not intend the missions to be permanent institutions, but rather beachheads of Spanish culture that would be developed and turned over to the local populace once they had learned to live, work, and worship like Spanish farmers and artisans. In the process the missions destroyed Native cultures, compelled thousands to live and work under regimented conditions, and inadvertently introduced diseases that killed thousands. Joining the mission was voluntary, but once converts were baptized, they were not allowed to leave without permission (though permission was regularly granted for visiting family villages). Mission soldiers forcibly returned runaways when they could, but some chose exile in the land of the Yokuts or lived like renegades in remote canyons of the Santa Lucias.

The Spanish did not have sufficient numbers to forcibly remove all the Natives from their villages, but they drew away enough young converts to sap the vitality of the old societies. The missions must have been exciting places, miniature cities with new foods, inventions, customs, stories, artwork, and music to beguile the young. Without people to fulfill all the jobs needed for the ancient communities to survive, the old village economies withered, forcing more to seek shelter in the mission system.

As mission residents learned new skills and cultivated new tastes that tied them tighter to the agricultural societies at the missions, they also forgot the hunting and gathering skills and mountain lore that had sustained the old culture for millennia. In short, they ceased to be able to survive as hunters and gatherers, and instead became herders, farmers, masons, tile makers, carpenters, threshers, millers, seamstresses, servants, kitchen workers, vintners, tanners, painters, musicians, and laborers dependent on an agricultural civilization.

Likewise, Native peoples from different districts and even different language groups mixed freely at the missions, advancing Spanish as a lingua franca and suppressing the distinctive cultural characteristics that made a person an Esselen, or a Salinan, or a Costanoan. The Natives became known collectively as Mission Indians. Some Costanoan and Salinan people retained fragments of their stories, language, and heritage, handed down orally, but the Esselen disappeared as a culture, though their descendants still live in the area.

One of the red-letter events of the Spanish era was the passage of the Juan Bautista de Anza expedition through what is now Monterey County in 1776. With a mandate to colonize San Francisco, de Anza led a party of 198 settlers north from Mexico, blazing a route that would later serve as California's first highway, El Camino Real. U.S. Highway 101 also parallels much of de Anza's route. The National Park Service has marked the route through Arizona and California with signs that read JUAN BAUTISTA DE ANZA NATIONAL HISTORIC TRAIL. The route passes through San Luis Obispo and into Monterey County along US 101, but turns west into the Santa Lucias where the San Antonio River meets the Salinas River. Marching up the San Antonio River, de Anza camped at Mission San Antonio, which he praised for its abundance of acorns, pine nuts, and hogs. The expedition then returned to the Salinas Valley by a different route and continued down to Monterey and Mission Carmel. Modern-day motorists can retrace de Anza's detour through the Santa Lucias by following the historical markers from Paso Robles northwest to Jolon along County Road G14. If you visit the mission, you will need to present a photo ID and proof of car registration and insurance to the guard at Fort Hunter Liggett's Jolon gate. To complete the tour, return to US 101 via the Jolon Road (County Road G14) to King City. www.cahighways.org.

Visiting the Missions

Mission Carmel

Founded near the mouth of the Carmel River on August 24, 1771, Mission San Carlos Borromeo de Río Carmelo is celebrated as Father Serra's chosen home and final resting place, even though the hard-driven old padre never saw any of the buildings that stand today. When Father Serra died in 1784, only humble wood-and-adobe structures stood here. The local Costanoan tribe called themselves the Rumsien.

Mission Carmel served both as headquarters for the mission's agricultural holdings in the Carmel Valley, and as command center for the statewide California mission chain. After the 1803 death of Father Serra's successor, Father Fermín Lasuén, the missions' governing offices moved to Santa Barbara, and Mission Carmel began its slow decay. (Exhibits in the little building on the north side of the courtyard in front of the church illustrate the facility's history, decline, and restoration.) Today the mission serves as a parish church, basilica, and school, and is a living, active part of the community. As the Vatican con-

Early headquarters of the California mission chain, Mission Carmel served as home and burial place for Father Serra.

siders Father Serra as a candidate for sainthood, the importance of Mission Carmel for religious pilgrimages is also increasing.

Widely considered the prettiest of California's mission chapels, the basilica was completed in 1797 under the direction of Father Lasuén. A Mexican master stonemason, Manuel Ruíz, directed a crew of Esselen and Costanoan workers in the extraordinary task of creating something reminiscent of nothing they had ever seen. They quarried the sandstone walls in the Santa Lucias, capped them with an arching roof, adorned them with a scalloped star window and two asymmetrical bell towers of Moorish inspiration, and surrounded them with courtyards, gardens, and fountains. Inside the heavy front door, the original stone baptismal font still stands in place. The statue of the Virgin Mary in the side chapel of Our Lady of Bethlehem is the same that Father Serra carried back from Mexico in 1769. Father Serra is buried beneath the floor of the sanctuary (near the altar) alongside his friends and fellow padres, Fathers Lasuén and Juan Crespí. The tranquil cemetery outside the north wall contains the remains of more than 3,000 neophytes, most of whom died in a series of epidemics.

Adjacent to the church, a reconstructed wing of the quadrangle houses a kitchen, a dining room, and California's first library. Different rooms display ornate, locally sewn vestments, antique books and silver altarpieces, a recreation of Father Serra's frugal bedchamber, and a twentieth-century sculpture by Jo Mora of Father Serra in death, being blessed by Fathers Crespí, Lasuén, and Julian Lopez.

The mission charges a moderate fee for the self-guided tour. To get there, turn west from Highway 1 onto Rio Road (the junction is just north of the Carmel River Bridge), and drive 0.7 mile to the corner of Lausen Drive. (831) 624–3600; www.carmelmission.org.

Mission San Antonio

Surrounded by Fort Hunter Liggett, the setting of Mission San Antonio de Padua is the least developed of any California mission. It is a mesmerizing sight, especially at dawn and dusk or during hot, still afternoons when cicadas drone unceasingly. The army holds the hill in front, but no newer buildings mar the view of fields and woodlands immediately surrounding the mission. The long view behind it, a vast, largely wild area empty of any modern commercial development, stretches 13 miles clear to Junipero Serra Peak, the summit of the Santa Lucias. Despite some remote ranches and a handful of cabins, the upper San Antonio Valley has a population smaller today than at any time over the past six millennia.

The present structures of Mission San Antonio are a very accurate reconstruction. The long-serving Father Buenaventura Sitjar oversaw construction

Mission San Antonio preserves one of the large music books that the old padres used to conduct the choir.

of the original church, finished in 1813. Headquarters of a vast rancho of 200,000 acres, Mission San Antonio at its height sheltered about 1,300 neophytes, mostly Salinan, and maintained a sophisticated irrigation system using aqueducts and a reservoir, the ruins of which are still visible. The mission was famous for its gristmill (the first in California) and herds of livestock, as well as its music. The church today is still active among local Salinan, Hispanic, and other Catholic parishioners. It comes to life for Sunday Masses and especially during the Mission San Antonio Fiesta, when the public gathers after Mass on the second Sunday in June for raffles, crafts, live music, a traditional oak-fired barbecue, and the distribution of St. Anthony's bread.

Around the front of the mission, visitors can investigate the ruins of its extensive irrigation system, the walled Indian burial ground (the graves unmarked), and a motley collection of scattered artifacts, including some Salinan mortars and metates (stone pestles) and two weathered ships' figureheads said to have been carried there by sailors grateful for surviving a rough sea passage. The front of the church is screened by a *campanario*, a wall designed to hold three bells; the middle one was the first bell to be cast in California. Within the entry porch, note the inscription commemorating California's first Catholic marriage, in 1773, when a Spanish soldier wed a Salinan woman from Lamaca.

The church interior is cool and musty, even on typically scorching summer days. The statues (except Saint Joseph) are original to this mission. When the mission was abandoned in 1882, local parishioners took them into their homes, returning them many decades later, after renovation.

The inner courtyard, surrounded by cloistered walkways, encloses a tangled garden. The public may use only one of the covered walkways—the one connecting the church to the museum in the south wing of the quadrangle. (The rest of the quadrangle is reserved for resident priests, caretakers, and guests.) The museum displays a plain but rich collection of Salinan tools, baskets, and projectile points, eighteenth-century vestments, Spanish armor and weaponry, a fully equipped kitchen, and assorted domestic crafts that maintained mission life. One exhibit preserves some dried medicinal plants known to the Salinan and cataloged by the padres. Models show how workers pressed olive oil and sawed timbers. A narrow passage leads into the dark, cool, two-level chamber where grapes were crushed and the juice poured into casks for fermentation.

The music room preserves some instruments, a choir book, and a replicated drawing of a hand on the wall, used by the padres to teach musical notation. Mission San Antonio was widely celebrated for its music. One early Salinan musician named José Carabajal built a violin from California laurel wood. Famed for its beauty and tone, and treasured for generations, it was stolen from this room in 2003. Before leaving the mission, go see the lively painting of five Salinan musicians on the wall above an archway in the covered outside walkway east of the church.

Mission San Antonio is reputed to be haunted. There is said to be a friendly phantom padre who greets residents at night in the back corridors. A ghostly little girl has been known to make childish mischief in the gift shop even in broad daylight. More baleful is a forlorn, headless woman, said to glide about the banks of the San Antonio River by night.

The mission caretakers request a modest donation for a self-guided tour. (Visitors will need to present photo identification and proof of auto insurance and registration when they enter Fort Hunter Liggett.) Contact (831) 385–4478; http://missiontour.org or www.californiamissions.com. You can also get in touch with the Friends of Historic San Antonio Mission, 2360 Alisal Road, Salinas, CA 93908; www.californiahistorian.com.

Mission San Luis Obispo

Founded by Father Serra in 1772, Mission San Luis Obispo de Tolosa stands at the center of a bustling college town. Linked to shops and restaurants by a network of footpaths and plazas along San Luis Obispo Creek, the mission today is tidier and more urbane than its neighboring counterparts. Fitting its strong connections to the Chumash people, the mission museum displays a large collection of Chumash stone tools, baskets, and weaponry, as well as historical pictures and household wares from the Spanish and American eras. Donations are accepted for self-guided tours. 782 Monterey Street, San Luis Obispo, CA 93401; (805) 543–6850; www.missionsanluisobispo.org.

Mission San Miguel

Founded by Father Lasuén in 1797, San Miguel was the home mission to a large population of Salinan, who built the canals and dams, planted and harvested the orchards and grain fields, and tended livestock on the vast ranchos. The mission church is remarkable for its interior frescoes, which have not been retouched since they were first painted in 1820 by Salinan artisans under the direction of Spanish artist Estévan Munras, who based his designs on pictures he saw in books in the mission library. Using pigments made from ocher, charcoal, cinnabar, and cobalt, the murals depict the architectural details of grand European buildings, with arches, draperies, fluted pillars, and a railed gallery. The All Seeing Eye of God, set in a triangle and surrounded by clouds and rays of light, stares down from above the altar. The great timbers from which the rafters were hewn were dragged 40 miles from the heights of the Santa Lucias.

The mission grounds also contain a museum, cactus garden, cemetery, and a monastery. Heavily damaged in an earthquake of December 2003, Mission San Miguel Arcángel is not likely to be reopened for public tours anytime soon. The mission is located on Main Street of the tiny town of San Miguel. (831) 467–3256; http://missionsanmiguel.org.

Mission Soledad

Founded by Father Lasuén in 1791, the thirteenth mission was named for María Santísima Nuestra Señora Doloroísima de la Soledad—Our Lady of Solitude. This proved an apt name, for there was no mission site in California more forsaken by comfort and prosperity. Hot and dry in summer, cold and damp in winter, prone to flooding, food shortages, and chronic rheumatism among residents, Mission Soledad was notorious for the death of one priest in 1835 from starvation. Salinan and Costanoan neophytes made up the main work force. After it was secularized and abandoned, the buildings melted over the decades into mounds of adobe clay.

Visitors today can see an adobe church, built in 1954 on a site adjacent to the original. The mission charges a moderate fee for the self-guided tour. Exit US 101, 29 miles south of Salinas at Arroyo Second Road; drive 1 mile southwest to Fort Romie Road; turn right and drive 1.5 miles northwest to the mission. (831) 678–2586; www.californiamissions.com or http://missiontour.org.

The Mexican and Californio Era

When Mexico won its independence from Spain in 1821, California became a Mexican state. Monterey remained the capital. Californios (as Hispanic residents had begun to call themselves) chafed for greater autonomy and economic opportunity. With the best grazing and farming lands held by the missions, ambitious residents demanded land reform. It came when Governor José Figueroa ordered the missions to be secularized in 1834.

The vast mission holdings were dismantled over the next two years. The missions themselves slid into a slow decline, and many of their buildings were sold or leased for homes, inns, stores, taverns, and other worldly establishments. In accord with the original plan of the Franciscan padres, the secularization program allowed for some of the lands to be distributed to the Mission Indians. The neophytes were not trained to manage private landholdings, and far less so to navigate legal hoops or wheedle politicians, lawyers, and judges to protect their interests. A very few kept their plots intact (mainly by marrying non-Indians), but most lost them to rogues and bullies in league with the powers-that-were, or through mismanagement born of being ill trained for the task, or through gambling and drunkenness. Mexican officials attempted to rectify this problem, lamely and belatedly, by granting title to settlements called *rancherías*, where dispossessed Mission Indians gathered. Two of the better-known *rancherías* were in Carmel Valley and on the Indians Ranch at the head of the San Antonio Valley, but there were others scattered throughout Big Sur.

Vast ranchos, many granted as political favors, spread out over the grassy flats and hills of California. From 1836 to 1842 Governor Juan Bautista Alvarado created twenty-eight land grants for friends and political allies in Monterey County alone. These were the best of the grazing lands, most of them prior mission lands of the Carmel, Salinas, San Antonio, and Nacimiento Valleys. Most of the Big Sur country was too rugged to bother with, aside from the coastal terraces around Point Lobos, which became Rancho San José y Sur Chiquito (Saint Joseph and the little south), and Point Sur, which became Rancho El Sur (the south). South of San Carpoforo Creek, where the coastal terraces broaden in San Luis Obispo County, Californios carved out Rancho Piedra Blanca (white stone) and Rancho San Simeon (Saint Simeon) from old Mission San Miguel holdings.

A tough-looking Californio hombre rides into the San Antonio Valley in the mural on the wall of the Hacienda dining hall.

These huge Mexican land grants still shape land-use patterns around Big Sur. Even when changing ownership during the two centuries following their creation, the ranchos were for the most part kept whole, or at least very large. William Randolph Hearst bought several of them when he amassed his property; he later sold some to Uncle Sam for a military base—Fort Hunter Liggett—which therefore owes its shape and size ultimately to Mexican-era land grants. Andrew Molera, Garrapata, and Point Lobos State Parks, and the lands of San Antonio and Nacimiento Reservoirs, were carved out from larger ranchos. Modern conservation easements still target large blocks of land that were initially granted by Governor Alvarado. When you drive the Old Coast Road and Highway 1 past Point Sur, you are crossing through the still-thriving, 3,000-acre section of Rancho El Sur, which will remain as private grazing land (but undeveloped in perpetuity) because of an agreement brokered by the Big Sur Land Trust in 1977.

California life in the twenty-odd years before the Mexican War and the gold rush uprooted Mexican rule has been portrayed for Californios as a kind of golden age. The land was perfect for cattle, and beef was so plentiful that when vaqueros harvested cowhides, they left behind hundreds of rotting carcasses (making this a golden age for grizzly bears, too). Merchants in Monterey traded these hides, known as California banknotes, for porcelain, silk, firearms, iron tools, and other luxuries imported from China and New England. California ranchos were so large, and pueblos so far apart, that Californios grew up riding horses and were famed for their great skill in the saddle. (The private Santa Lucia Preserve celebrates the long traditions of California horsemanship in its annual Fall Fandango, but you'll need an invitation from a resident to attend.) Ranchers broke the monotony of country life with weeklong fiestas, and many large families kept town houses in Monterey. Many Americans settled in Monterey County during the Mexican era, marrying into Californio families and prospering; by law they adopted the Catholic religion and pledged allegiance to the Mexican government.

Mission Indians living on *rancherías* (Indian villages) in the midst of the ranchos provided much of the labor to run these sprawling concerns, but it was not a prosperous life for them. Many weakened and died, or fled inland to seek refuge among the Central Valley and Sierra foothill tribes. Some of the Esselen, and perhaps the Salinan, retreated back into the high interior of the Santa Lucias during the Mexican era, eking out meager livings there. Archaeologists in 1952 uncovered the grave of a six-year-old girl from a site above Church Creek known as the Isabella Meadows Cave (on private property with no public access). She died about 1825 and was buried with shell and glass beads. Poignant also were the nearby remains of an older person who died some fifteen to twenty years later, but received no burial. (The Pacific Grove Museum of Natural History has a small exhibit on the Native peoples of the Big Sur area, including a display about the Isabella Meadows Cave.) Ranchers reported seeing "wild Indians" in the higher mountains even as late as the 1850s, stories that perhaps kindled the legends of the "Dark Watchers of the Santa Lucias."

The American Era

The United States seized California in 1846 as the spoils of the Mexican War. Change came quickly after the 1849 gold rush, when thousands of people flooded into California from all parts of the world, transforming the state's economy, government, and social order. Many old Spanish ranchos and Indian *rancherías* throughout the state fell into turmoil. Although the Treaty of

Santa Lucia Desperadoes

Many of the Californios chafed under their newly imposed second-class citizenry. Tiburcio Vásquez and Anastacio Garcia, two of Monterey County's most famous desperadoes, both claimed to have taken up their bandit careers out of revenge. Certainly many of Vásquez's downtrodden contemporaries considered him a hero, a rebel who stole from the rich and gave to the poor. Despite his undisputed record of crime and violence, many people still do.

Anastacio Garcia fought against the Americans during the Mexican War. Handy with a gun, he later served as a deputy constable in Monterey County under the Americans, while rustling cattle on the side. Garcia boasted of having killed fourteen men and professed to have ridden with the legendary gold rush bandit Joaquín Murrieta. Local lore claims that during hot times he would take refuge in a Santa Lucia mountain hideout still named, apparently in his honor, Anastasia Canyon. Hikers can explore Anastasia Canyon today by trail from Tassajara Road. While detained for murder in the Monterey jail in 1857, unknown assailants overpowered the guard and lynched Garcia in his cell.

Tiburcio Vásquez was a younger protégé of Garcia. Born in Monterey in 1835 (the family home still stands today behind Colton Hall), Vásquez crossed over to the desperado life after killing an American troublemaker at a Monterey fandango. No other California bandit, save Murrieta himself, achieved greater notoriety, not only for his bravado but also for his generosity to the poor, his handsome demeanor, and his popularity among the ladies. Tiburcio was active in Jolon, where he robbed the stage from King City and then joined the posse to track the robber. He rustled cattle and was known to drink at the bar of the Dutton Hotel. He knew Arroyo Seco well, and reportedly hid stolen horses in the upper reaches of Horse Canyon, whose narrow mouth is on private property opposite the junction of the Jamesburg and Arroyo Seco Roads. (The upper canyon lies in the national forest.) Legend says he had other hideouts at Wagon Cave and on the Big Sur coast near Lucia. Betrayed by a girlfriend, Tiburcio Vásquez was captured and hanged in San Jose in 1875.

Guadalupe Hildalgo was supposed to protect these lands, interlopers squatted on the rich pastures and refused to move. American courts ground slowly through the ensuing swamp of land-claim cases. Many Californios died of old age before receiving verdicts, while others had to sell off parcels to pay their lawyers. California Indians fared even worse. To stave off maltreatment, violence, and wanton murder, for which they had no legal recourse, many Mission

Indians took on Hispanic identities, which at least provided some basic protections against cold-blooded murder.

American and British speculators eventually bought up most of the sprawling rancho lands in the Santa Lucias. The U.S. government, de facto owner of the unclaimed West, hoped to populate vast, vacant lands through the Homestead Act of 1862, which offered free plots for individuals or families to settle and develop as farms and ranches. The Homestead Act successfully enticed settlers to the Arroyo Seco and Big Sur Valleys, while more reclusive ranchers

Santa Lucia Gold

Miners found gold in Willow Creek placers in the 1850s, but they were not rich enough to spark much interest until the 1870s. By 1875 miners prospecting on the western slope established Los Burros Mining District to sort out claims and mining disputes. Gorda and Jolon boomed (in their very small ways) as jumping-off points for pack trains supplying the mines, while the mouth of Willow Creek developed (also in a very small way) as a dog-hole port for shipping in mining supplies and equipment.

The hard-rock Last Chance Mine, discovered by W. D. Cruikshank in 1887 and later consolidated as the Buclimo Mine, produced more gold than any other mine in the Santa Lucias. Among the more than 2,000 other mines in the Los Burros District were the Lucky Cuss, the Fighting Chance, the Pansy, the Humbug, and Old Man of the Mountains. The rough-and-ready town of Manchester, at one time also known as Mansfield, sprouted up nearby. In its heyday it sported a hotel, stores, barbershop, blacksmith, one-room schoolhouse, dance hall, several saloons, a cemetery, and about 150 residents. When the town burned down in 1892, the mines' declining fortunes did not encourage rebuilding.

Motorists can still drive to the site of Manchester from Highway 1 via the unpaved Willow Creek Road and the even rougher spur road toward Alder Creek Camp. There isn't much to see. A handful of backwoods folk still live there, some working hobby claims. Judging by the many NO TRESPASSING signs, they (like most miners) like their privacy.

In the 1850s miners also found small amounts of placer gold in streams flowing east into the San Antonio Valley. They established the Jolon Mining District there in the 1870s, but the Santa Lucia's eastward-flowing streams were even stingier than those of the western slope. Most of the Jolon District today is off-limits because of Fort Hunter Liggett, but Jolon itself still contains many reminders of the era, including the Tidball Store and the ruins of the Dutton Hotel.

staked out isolated homesteads on scattered ridges and in remote pockets of the Santa Lucias. Still, most of the mountain lands were too poor and rugged for permanent settlement. The Santa Lucias' steepest canyons and highest mountains remained in federal hands, eventually to become the Monterey District of the Los Padres National Forest.

Big Sur's homesteaders were a self-sufficient breed. They ran cattle and horses, made cheese, kept bees, planted orchards, and raised poultry, hogs, hay, and vegetables. Some hunted game and trapped for pelts. For shipping crops to market and importing supplies, coastal residents built jerry-rigged hoists and ramps to get their goods up and down the coastal bluffs to schooners anchored offshore. Inland homesteaders maintained old trails that ran north and south along the coast, and eastward over the Santa Lucias to the San Antonio and Salinas Valleys. Some lived as hermits, but most cultivated a strong sense of community, with neighbors joining together for cattle roundups and throwing all-night dances and barbecues when they could. Coast-siders commonly married among themselves—Indian, Hispanic, American, and European immigrants—thoroughly mixing the heritage of the old settlers. Their names still march down the coast, preserved in the monikers of canyons, headlands, and other features: Soberanes, Molera, Cooper, Pfeiffer, Post, Castro, Lafler, Torre, Burns, Dolan, Gamboa, and so on.

Not all of Big Sur's new settlers were homesteaders. Others arrived as part of business ventures to harvest the natural resources, especially lime for making cement, tanbark for making tannin (used in tanning leather), and redwood timber for lumber, shakes, railroad ties, and grape stakes. There were coal mines in the Carmel Highlands above Malpaso Creek, an abalone cannery at Point Lobos, and shore-based whaling stations at San Simeon Point, Piedras Blancas Point, and Point Lobos. As shipping increased along the Big Sur coast in the 1860s, the government built two light stations, at Point Sur and Piedras Blancas.

In the 1880s, after Monterey County built a wagon road from Monterey to Castro Canyon (home of Deetjen's Big Sur Inn), the Big Sur Valley became the main population center of the coast. A school, saloons, and stores followed in its wake, creating a diverse and fluid community of ranchers, fishermen, dairy workers, lumberjacks, miners, lighthouse keepers, blacksmiths, teamsters, laborers, and adventurous tourists. Motorists can still drive sections of this old corridor along the Old Coast Road between Bixby Creek and Molera State Park (see chapter 4, Driving the Back Roads). Southward from Castro Canyon the county built and maintained a pack trail. The Coast Trail, aka South Coast Trail, was the only public thoroughfare there until the 1930s.

The *Pfeiffer* name is especially prominent around Big Sur. Michael and Barbara Pfeiffer settled at Sycamore Canyon in 1869. Their original ranch house still stands on private property near Pfeiffer Beach. Pfeiffer Big Sur State Park was part of the family ranch and the site of the first tourist lodge at Big Sur, the Pfeiffer Ranch Resort. Julia Pfeiffer Burns State Park is named for their daughter, who married into the Burns family. Almost everyone pronounces Pfeiffer as *FI-fer*, and that's fine. But sometimes you might meet an old-timer who pronounces it the way the Pfeiffers used to do, with a hard *P*. As Florence Pfeiffer used to instruct early tourists at her Pfeiffer Ranch Resort: "Just remember—*Pie fer* breakfast, *Pie fer* lunch."

In Search of Old-Time Big Sur

The Santa Lucias are rich with reminders of old homesteads, ranches, logging camps, and lime works. You can glimpse many from the road, some still occupied, but the most haunting of them are more remote. Hiking through the backcountry, you can find many a weathered fence line, road cut, or strand of barbed wire ingrown on a tree trunk. There are corrals, tree stumps, old debris, sagging barns and sheds, water troughs, piped springs, and even grave sites to remind us of past visitors. Eucalyptus trees are a good clue to a homesteader heritage, since they are native to Australia and were planted by Big Sur ranchers mainly for windbreaks. Sometimes hikers come across old orchard trees gone to pot, still hung (in season) with stunted, scraggly, disreputable-looking fruit.

Such places are among the most mesmerizing in the Santa Lucias, inviting you to linger and reflect on the people who used to live there. They did not tread lightly across the property, as we do. Their contest was a formidable match, no punches pulled, no quarter given. Trees fell without anguish; buildings rose without permits; people stamped the mud off their boots with no worry of shaking down the flimsy wreck that you see today. These pioneers knew firsthand that nature reclaims everything not guarded with vigor and vigilance, secretly drawing the nails from their houses, caving in their wells, seducing their pigs and orchards to barbarous states. For those of us who buy our bread at the store, such old ruins are very picturesque. For the pioneers who built them, they were both home and livelihood.

Homesteads

John Pfeiffer's 1869 homestead cabin sits on high ground above the Big Sur River in Pfeiffer Big Sur State Park, a short stroll on the Gorge Trail from the picnic area. Manuel Innocenti and his family lived in an adjacent homestead, now vanished except for the graveyard where Mrs. Innocenti and their seven children (none of whom survived childhood) are buried. Manuel himself, a Mission Indian, survived to old age and died in an insane asylum.

The old Post Ranch house still stands at the junction of the Ventana Inn entrance and Highway 1. You can still see some of the old orchards and fence

Sebastian's Store

The oldest continually operating store in San Luis Obispo County, Sebastian's Store started life as a ship's store on the brigantine *Ayochucho*. The goods were hauled ashore to set up a makeshift supply center near San Simeon Point in 1852, when it was a dry-land whaling station. The store was pulled on sleds to its present location in tiny San Simeon in 1878, after George Hearst built the warehouses that still stand across the street. The store went through many owners until Manual Sebastian bought it in 1914. The Sebastian family still owns it, running a post office, gift shop, and coffee bar. Harpoons on the wall recall its wild youth. (805) 927–4217.

Operating since 1852, Sebastian's Store in old San Simeon is the oldest business still in operation along the Big Sur–San Simeon coast.

lines on the Post Ranch Inn property. The present-day Lucia Lodge traces its roots to the old Harlan Ranch, where travelers enjoyed pies and desserts that Mrs. Harlan made from ranch-grown lemons and pears. The Harlan family still owns the lodge.

Garland Ranch Regional Park is assembled of several old ranches. The most complete homestead sits on the Cooper Ranch addition, once famous for its walnuts, apricots, pears, lettuce, and hay. Immigrant Martin Tomasini, an

Molera's Ranch

The best-preserved homestead open to the public at Big Sur is the Molera Ranch House Museum at Andrew Molera State Park. The house is furnished in a time warp straddling 1937, the year that Highway 1 pushed past the front door and carried the twentieth century into the Big Sur country. In addition to period furnishings, clothing, old newspaper clippings, kerosene lamps, a hand-cranked ice cream maker, and a stereoscopic viewer, the museum exhibits photos of local pioneer families. Scattered outbuildings shelter the Point Reyes Bird Observatory and the Molera Riding Stables. The Molera Ranch House is open weekends from 11:00 A.M. through 3:00 P.M., when docents are available.

The Molera Ranch was originally part of Rancho El Sur, granted to Juan Bautista Alvarado in 1834. (Alvarado later served as California governor.) In 1840 he traded the El Sur to his uncle Don Juan Bautista Rogerio Cooper for a ranch in the Salinas Valley. A Yankee sailor who Hispanicized his name as a precondition to marrying into the Vallejo family, Captain Cooper (as he was also known) is the namesake of the Cooper Cabin, built in the 1860s and still standing near the park's walk-in campground.

Rancho El Sur is illustrious as the birthplace (or one of the birthplaces) of Monterey Jack cheese. The origin of the cheese's name is disputed. One story says that ranch hands used a jack to press the whey from the curds. Another says that the cheese was marketed by David Jacks, a Monterey business scion. A third says that a drunken Molera ranch hand named Jack goofed up a recipe, whereupon the angry ranch manager scornfully christened the resulting failure as "Jack's cheese." The cows from whose milk the cheese was made once grazed in Creamery Meadow, where hikers can still find evidence of irrigation canals.

The great ranch, famous for its multiday fiestas, was divided among heirs in 1899. The Moleras, who were related to the Coopers, took over this section in 1915. (For a look at old-time Californio city life, visit the Cooper-Molera Adobe in Monterey.)

Italian Swiss, received the ranch as a dowry when he married Concepcion Mariano Soberanes. The old barn (1875), outbuildings, and ranch house are an easy 0.3-mile walk from the main entrance of the park; the house itself is open and displays a collection of mounted birds and mammals from the area.

Christopher McWay and his wife homesteaded along McWay Creek in 1887, calling it the Saddle Rock Ranch. Built of hand-split redwood, his barn still stands (though rickety) above the Canyon Trail a little upstream from the main parking area of Julia Pfeiffer Burns State Park. The McWays' grave sites are close by. Ranch foreman Han Ewoldsen built Big Sur's first power station in 1932 along McWay Creek, a little downstream from the parking lot, but its Pelton waterwheel dates from 1940.

Many old settlements are reached only on foot. The crumbling ruins of the Pico Blanco Hunting and Fishing Lodge, a hunting camp built in the early twentieth century, still stand near Launz Ridge on the Little Sur Trail. Hikers in Miller Canyon pass the site of the Nason Cabin, a former cow camp on the Middle Fork of the Carmel River. Hikers on the Church Creek Trail pass near the Church Ranch, homesteaded by the Church family in 1888 and still a private ranch (not open to the public). Among the old homesteads that now serve as National Forest campsites are Comings Camp, Upper Cruikshank, Vicente Flat, and Dutra Flat, all reached only by trail. Lottie Potrero Campground, on the ridge east of the San Carpoforo watershed, commemorates Lottie Woodworth, who homesteaded 160 acres on nearby pastures between 1886 and 1910.

José Maria Gil built an adobe and mud-mortared stone ranch house in the San Antonio Valley around 1865. After the military took it over in the 1940s, it briefly served as housing for unmarried officers. Presently dilapidated, it is slated for restoration.

Dog-Hole Ports

With no road or good harbors between Point Lobos and San Simeon, farmers, ranchers, lumber companies, miners, and homesteaders along the Big Sur coast had no economical access to markets. Shippers filled the void with makeshift landings in tiny coves, called dog-hole ports because they were so small "a dog could hardly turn around in them." Ships usually floated offshore while longshoremen lowered cargoes down cliffs on cables, swung them out with primitive cranes, slid them down greased ramps, or rowed them out on small boats. Smugglers were said to make good use of these ports for moonshine, a popular product of Big Sur.

The following list of Big Sur's dog-hole ports runs from north to south. Some are on private property. Whalers Cove and San Simeon are still used for recreation, but Partington Landing is by far the most interesting.

- **Whalers Cove:** On the north side of Point Lobos. It's still heavily used for recreation. It once shipped coal, granite, sand, redwood lumber, whale oil, tanbark, and fruit.
- **Straders Landing:** At the mouth of Malpaso Creek. It shipped coal.
- **Notley's Landing:** Remains include the occupied ranch at the junction of Palo Colorado Road and Highway 1. It shipped lumber and tanbark.

- **Bixby Landing:** On the headland north of Bixby Bridge. From a turnout near the bridge, you can still see ruins of the cable system that brought lime from 3 miles inland to ships offshore. It shipped lime, tanbark, and lumber.
- **Cooper Landing:** South of Point Sur. It shipped lumber and cheese.
- **Partington Landing (aka Seaview Landing):** This port shipped tanbark, lumber, firewood, mica, and coal; according to local legend it also smuggled booze.
- **Saddle Rock Landing:** In a cove to the south of Saddle Rock (near McWay Falls), Julia Pfeiffer Burns State Park. It shipped lumber and tanbark.
- **Anderson Landing:** Between Anderson and Burns Creeks. It shipped lumber and tanbark.
- **Gamboa Point:** Tanbark and lumber.
- **Harlans Landing:** A cable strung between shore and an offshore rock, near Lucia. It shipped lumber.
- **Rockland Landing:** At the mouth of Limekiln Creek. It shipped lumber and lime from upstream kilns now in Limekiln State Park.
- **Mill Creek:** Lumber and tanbark.
- **Pacific Valley Landing:** South of Prewitt Creek. It shipped lumber.
- **Willow Creek:** Gold-mining equipment.
- **San Simeon:** The largest harbor between Carmel and Morro Bay, it's still heavily used for recreation. It once shipped lumber, farm produce, and cinnabar ore, as well as building materials, artwork, furnishings, and supplies for Hearst Castle.

Modern Times

Highway 1

The twentieth century arrived at Big Sur in June 1937, when dignitaries cut the ribbon that officially opened Highway 1 down the coast. The road had been a long time coming. State highway engineers did their first survey in 1918. Work started in 1922 but stopped soon after for lack of funds. Road crews were bolstered by convict laborers, who received small wages and reductions in their prison sentences of 1.5 days of jail time for every day of road work They also enjoyed a measure of freedom, both at work and in their camps at the Little Sur River, Salmon Creek, Anderson Creek, Kirk Creek, and Point Gorda.

Construction was fraught with difficulties. The route was a succession of deep canyons and unstable cliffs. Engineers sweated bullets as 2,000 feet of survey line slid 2 feet west and 8 vertical feet downward over the course of two

Whalers Cabin Museum

The little shack above Whalers Cove, in Point Lobos State Reserve, is a humble monument to those who have made their livings from the surrounding sea. Whale bones piled outside recall the 1862 colony of Portuguese shore whalers who spied for passing whales from Whalers Knoll, ready at a moment's notice to put to sea with harpoons. The parking lot on the shore just downhill occupies the site of their old whale-rendering factory.

When whales disappeared, abalone filled the economic void. The museum houses a motley collection of seafaring tools, fishing gear, ship parts, news clippings, and a diving suit recalling the local abalone fishery pioneered at Whalers Cove by Gennosuke Kodani and other Japanese divers in 1898. The tough but tasty mollusk was dried and shipped to Japan at first, but after investors built a cannery atop the site of the old blubber factory, Americans learned to enjoy canned abalone. It, too, was soon depleted.

The so-called Whalers Cabin itself is apparently older than either the Portuguese or Japanese colonies. It was built by Chinese fishermen who landed at the mouth of the Carmel River in 1851, having crossed the Pacific in a junk. Nursed back to health by the local Rumsien tribe, they settled on the shore of Whalers Cove and took up fishing. This building is the last remnant of their fishing village. A girl named Quock Mui was

An old diving suit and other maritime equipment grace the humble walls of the old Whalers Cabin in Point Lobos State Reserve.

born here in 1859, possibly in this very cabin. She learned to speak Chinese, Rumsien, Portuguese, Japanese, Spanish, and English just by mixing with her neighbors—a remarkable tribute to the cosmopolitan heritage of Monterey County. Quock Mui died in 1930, and her house still stands near Cannery Row in Monterey.

years. While working with a highway crew at Hurricane Point in the winter of 1934, Barbara Pfeiffer's son, Frank, was killed in a slide. Bridges were especially challenging, since most of the canyons were too deep to allow for central piers. Engineers solved that problem with a series of graceful arches anchored between two canyon walls, a perfect union of function and beauty. The two most photographed of these engineering marvels are the Bixby Bridge (1932), soaring 260 feet above the creek, and the double-arch Big Creek Bridge (1937).

Highway 1 brought great changes to Big Sur. Many residents appreciated the economic boost and easy access to the outside world, not to mention the electricity and telephones that eventually followed the road down the coast. But Highway 1 was not universally welcomed. Big Sur residents dreaded blasted hillsides, bulldozed canyons, the influx of people, and rises in real estate prices.

The Hearst Legacy

Senator George Hearst bought a 45,000-acre ranch on the San Simeon coast in 1865. His family enjoyed rustic vacations in the Santa Lucia Mountains. The senator's son, newspaper magnate William Randolph Hearst, loved the area and began to develop it in 1919. He bought up scores of ranches in the Santa Lucias, especially in the San Antonio Valley, consolidating his holdings into one enormous ranch of about 200,000 acres, half as large as the state of Rhode Island. Meanwhile he commissioned architect Julia Morgan to design a private home unlike anything ever seen before, and he commenced to build it in the hills above San Simeon, a place they called La Cuesta Encantada—the enchanted hill. Besides the palatial mansion, Morgan built Hearst an astounding complex of guest houses, pools, a zoo, and terraced gardens. Hearst's "castle" was lavishly furnished with art and antiques from Europe. Scores of celebrities and Hollywood stars came to partake of Hearst's celebrated parties. The castle and Mr. Hearst served as inspiration for Xanadu and Mr. Kane in Orson Welles's classic film *Citizen Kane*.

Hearst's workforce continued to ranch his property. His cattle company established a northern base of operations in the San Antonio Valley on a hill above the mission. Julia Morgan designed the ranch headquarters, called the Hacienda, building another fantasy that looked more like an idealized Spanish mission than it did a Santa Lucia ranch house, barn, or bunkhouse. Ranch hands were intimidated by it. Instead of bunking in the fancy Hacienda, Hearst's cowpunchers preferred to camp out in the field in front. Hearst still made good use of the property for entertaining guests with lavish picnics, as well as for housing his mistress, Marion Davies.

As his debts mounted in 1940, Hearst decided to part with the northern section of his ranch, selling 153,830 acres to the U.S. Army for a military base. Named for a World War I commander, the Hunter Liggett Military Reservation

Hearst Castle looms on the hillside above the old village schoolhouse in San Simeon.

(or Fort Hunter Liggett as it has been known since 1975) became a vast training ground for infantry bound for the European theater of World War II. (In 1957 Congress transferred 45,700 acres of Forest Service land east of the coast ridge to the army, and 26,050 acres on the west slope from the military to the Forest Service.) Tank crews and other units still train there.

After William Randolph Hearst's death in 1951, the family also parted with their castle. Transformed into a state park, Hearst Castle opened for public tours in 1958. Other parcels were sold to make San Simeon State Park and William Randolph Hearst State Beach. The Hearst Corporation even more recently sold or transferred some 14 additional miles of coastline to San Simeon State Park, but still owns an 82,000-acre cattle ranch in the Santa Lucias.

Tourists, Beats, Hippies, Yuppies

Tourism to Big Sur increased when gasoline rationing ceased after the end of World War II. Most of the growth was in Big Sur Valley stores and lodges. Other landowners sold land for state parks. The fame of Highway 1 as a scenic spectacle and engineering marvel spread. In 1966 Lady bird Johnson, the first lady, officiated at a ceremony declaring Highway 1 as California's first federal Scenic Highway.

Big Sur had always been home to hermits and eccentrics. The new highway bolstered their numbers with artists, writers, and bohemians. After Henry Miller arrived in 1944, his writing spread Big Sur's reputation for artistic freedom and natural beauty to an even wider public. The 1958 publication of his *Big Sur and the Oranges of Hieronymus Bosch* in particular regaled the public with its chronicle of local characters, poets, artists, crackpots, and neighbors, and inspired a number of Beat Generation writers to make their way to Big Sur. Cultural offspring of the beatniks, hippies also took a shine to Big Sur in the 1960s, adding a heady whiff of communal life, free love, pot smoking, and footloose ways to the Big Sur reputation. Some riled locals by squatting on private property. The countercultural interest in Big Sur continues to thrive in the area's continuing flirtation with New Age mysticism and self-empowerment movements.

As Big Sur's fame has spread, so has the desire to preserve it. In the wake of the Wilderness Act of 1964, the federal government set aside large tracts of the Los Padres National Forest as designated wilderness areas. Talk comes and goes of establishing a national park there. Private conservation groups have bought large ranches for nature preserves.

Protection is a double-edged sword. Conservation-minded Californians, including many locals, view the public acquisition of land as a good thing, but some locals also worry that it threatens the vitality of their community. People who choose to live at Big Sur want to see the land preserved, but they also want to see their community preserved. As more land is protected, the pool of local real estate shrinks even as its desirability rises, forcing land prices ever upward. The result is that wealthy buyers who live (and earn!) in the outside world wield ever greater clout in the Big Sur real estate market. Big Sur is seeing an influx of wealthy people who buy or build second homes but spend most of their time elsewhere. This could become a serious problem for a small community like Big Sur, which depends on volunteers for the fire department, youth sports programs, and helping neighbors clean driveways and side roads of winter storm debris.

Reading Local History

Coyote Press specializes in archaeology and Native American studies in the western United States, and offers a wide array of publications on the Ohlone, Esselen, and Salinan. It has a catalog. P.O. Box 3377, Salinas, CA 93912; (831) 422–4912; www.coyotepress.com.

Breschini, Gary S., and Trudy Haversat. *The Esselen Indians of the Big Sur Country: The Land and the People*. Salinas, Calif.: Coyote Press, 2004.

Chase, J. Smeaton. *California Coast Trails: A Horseback Ride from Mexico to Oregon*. Boston: Houghton Mifflin, 1913.

Clark, Donald Thomas. *Monterey County Place Names: A Geographical Dictionary*. Carmel Valley, Calif.: Kestrel Press, 1991.

Coelho, Albert J. *The Arroyo Seco: The Central Coast's Grand Canyon*. San Francisco: Monterey Pacific Publishing, 2001.

Durham, David L. *Place-Names of California's Central Coast*. Clovis, Calif.: Word Dancer Press, 2000.

Jones, Terry L. *Prehistoric Human Ecology of the Big Sur Coast, California*. Berkeley: University of California Press, 2003.

Norman, Jeff. *Images of America: Big Sur*. Charleston, S.C.: Big Sur Historical Society and Arcadia Publishing, 2004.

Smith, F. R. *The Mission of San Antonio de Padua (California)*. Stanford, Calif.: Stanford University Press, 1932.

Wall, Rosalind Sharpe. *A Wild Coast and Lonely*. San Carlos, Calif.: World Wide Publishing/Tetra, 1989.

Chapter 9
Big Sur Culture

B ig Sur is a place that promotes thought, wonder, contemplation. This chapter presents some opportunities for enjoying the literary, artistic, spiritual, and cultural landscape of this unique countryside.

Big Sur Lore

Big Sur and the Santa Lucias seem to generate mysteries. Old tales of buried gold and shadowy beings, the Dark Watchers, have been around for decades, but even in this age of Internet communications, a quick Web search shows that new tales are still being generated. A case in point is Drum Rock, located near the headwaters of the North Fork of the Little Sur River. Drum Rock's powers remain (in time-honored fashion) vague and mysterious, but one awestruck witness claims that it caused the flesh on a companion's hands to "boil."

I have not myself experienced any unexplained phenomena at Big Sur. I report the following examples as part of Big Sur's cultural heritage, without any intent to debunk or endorse.

The Ventana

Ventana Wilderness is named for a natural notch along the granite ridge between Ventana Double Cone and Peak 4653 (also known as Kandlbinder Peak). Legend says that it used to be roofed over with rock to make a natural "window," which is what purportedly first inspired the Spanish to call it *Ventana*. Climbers call this sheer-walled, squared-off, 200-foot-deep notch "the Slot." You can see it looking west from Ventana Double Cone, looking north from the Coast Ridge Road, or looking northeast from Post Ranch Inn. New Age mystics still attach great importance to the "window," but geologists argue that the notch does not contain the rubble of a collapsed arch.

The Dark Watchers

The old story that a race of small, dark humanlike beings inhabit the forests and high country of Big Sur has received backing from some notable witnesses. John Steinbeck's mother claimed to have seen them, and they actually appear in Steinbeck's short story "Flight." Longtime Big Sur resident Rosalind Sharpe Wall claims to have seen them near Bixby Creek. Robinson Jeffers described them, too. More recently Thomas Steinbeck published a book of short stories, *Down to a Soundless Sea*, in which the Dark Watchers appear.

The prevailing wisdom is that you should not look at a Dark Watcher. They do not harm you, and in fact they disappear as soon as you accidentally glimpse one of them. Regardless, someone who sees a Dark Watcher is supposed to look away immediately.

Point Lobos Spiritualism

Rosalind Sharpe Wall cites a long history of supernatural speculation at Point Lobos. The Rumsien neophytes at Mission Carmel told a priest that fog spirits came ashore at night, lonely and forlorn, and required the Indians to go to Point Lobos to cheer the spirits up. To stop the pagan rituals, a priest followed them out one night to perform an exorcism. The angry spirits flew off, but the priest went mad and jumped to his death from a cliff.

Ella Young, a professor of Celtic lore at the University of California at Berkeley in the 1930s, claimed that Point Lobos (like Mount Shasta) is a sacred "mountain," the center of great psychic power, a place where fairies still dwell. The power isn't malicious, but it is dangerous. Many other people, including marine biologist Ed Ricketts—a close friend of John Steinbeck—have reported strange and inexplicable feelings of terror in and around Point Lobos.

A Tibetan lama visiting the 1915 Panama-Pacific International Exposition in San Francisco passed through Point Lobos on a journey south. After seeing the cypress grove, he determined that they were sacred trees planted by three Buddhist missionaries 1,000 years before, from seeds gathered at his monastery in Lhasa.

The strange beauty and haunting atmosphere of the cypress grove at Point Lobos has given birth to many supernatural stories.

Big Sur Shipwrecks

Big Sur has a long history of shipwrecks. Salvaging cargoes proved to be a profitable side-business for many of the old, coastal residents. Local lore claims that Wreck Beach, south of Pfeiffer Point, exerts a strong magnetic pull on ships' compasses because of a high occurrence of iron sands.

Music in the Air

At the artists' colony where he lived in his early days at Big Sur, Henry Miller wrote that "everyone who goes to live at Anderson Creek hears things. Some hear Beethoven symphonies, some hear military bands, some hear voices, some hear wails and shrieks. Particularly those who live near the canyon creek, which is the source of these eerie, disturbing sounds." The hermit Al Clark also claimed to hear symphonies in the air up where he lived on the Little Sur River.

UFOs

In *Big Sur and the Oranges of Hieronymus Bosch*, Henry Miller recounted several secondhand accounts of UFOs at Big Sur, and one that he witnessed firsthand. The latter he observed for twenty minutes, and said it looked "like twin stars gyrating about an invisible pivot." Esalen Institute has hosted seminars on the very subject.

Al Clark's Hidden Gold Mine

The eccentric Al Clark had a degree from Columbia but posed as an illiterate. He dug a mine on Pico Blanco and claimed that it opened into a huge limestone cave with an underground river. He claimed that it also contained ancient cave paintings of prehistoric mammals on the walls. Rumors were that he also found a hoard of Rumsien gold. He had no use for money, however, and left it alone, keeping the mine's location a secret. Before his death he sealed the mine with a dynamite blast.

New Age Big Sur

Some people claim that Big Sur is a "vortex"—an area where powerful energy from spiritual or unknown forces is concentrated. Other acclaimed vortex centers include Mount Shasta, Stonehenge, the Great Pyramid of Egypt, and Sedona, Arizona. Mystics seeking to tap into this energy often employ vision quests in the Ventana backcountry, with the aid of fasting and solitude. Some claim that Big Sur is a portal for souls entering and departing the planet, a gateway to different worlds or other dimensions. Seminar programs at the Esalen Institute have been both generators and magnets for much of Big Sur's reputation as a New Age center.

Big Sur Literature

Literary pilgrims find a few prominent (and a great many obscure) reasons to visit Big Sur. The two biggest names—well-known writers who lived on this coast and wrote about it intimately—are Robinson Jeffers and Henry Miller. The list of other authors associated with Big Sur to lesser degrees is long and includes Lynda Sargent, Jaime DeAngulo, Ruth Comfort Mitchell, Dennis Murphy, Jack London, Mary Austin, George Sterling, Ken Kesey, and Nicholas Roosevelt.

Robert Louis Stevenson was one of the earliest to celebrate the coast south of Monterey in literature. Some think Point Lobos was the inspiration for *Treasure Island*.

Gertrude Atherton, who fictionalized and romanticized old Californio life, set a novel in the San Antonio Valley. She gained firsthand knowledge of the area when her husband, George Atherton, inherited the Rancho Milpitas, and the couple went down to manage it in 1877. Milpitas Ranch covered 43,000 acres, stretching from Jolon to The Indians, including Mission San Antonio. Many settlers had already staked claim to parcels on the ranch, including descendants of displaced Mission Indians. The Athertons, with the help of the sheriff, set out to evict them. When Gertrude ran into a cold and hapless throng of evicted families gathered at Mission San Antonio, she expressed shock at the turmoil she had helped to cause—and used the incident in her novel *Los Cerritos*.

The Beat Generation knew Big Sur intimately. Lawrence Ferlinghetti had a cabin in Bixby Canyon, and many writers visited in the 1950s and 1960s, including Neal Cassady, Michael McClure, and Jack Kerouac. Kerouac came to stay in the summer of 1961. At that stage of life, he was ravaged by alcoholism, and the stark, primordial wildness of the place unhinged him. He left after a week and described the experience in his novel *Big Sur*. Richard Brautigan was inspired to write *Confederate Yankee from Big Sur* after staying in a ramshackle cabin north of Gorda in 1957. This whimsical, surreal novel was published in 1965.

The late Lillian Bos Ross, a local writer known to friends as Shanagolden, coined the famous saying, "Big Sur is a state of mind." She also wrote "The Ballad of the South Coast." Her novel *The Stranger* was set at Notley's Landing. Liv Ullmann and Gene Hackman starred in the Hollywood version, which was called *Zandy's Bride*.

John Steinbeck is well known as a Salinas Valley writer. Less well known is that he worked at least one summer at the Post Ranch. His short story "Flight" was set in a coastal canyon "about 15 miles below Monterey." The San Antonio Valley near Jolon was the setting for *To a God Unknown*.

John Steinbeck's son, Thomas, is both a writer and a Central Coast resident. His collection of short stories *Down to a Soundless Sea* (published in 2002) makes many fascinating references to the local characters, lore, and history, much of it inspired by his father's own life. Among the seven stories, "The Night Guide" and "The Wool Gatherer" are both set on the Post Ranch. "The Dark Watcher" concerns an anthropology professor who meets a Dark Watcher while exploring in the Santa Lucia Mountains. The wreck of the *Los Angeles* near Point Sur is featured in "Blind Luck."

Robinson Jeffers

The austere doyen of Big Sur writers wrote extensively of people and places along the Big Sur coast. With the love of his life, Una, he built a home from native granite above Carmel Bay. They moved into Tor House in 1925 and lived there the rest of their lives. Jeffers died in 1962.

Jeffers had little faith in humanity. He felt civilization to be trivial in the larger scheme of things, and all human endeavors doomed to ultimate futility. The natural world is regal and longer lasting than anything human-made, but even nature changes. Jeffers's most famous long works were *Tamar*, *The Roan Stallion*, *The Women of Point Sur*, and the verse-drama *Medea*, but he wrote many shorter lyrics. His narrative works have tragic themes, and all his poetry is heavily symbolic. He shocked a lot of readers by writing about incest, but he had acquired a national stature by the 1920s and 1930s. Of lasting interest to the book-toting Big Sur traveler, Jeffers makes scores of references to real places throughout the region, and most of his fictitious names are easily identified with real places.

Located in a Carmel neighborhood, Tor House is one of the most intimate monuments to any poet on the West Coast. Built by hand of redwood and stone, it is open for tours by arrangement. Visitors browse through the bookstore and wander the low-ceilinged cottage contemplating Jeffers's family photos and books. Look for the bed by the window where Jeffers died, as he foresaw in an early poem. Climb 40 feet to the top of Hawk Tower, where you can look out over Carmel Bay and Point Lobos. Among the famous artists, actors, musicians, and writers who visited Jeffers at Tor House were George Sterling, Edgar Lee Masters, Edna St. Vincent Millay, Lincoln Steffens, Irvin Cobb, Krishnamurti, James Cagney, Ralph Bellamy, Charlie Chaplin, George Gershwin, Bennett Cerf, Thornton Wilder, Langston Hughes, William Saroyan, Aldous Huxley, Toscanini, Salvador Dali, Joseph Campbell, and Martha Graham. A home truly worthy of a poet, Tor House is a National Historic Landmark. For tours, contact the Robinson Jeffers Tor House Foundation, P.O. Box 2713, Carmel, CA 93921; (831) 624–1831; www.torhouse.org.

Boon Hughey and others have published interesting articles on Jeffers in the *Double Cone Register* (www.ventanawild.org). Jeffers fans should also know the *Robinson Jeffers Newsletter* (www.jeffers.org). The Poetry Speaks series publishes Jeffers recordings on CD.

Henry Miller

Miller came to Big Sur in 1944, already famous (notorious in some circles) for his autobiographical writings, and particularly *Tropic of Cancer*. His French publisher was unable to pay royalties because of World War II, and Miller was virtually penniless. He stayed first with novelist Lynda Sargent at what is now Nepenthe. The two did not get along, and he soon moved to an artists' colony at Anderson Creek, taking up residence in cabins built to house convicts working on Highway 1. Later he took up a home on Partington Ridge, where he raised two children, Valentine and Tony. During these years he painted and wrote, publishing *Big Sur and the Oranges of Hieronymous Bosch* and the Rosy Crucifixion trilogy of *Sexus*, *Plexus*, and *Nexus*. A fascinating autobiographical

Henry Miller Library

The Henry Miller Library serves as a community center, art gallery, and venue for lectures, concerts, and literary events—in short, almost anything except a *lending* library. It does store and sell rare books by Miller and other local writers, however, and Miller's paintings hang on the walls. Built in 1966 as a home by Emil White, Miller's personal secretary, it keeps a cozy fireplace and photographs of Miller's home on Partington Ridge. Local folks drop in to talk. Even when nothing special is going on, it's a nice place to relax. It's located just south of Nepenthe in the redwoods of Graves Canyon. Highway 1, Big Sur, CA 93920; (831) 667-2574; www.henrymiller.org.

account of his many acquaintances and experiences around Big Sur, the *Hieronymous Bosch* book regales the reader with stories about local artists, writers, musicians, and other Big Sur characters.

Miller's writings inadvertently spread Big Sur's reputation around the country and beyond, attracting attention from other artists and writers, and inadvertently sparking the beatniks' (and, through them, the hippies') "discovery" of Big Sur. Miller left Big Sur in 1962, but his ashes were scattered there after his death in 1980.

Big Sur Literary Links

Anderson Creek
In the 1940s Henry Miller resided in an artists' colony here.

Bixby Canyon
This is the site of Lawrence Ferlinghetti's cabin, where Beat Generation icons Neal Cassady, Michael McClure, and Jack Kerouac visited. Kerouac's novel *Big Sur* was hatched here. Bixby's Landing was the inspiration for Robinson Jeffers's 1932 poem "Thurso's Landing."

Bottchers Gap
The area is mentioned in Jeffers's "The Inquisitors." In "All the Little Hoofprints," he calls it Pigeon Gap.

Brazil Ranch
A pair of eagles roosting here inspired Jeffers's "Beaks of Eagles."

Church Creek Canyon
Robinson Jeffers visited the caves, where he saw the Esselen handprints that inspired his poem "Hands."

Deetjen's/Big Sur Inn
Henry Miller and Robinson Jeffers were both guests of Grandpa Deetjen.

Esalen Institute
Old Slates Hot Springs appeared in Jeffers's poem "Solstice" (as did nearby Devils Canyon). Miller called them Sulphur Springs and was a frequent guest. Among the famous speakers here were Aldous Huxley, Arnold Toynbee, Linus Pauling, Carlos Castaneda, and LSD guru Dr. Timothy Leary. Well-armed Hunter S. Thompson once worked as a guard. Charles Manson played a concert at Esalen three days before his "family" murdered Sharon Tate. Tom Wolfe recounts a Merry Pranksters visit to the institute in his novel *Electric Kool-Aid Acid Test*.

Hearst Castle
Literary guests included George Bernard Shaw, Winston Churchill (a historian, after all), Irving Cobb, and gossip columnists Hedda Hopper and Louella Parsons. Aldous Huxley's *After Many a Summer Dies the Swan* (1939) satirizes Hearst and his castle, transplanting it to the San Fernando Valley, with Okies working as serfs.

Lafler Canyon
Henry Lafler edited the *Blue Mule*, a literary magazine. Jack London and George Sterling stayed at Lafler's cabin.

Lime Creek
Lillian Bos Ross lived at Livermore Ledge, now part of John Little State Reserve near the mouth of Lime Creek. Henry Miller was a guest for dinner on his first night in Big Sur.

Little Sur River
Poet Eric Barker lived as a caretaker near the mouth of the river. Jeffers set Hanlon's Camp upstream near the Old Coast Road crossing in his poem "A Woman Down the Coast."

Malpaso Creek
Jeffers set "Tamar" in upper Malpaso Creek Canyon. His poem "The Wind-Struck Music" takes place in the hills above.

Manchester
When botanist Alice Eastwood visited in 1893, she noted that the rough mining town had a literary and debating society and an excellent library.

Nepenthe
Novelist Lynda Sargent owned a log house here and hosted Henry Miller, who often visited after the Fassetts built Nepenthe.

Notley's Landing
The Stranger, by Lillian Bos Ross, was set in this now vanished community.

Old Coast Road
Many of Jeffers's characters lived or traveled along this old highway.

Partington Ridge
Jaime de Angulo, Nicholas Roosevelt, and Henry Miller all lived here. Driving past in *Confederate General from Big Sur*, Brautigan's alter ego, Jesse, spotted Miller in his car waiting at the row of mailboxes on Highway 1.

Point Lobos
This rich scene has inspired much literature, possibly including Robert Louis Stevenson's *Treasure Island*, and many poems by Robinson Jeffers. George Sterling and Jack London used to enjoy abalone roasts with their Carmel friends here. Sterling started a tradition of making up stanzas to a song while they beat the mollusks to tenderize them. A sample verse:

> Oh some folks boast of quail on toast
> Because they think it's toney
> But I'm content to owe my rent
> And live on abalone.

Point Sur Light Station
Jeffers's "The Women of Point Sur" was published in 1927.

Posts
As a young man, John Steinbeck worked on the ranch for Frank Post. Thomas Steinbeck set some of his stories here.

Robinson Canyon
Robert Louis Stevenson took sick while roaming through the northern Santa Lucias; he was nursed back to health here by a bear hunter named Jonathan Wright. A cabin in this canyon inspired "The Roan Stallion."

Rocky Creek

This is the canyon where Robinson Jeffers's Cawdor lived.

Rocky Point

You can buy a copy of *The Rocky Point Murders*, a book of short stories from a creative writing class, at the restaurant.

San Antonio Valley

Steinbeck's *To a God Unknown* was set in the "Valley of Nuestra Senora," based on the country around Jolon. Gertrude Atherton set her novel *Los Cerritos* here. The Athertons owned Rancho Milpitas but returned to San Mateo County after one winter's stay, during which time George Atherton took to drinking and gambling in Jolon.

Soberanes Point

This was the setting for Jeffers's poem, "Place for No Story."

Ventana Creek

"Oh Lovely Rock," "Beaks of Eagles," and "Night Without Sleep" all mention this wilderness stream, where Jeffers once backpacked with his son and a friend.

Big Sur Movie Links

The dramatic scenery of Big Sur has attracted many filmmakers. Point Lobos is the favorite location by far. Many of the location shots listed below amounted to only one fleeting moment on the big screen.

Andrew Molera State Park
- *Zandy's Bride* (1974).

Big Creek
- *Poetic Justice* (1993).

Big Sur (unspecified locations)
- *A Woman Rebels* (1936).
- *Suspicion* (1941). Look for Alfred Hitchcock's cameo as he motors down Highway 1.
- *Deep Valley* (1947).
- *From Here to Eternity* (1953). Though mostly shot in Hawaii, one Big Sur beach made the cut.
- *The Terror* (1963).
- *Incubus* (1966).

- *Chandler* (1972).
- *Escape to Witch Mountain* (1975).
- *The Cat from Outer Space* (1978).
- *Junior* (1994).

Bixby Creek Bridge
- *Brainstorm* (1983). Look for the truck driving over the cliff.

Carmel Highlands
- *Play Misty for Me* (1971). Clint Eastwood's character lives in a house on Spindrift Road.
- *Basic Instinct* (1992). Sharon Stone's character lives in the *same* house on Spindrift Road (except that it's supposed to be in San Francisco).

Deetjen's Big Sur Inn
Legend has it that Greta Garbo and "Grandpa" Deetjen were good friends, and that she often visited.

Doud Ranch, Santa Lucias
- *Doctor Dolittle* (1967).

Esalen Institute
- *Celebration at Big Sur* (1971). Esalen resident Joan Baez, as well as visiting band Crosby, Stills, Nash and Young, make appearances.

Fort Hunter Liggett
- *We Were Soldiers* (2002). The War Room and most of the Vietnamese village scenes were shot here.

Garrapata State Park
- *Salome, Where She Danced* (1945).
- *The Master Gunfighter* (1975).
- *Basic Instinct* (1992).

The Hacienda
Among the famous Hollywood guests at Hearst's home away from home were Spencer Tracy, Clark Gable, Dick Powell, Will Rogers, Jean Harlowe, Errol Flynn, and, of course, Marion Davies. Local residents recall fiestas with Mariachi bands playing from the dining room balcony.

Hastings Natural History Reservation
- *Poco Loco* (1994).

An artist at Garrapata State Park attempts to capture Soberanes Point and Whale Peak on canvas.

Hearst Castle

The list of Hollywood guests is long: John Barrymore, Lionel Barrymore, David Niven, Barbara Stanwyck, Mary Pickford, Dick Powell, Carole Lombard, Greta Garbo, Cary Grant, Jean Harlow, John Gilbert, Buster Keaton, Harpo Marx, Joel McCrea, Harold Lloyd, Errol Flynn, Douglas Fairbanks Jr., Gary Cooper, Charlie Chaplain, Joan Crawford, Dolores del Rio, Clark Gable, Marie Dressler, Hal Roach, Louis B. Mayer, Jack Warner, and Howard Hughes. Orson Welles's most famous film, *Citizen Kane*, was inspired by Hearst and his castle, even though Kane's castle (Xanadu) is in Florida.

Little Sur River

• *The Master Gunfighter* (1975).

Monastery Beach
- *Play Misty for Me* (1971).

Nepenthe
Orson Welles bought this property for his bride Rita Hayworth, but they never lived here. Richard Burton and Elizabeth Taylor relaxed here while filming *The Sandpiper* in 1963. A folk-dancing scene filmed here appears in the movie.

Notley's Landing
- *My Son* (1925).

Pfeiffer Beach
- *One-Eyed Jacks* (1961), directed by Marlon Brando.
- *The Master Gunfighter* (1975).

Point Lobos
More than forty Hollywood films and TV commercials have had scenes shot here, starting as far back as 1914. Point Lobos has stood in for Cornwall, Elba, Massachusetts, and France. Among the movie greats involved were Greer Garson, Robert Mitchum, Erich von Stroheim, James Cagney, Shirley Temple, Claudette Colbert, Fred MacMurray, Charles Boyer, Roddy McDowell, Elizabeth Taylor, James Dean, Jack Lemmon, Kim Novak, and Fred Astaire.

Point Sur
- *Green Dolphin Street* (1947).

Rancho San Carlos
- *Sleeper* (1973).
- *The Muppet Movie* (1979).
- *Poco Loco* (1994).

San Antonio Valley
Born on a homestead here in 1890, character actor Edgar Kennedy appeared in more than 400 films. Clint Eastwood starred as Rowdy Yates in the TV series *Rawhide* (1958–1965), which filmed boilerplate location shots of cattle drives in this valley.

Art and Craft Galleries

An artist himself (as well as an author), Henry Miller observed of the Big Sur community, "If you are an artist and think to muscle in here, it would be wise to first find a patron, because the artist cannot live off the artist, and here every other individual, seemingly, is an artist of one sort or another. Even the plumbers."

The Central Coast is steeped in artistic tradition. Carmel, of course, was an early artists' colony, a muse to William Ritschel, Paul Dougherty, Arthur Hill Gilbert, Mary Morgan, Jo Mora, and Armin Hansen. Edward Weston was a pioneer photographer of Point Lobos, and Ansel Adams lived at Yankee Point in the Carmel Highlands. Among the artists who lived farther down the coast in Big Sur were Benny Bufano, Gordon Newell, Jean "Yanko" Varda, Edmond Kara, Emile Norman, Rog Rogway, Helen Flemming, and Harry Dick Ross. (You can see an example of Ross's painted wood carving at Molera Ranch House Museum—the monkey next to the fireplace.) Among contemporary local artists whose work you can find in Big Sur galleries are painters Erin Lee Gafill, Holly Fassett, Tom Davies, Ronna Rio, Lygia Chappellet, Heidi Hybl, Branham Rendlen, and Erlinda Montano Hiscock; sculptors Barbara Spring, Loet Vanderveen, Ann Seifert, Micah Curtis, Hans Apelqvist, and Michael Emmons; ceramic artist Embree de Persiis; and painter and sculptor Greg Hawthorne.

- **Big Sur Arts Center:** Located upstairs in the Village Shops of Big Sur Center, this fine-arts gallery is home to the Big Sur Arts Initiative, which coordinates arts programs and events around Big Sur. This place is an excellent source of information on Big Sur artists and events. P.O. Box 459, Big Sur, CA 93920; (831) 667–1530; www.bigsurarts.org.
- **Heartbeat Gift Gallery:** Next to the Big Sur River Inn in Big Sur Center, this is the place to go for unusual, exotic, or erotic gifts, including magic wands. (831) 667–2557; www.heartbeatbigsur.com.
- **Local Color:** This shop displays handmade goods from local artisans. Village Shops in Big Sur Center; (831) 667–0481.
- **Sofanya's Art Gallery:** Portraiture, paintings, sculpture, and gifts at Fernwood Resort. (831) 667–2130; www.sofanya.com.
- **Big Sur Bazaar:** At Loma Vista near the post office, this store offers an assortment of gift items, jewelry, books, and pottery. (831) 667–2197.
- **The Garden Gallery:** Local arts and crafts, sculpture, jewelry, and more in Loma Vista. (831) 667–2818.
- **Gallery Ventana:** This gallery features fine art by local artists; it's located in the Ventana Inn. (831) 667–2787.
- **Post Ranch Mercantile:** Tableware, home accessories, and natural clothing at the Post Ranch Inn. (831) 667–2795; www.postranchmercantile .com.
- **Phoenix Shop:** Located at Nepenthe, this is one of the most fascinating stores along the coast. Look for unique gifts, clothing, and a wide selection of books. (831) 667–2347; www.nepenthebigsur.com.

Art-Themed Tours

- **Artists' Studio Tours:** Artists Equity sponsors self-guided tours all over Monterey County every September. (831) 754-2787; www.artists-equity.org.

- **Big Sur Artisans Fair:** This "neighborhood" gathering pulls artists and artisans from all along the Big Sur coastline for booths and fun every November. (831) 667-2557.

- **Esalen Arts Festival:** This annual event, held at the Esalen Institute during the week of July 4, includes world music, a poetry slam, displays of art, and artist workshops. Buy tickets online. (415) 609-8707; www.esalen.org.

- **Hidden Gardens Tour:** Here's a chance to see gardens and artists' studios not usually open to the public. Some are private homes, but the tour also visits the organic gardens at Esalen Institute and the cutting garden at Post Ranch Inn. Reservations are required. (831) 667-1530; www.big surarts.org.

- **Hawthorne Gallery:** This spectacular showroom and outdoor sculpture garden showcases the work of local artists, and is particularly strong in granite, wood, steel, glass, and bronze sculpture. It's located across Highway 1 from Nepenthe. (831) 667-3200; www.hawthornegallery.com.

- **Coast Gallery:** This complex houses six galleries displaying the works of more than 250 American artists and artisans. Upstairs you will find a permanent exhibition of paintings by Henry Miller. (831) 667-2301; www.coastgalleries.com.

Spiritual and Contemplative Retreats

Esalen Institute

This famous conference center on a cliff above the ocean along an isolated stretch of Big Sur coastline is the birthplace of the Human Potential Movement—a phrase inspired (if not actually uttered) by Aldous Huxley, who taught here in the 1960s. The institute offers seminars and workshops on mysticism, religion, psychic phenomena, psychology, Gestalt therapy, quantum physics, UFOs, shamanism, acupressure, art, economics, dance, yoga, massage, bodywork, couples therapy, and a hundred other topics. Although it attracts celebrities, it's not a fancy place; it started its present life as the most humble of hot-springs resorts.

The contemporary hot-springs bathhouse at Esalen Institute replaces several earlier structures that were destroyed by slides, but it still retains the famous cliffside views.

Esalen's hot springs were well known to the Esselen people. Thomas Benton Slate and his wife, Bersabé, built a modest resort here in the 1880s. J. Smeaton Chase soaked his aching bones when he rode through in 1911 and described it thus: "Here I found a comfortable, old-fashioned house where I could put up for the night. . . . A quarter of a mile from the house I found a couple of tents pitched on a ledge of rock halfway down the hundred-foot bluff. In them were bath-tubs to which hot sulphur water was led from springs that break out all along the cliff. . . . It was an enjoyable experience to bathe thus, as it were, in mid-air, with gulls screaming all around and breakers roaring fifty feet below."

The Esalen Institute itself was established by Mike Murphy and Dick Price in the early 1960s. Sharing a mutual interest in psychology, the pair began inviting an ever expanding list of speakers on an ever expanding array of topics. Guests soaked in the hot springs and attended seminars by Alan Watts, Aldous Huxley, Gregory Bateson, Gerald Heard, Arnold Toynbee, Paul Tillich, Carl Rogers, B. F. Skinner, Ida Rolf, Abraham Maslow, Timothy Leary, Linus Pauling, and Buckminster Fuller. The institute's transforming interests readily embraced Fritz Perls's Gestalt movement therapy, mysticism, Indian philosophy, meditation, and all forms of bodywork. The springs and alternative thinking attracted countercultural types as well as 1960s hipsters and musicians. Esalen helped popularize many cultural notions that have since gone mainstream, including Eastern philosophy, holistic health, and bodywork.

The Esalen Institute continues to offer a diverse range of classes, seminars, and workshops year-round. Facilities are available for use only by registered guests; casual drop-in visits are a thing of the past. Among the ways that you can visit Esalen without taking a class, the easiest might well be arranging to have a massage, buying tickets to the Esalen Arts Festival, setting up a middle-of-the-night visit to the hot-springs baths, or arranging a personal retreat. Reservations are required for all of these.

The famous baths themselves were wrecked by landslides in the 1950s and again in 1998. The present structure contains dressing rooms, massage tables, a sundeck, heated sandstone floors, and seven tubs able to hold about sixty people. The spectacular view of waves and cliffs, of course, is as good as ever. Esalen Institute, 55000 Highway 1, Big Sur, CA 93920; (831) 667–3000; www.esalen.org.

New Camaldoli Hermitage

This community of Catholic Benedictine monks occupies a shelf about 1,300 feet above the Pacific at Lucia. You reach the hermitage by a paved, winding, 1.9-mile road that starts next to a white cross about 0.5 mile south of the Lucia store on Highway 1. This facility is not geared for tourism, but drop-in visitors are very welcome at the store, which sells religious books, crafts, and fruitcake and date bread baked by the monks.

Founded in 1958, the order traces its beginnings to the original Camaldolese community in Italy, founded by a monk now known as Saint Romuald in 1027. The monks themselves observe vows of silence. Their lives revolve around work, meditation, prayer, and the duties of worship. "Sit in your cell as in paradise," says Saint Romuald's *Brief Rule*. "Watch your thoughts like a good fisherman watching for fish. The path you must follow is in the Psalms; never leave it."

Guests on retreat may stay for up to three days. Retreatants stay in single rooms or trailers, and may participate in liturgical prayer services in the church.

The hermitage requests a modest payment, which includes vegetarian meals. New Camaldoli Hermitage, 62475 Coast Highway 1, Big Sur 93920; (831) 667–2456; www.contemplation.com.

Tassajara Zen Mountain Center

For centuries Tassajara Hot Springs was one of the glories of the Esselen heartland. The springs, which bubble out of the bank on Tassajara Creek, are now part of the Tassajara Zen Mountain Center, a Buddhist monastery. From late fall to late spring, the monastery is home to priests, masters, and novice students who come for study and rigorous training in meditation. From May to Labor Day, however, the temple opens for guests to come and enjoy the peaceful beauty of Tassajara Canyon and its therapeutic hot springs.

The hot springs became a tourist resort in the 1860s after developers built a 14-mile stage road from Jamesburg over Chews Ridge. (Travelers still use the same road.) The resort declined in the twentieth century. When a Japanese Buddhist priest, Shunryu Suzuki, started searching for a rural spot to build a retreat for the San Francisco Zen Center, he found it at Tassajara Hot Springs. In July 1967 he opened the first rural Zen monastery outside Asia, calling it Zenshinji, Zen heart-mind temple.

Some fifty to sixty students in residence follow some basic rules: Keep to the schedule of prayer and meditation, no drugs, no alcohol, and no new sexual relations. The monastery can be very isolated in winter, when temperatures drop, storms turn the road into mush, and the local creeks rise into rivers. Days are divided by a strict regimen of prayer and meditation, a schedule that dates back to China's Tang dynasty (A.D. 618–907), opening with the wake-up bell at 5:30 A.M., and closing after the 8:40 P.M. *zazen* (meditation) session in the *zendo* (temple building). Winter is rough on buildings, so there's always work to perform around the monastery. The extensive vegetable gardens need to be worked and planted.

The monastery is a handsome place, well wooded with oak and sycamore, threaded by paths, the buildings mostly of stone or wood. Occasional bells, drums, and chanting drift quietly over the scene. Visitors who book humble rooms during the summer open season come to Tassajara for many reasons. Some participate in meditation or religious services. Some come for the famously delicious vegetarian meals and bread. Some come to soak in the hot springs or the spring-heated swimming pool. Others come to take classes or attend lectures or workshops on Zen, painting, calligraphy, and other topics. Some spend their days peacefully reading, and others hike or go swimming in Tassajara Creek. At night all is lit by kerosene lanterns. The atmosphere is

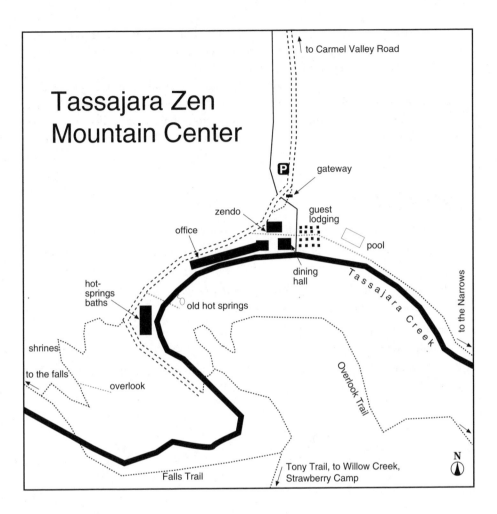

relaxing and quiet, the schedule for guests dictated only by mealtimes and the 10:30 fire-watch, when all lamps must be extinguished for the night.

The bathhouse is an elegant new building in the Japanese style, with sun-deck, outdoor and indoor pools, showers, dressing room, steam room, hot (106 degrees Fahrenheit) and warm tubs, and steps down to the creek for a cooler dip. The bathhouse is separated into men's and women's sections, though there are hours posted when that distinction is ignored. Clothing is always optional; some do, some don't. Day-use visitors are allowed to use the hot springs in summer if they make reservations *in advance;* (415) 865–1899.

Hiking trails around the grounds lead to the Narrows and into the Ventana Wilderness. One path winds up a knoll to a shrine to Suzuki, the temple founder. You can follow the Falls Trail to see a slender waterfall upstream from the monastery; go in May before it dries up. Hikers may pass through the monastery grounds en route to Forest Service trails at any time of year, but nonguests are encouraged not to linger.

Prospective guests need to make reservations starting in March. Places fill up fast. For those who do not want to drive the mountainous Tassajara Road, the monastery runs a shuttle service (fee) from Jamesburg. Tassajara Zen Mountain Center, 39171 Tassajara Road, Carmel Valley, CA 93924; (415) 865–1899 or (415) 865–1895; www.sfzc.com.

Further Reading

The following books have strong Big Sur connections.

Mayo, Gui. *The Old Coyote of Big Sur: The Life of Jaime DeAngulo*. Berkeley, Calif.: Stonegarden Press, 1995.

Miller, Henry. *Big Sur and the Oranges of Hieronymus Bosch*. New York: New Directions Publishing Corporation, 1957.

Reinstedt, Randall A. *Ghosts of the Big Sur Coast*. Carmel, Calif.: Ghosts Town Publications, 2002.

Wall, Rosalind Sharpe. *A Wild Coast and Lonely*. San Carlos, Calif.: World Wide Publishing/Tetra, 1989.

Highway 1 Mileage Chart: From Point to Point

	Carmel River	Point Lobos SR	Malpaso Creek	Palo Colorado Road	Bixby Bridge	Little Sur River	Point Sur Light Station	Andrew Molera SP	Pfeiffer Big Sur SP	Big Sur Station	Old Post Ranch	Nepenthe	Pfeiffer Burns SP	Esalen Institute	Lucia	Limekiln SP	Nacimiento Road	Pacific Valley Station	Gorda	Salmon Creek	Ragged Point Inn	San Carpoforo Creek	Piedras Blancas settlement	Hearst Castle	San Simeon Creek Bridge	Cambria turnoff
Carmel River	0	1.9	4.5	11	13.1	16.4	18.5	21.5	26	26.4	28.3	29	37.1	40.3	50	52.1	54.2	58.5	63	71.1	75	76.4	82.7	90.2	95.1	97.5
Point Lobos SR	1.9	0	2.6	9.1	11.2	14.5	16.6	19.6	24.1	24.5	26.4	27.1	35.2	38.4	48.1	49.5	52.3	56.6	61.1	69.2	73.1	74.5	80.8	88.3	93.2	95.6
Malpaso Creek	4.5	2.6	0	6.5	8.6	11.9	14	17	21.5	21.9	23.8	24.5	32.6	35.8	45.5	47.6	49.7	54	58.5	66.6	70.5	71.9	78.2	85.7	90.6	93
Palo Colorado Road	11	9.1	6.5	0	2.1	5.4	7.5	10.5	15	15.4	17.3	18	26.1	29.3	39	41.1	43.2	47.5	52	60.1	64	65.4	71.7	79.2	84.1	86.5
Bixby Bridge	13.1	11.2	8.6	2.1	0	3.3	5.4	8.4	12.9	13.3	15.2	15.9	24	27.2	36.9	39	41.1	45.4	49.9	58	61.9	63.3	69.6	77.1	82	84.4
Little Sur River	16.4	14.5	11.9	5.4	3.3	0	2.1	5.1	9.6	10	11.9	12.6	20.7	23.9	33.6	35.7	37.8	42.1	46.6	54.7	58.6	60	66.3	73.8	78.7	81.1
Point Sur Light Station	18.5	16.6	14	7.5	5.4	2.1	0	3	7.5	7.9	9.8	10.5	18.6	21.8	31.5	33.6	35.7	40	44.5	52.6	56.5	57.9	64.2	71.7	76.6	79
Andrew Molera SP	21.5	19.6	17	10.5	8.4	5.1	3	0	4.5	4.9	6.8	7.5	15.6	18.8	28.5	30.6	32.7	37	41.5	49.6	53.5	54.9	61.2	68.7	73.6	76
Pfeiffer Big Sur SP	26	24.1	21.5	15	12.9	9.6	7.5	4.5	0	0.4	2.3	3	11.1	14.3	24	26.1	28.2	32.5	37	45.1	49	50.4	56.7	64.2	69.1	71.5
Big Sur Station	26.4	24.5	21.9	15.4	13.3	10	7.9	4.9	0.4	0	1.9	2.6	10.7	13.9	23.6	25.7	27.8	32.1	36.6	44.7	48.6	50	56.3	63.8	68.7	71.1
Old Post Ranch	28.3	26.4	23.8	17.3	15.2	11.9	9.8	6.8	2.3	1.9	0	0.7	8.8	12	21.7	23.8	25.9	30.2	34.7	42.8	46.7	48.1	54.4	61.9	66.8	69.2
Nepenthe	29	27.1	24.5	18	15.9	12.6	10.5	7.5	3	2.6	0.7	0	8.1	11.3	21	23.1	25.2	29.5	34	42.1	46	47.4	53.7	61.2	66.1	68.5
Pfeiffer Burns SP	37.1	35.2	32.6	26.1	24	20.7	18.6	15.6	11.1	10.7	8.8	8.1	0	3.2	12.9	15	17.1	21.4	25.9	34	37.9	39.3	45.6	53.1	58	60.4
Esalen Institute	40.3	38.4	35.8	29.3	27.2	23.9	21.8	18.8	14.3	13.9	12	11.3	3.2	0	9.7	11.8	13.9	18.2	22.7	30.8	34.7	36.1	42.4	49.9	54.8	57.2
Lucia	50	48.1	45.5	39	36.9	33.6	31.5	28.5	24	23.6	21.7	21	12.9	9.7	0	2.1	4.2	8.5	13	21.1	25	26.4	32.7	40.2	45.1	47.5
Limekiln SP	52.1	49.5	47.6	41.1	39	35.7	33.6	30.6	26.1	25.7	23.8	23.1	15	11.8	2.1	0	2.1	6.4	10.9	19	22.9	24.3	30.6	38.1	43	45.4
Nacimiento Road	54.2	52.3	49.7	43.2	41.1	37.8	35.7	32.7	28.2	27.8	25.9	25.2	17.1	13.9	4.2	2.1	0	4.3	8.8	16.9	20.8	22.2	28.5	36	40.9	43.3
Pacific Valley Station	58.5	56.6	54	47.5	45.4	42.1	40	37	32.5	32.1	30.2	29.5	21.4	18.2	8.5	6.4	4.3	0	4.5	12.6	16.5	17.9	24.2	31.7	36.6	39
Gorda	63	61.1	58.5	52	49.9	46.6	44.5	41.5	37	36.6	34.7	34	25.9	22.7	13	10.9	8.8	4.5	0	8.1	12	13.4	19.7	27.2	32.1	34.5
Salmon Creek	71.1	69.2	66.6	60.1	58	54.7	52.6	49.6	45.1	44.7	42.8	42.1	34	30.8	21.1	19	16.9	12.6	8.1	0	3.9	5.3	11.6	19.1	24	26.4
Ragged Point Inn	75	73.1	70.5	64	61.9	58.6	56.5	53.5	49	48.6	46.7	46	37.9	34.7	25	22.9	20.8	16.5	12	3.9	0	1.4	7.7	15.2	20.1	22.5
San Carpoforo Creek	76.4	74.5	71.9	65.4	63.3	60	57.9	54.9	50.4	50	48.1	47.4	39.3	36.1	26.4	24.3	22.2	17.9	13.4	5.3	1.4	0	6.3	13.8	18.7	21.1
Piedras Blancas settlement	82.7	80.8	78.2	71.7	69.6	66.3	64.2	61.2	56.7	56.3	54.4	53.7	45.6	42.4	32.7	30.6	28.5	24.2	19.7	11.6	7.7	6.3	0	7.5	12.4	14.8
Hearst Castle	90.2	88.3	85.7	79.2	77.1	73.8	71.7	68.7	64.2	63.8	61.9	61.2	53.1	49.9	40.2	38.1	36	31.7	27.2	19.1	15.2	13.8	7.5	0	4.9	7.3
San Simeon Creek Bridge	95.1	93.2	90.6	84.1	82	78.7	76.6	73.6	69.1	68.7	66.8	66.1	58	54.8	45.1	43	40.9	36.6	32.1	24	20.1	18.7	12.4	4.9	0	2.4
Cambria turnoff	97.5	95.6	93	86.5	84.4	81.1	79	76	71.5	71.1	69.2	68.5	60.4	57.2	47.5	45.4	43.3	39	34.5	26.4	22.5	21.1	14.8	7.3	2.4	0

*Distances are in miles

Index

W

About the Author

Born and raised in the San Francisco Bay Area, Barry Parr especially enjoyed his boyhood camping trips to the wilds of California. Now a high school English teacher in the East Bay area, Parr still enjoys backpack trips with family and friends as often as he can.